BLOCKCHAIN DEMOCRACY

In *Blockchain Democracy*, William Magnuson provides a breathtaking tour of the world of blockchain and bitcoin, from their origins in the online scribblings of a shadowy figure named Satoshi Nakamoto, to their furious rise and dramatic crash in the 2010s, to their ignominious connections to the dark web and online crime. Magnuson argues that blockchain's popularity stands as a testament both to the depth of distrust of government today and also to the fervent and undying belief that technology and the world of cyberspace can provide an answer. He demonstrates how blockchain's failings provide broader lessons about what happens when technology runs up against the stubborn realities of law, markets and human nature. This book should be read by anyone interested in understanding how technology is changing our democracy, and how democracy is changing our technology.

William Magnuson is an associate professor at Texas A&M Law School. He teaches and writes about corporations, technology and finance. Prior to joining Texas A&M, he taught law at Harvard, worked as an associate at Sullivan & Cromwell in New York and served as a journalist in the Rome bureau of the *Washington Post*.

Blockchain Democracy

TECHNOLOGY, LAW AND THE RULE OF THE CROWD

WILLIAM MAGNUSON

Texas A&M Law School

CAMBRIDGE
UNIVERSITY PRESS

University Printing House, Cambridge CB2 8BS, United Kingdom

One Liberty Plaza, 20th Floor, New York, NY 10006, USA

477 Williamstown Road, Port Melbourne, VIC 3207, Australia

314–321, 3rd Floor, Plot 3, Splendor Forum, Jasola District Centre, New Delhi – 110025, India

79 Anson Road, #06–04/06, Singapore 079906

Cambridge University Press is part of the University of Cambridge.

It furthers the University's mission by disseminating knowledge in the pursuit of education, learning, and research at the highest international levels of excellence.

www.cambridge.org
Information on this title: www.cambridge.org/9781108482363
DOI: 10.1017/9781108687294

© William Magnuson 2020

First published 2020

A catalogue record for this publication is available from the British Library.

Library of Congress Cataloging-in-Publication Data
NAMES: Magnuson, William J., 1982– author.
TITLE: Blockchain democracy : technology, law and the rule of the crowd / William Magnuson, Texas A&M Law School.
DESCRIPTION: Cambridge, United Kingdom ; New York, NY, USA : Cambridge University Press, 2020. | Includes bibliographical references and index.
IDENTIFIERS: LCCN 2019032014 (print) | LCCN 2019032015 (ebook) |
ISBN 9781108482363 (hardback) | ISBN 9781108687294 (epub)
SUBJECTS: LCSH: Cryptocurrencies – Law and legislation. | Blockchains (Databases) – Law and legislation.
CLASSIFICATION: LCC K4431 .M34 2020 (print) | LCC K4431 (ebook) | DDC 343/.032–dc23
LC record available at https://lccn.loc.gov/2019032014
LC ebook record available at https://lccn.loc.gov/2019032015

ISBN 978-1-108-48236-3 Hardback
ISBN 978-1-108-71208-8 Paperback

Contents

Preface

As the nineteenth century belongs to literature, and the twentieth to war, the twenty-first century belongs to technology. Its steady march into the fabric of our daily lives has been swift and utterly complete. For many of us in the Western world, we can hardly imagine a day in which we do not chat with friends, read the news, go shopping and watch movies, all through the internet, and often on our phones. Technology is everywhere, and looks likely to stay there. Thus, if we are to understand the great movements in politics and society today, we must begin by understanding technology.

In recent years, understanding technology has largely meant understanding Big Tech. A few giant corporations, easily countable on a single hand, dominate the tech industry to an extent rarely before seen in the history of capitalism. Their names are familiar to us all: Facebook, Apple, Amazon, Netflix, Google. Their dominance is remarkable. Social media *is* Facebook. Online search *is* Google. Online shopping *is* Amazon. Apple and Netflix have competitors, but they still manage to exert unrivaled control over their industries. These companies rule technology and, consequently, our lives. One cannot partake in the wonders of modern technology without going through them. Technology is, in a word, centralized.

There is, however, an exception.

The blockchain is famously the technology underpinning bitcoin, the virtual currency that took the world by storm in the mid-2010s, launching a generation of bitcoin billionaires and blockchain fanatics along with it. But unlike so much of the tech industry, bitcoin and the blockchain are based, not around a central company or product, but around an idea of radical decentralization. Instead of entrusting our technological lives and fortunes to a single large corporation, the blockchain allows us to entrust them to a network of peers. Instead of relying on a Silicon Valley monopoly to keep our data private and safe, we rely on ourselves. By creating a single, immutable document that is shared and maintained by everyone, the blockchain is purpose-built to avoid the perils of Big Tech.

It is for these reasons that I first became interested in the blockchain. As a legal scholar, I was curious about how our laws might govern a decentralized technology of the likes of blockchain. What laws would apply to it? Who would apply them, and to whom? With Big Tech, these questions are easy. With blockchain, they are hard. As a citizen, I was curious about how blockchain might affect government. Would it reduce government's role in society? Would it circumvent democratic processes? Or would it, conversely, improve democracy's ability to reflect and promote the public good? As a tech devotee, I was curious about whether the blockchain could make inroads into the broader technology universe. How would businesses make use of it? How might it affect the financial industry? What risks did it pose for companies that adopted it, and for individuals that invested in it?

As I would learn as I began my research for this book, these are questions about which people have strong opinions. Asking people what they think about blockchain is not unlike asking them if they believe in God. Some say yes. Some say no. Some turn red in the face and tell you that you shouldn't be discussing such things around the dinner table. All have something to say. In fact, it is tempting to say that no technology has ever generated so much hype, either negative or positive, as has the blockchain.

I have attempted to approach these questions with an open mind. When I began my research, I had no strong preconceptions or material interests. I didn't have a grand theory. I was aware of the fierce debates on both sides, but I had no stake in them. I was simply fascinated by the phenomenon that was blockchain, from its origins in the online scribblings of a shadowy figure named Satoshi Nakamoto, to its furious rise and sudden crash in the mid-2010s, to its ignominious connections to the dark web and online crime.

In the course of writing the book, I bought an espresso using bitcoin, I stayed in a bitcoin hostel and I visited a bitcoin mine in dusty East Texas. I played ping-pong with fervent blockchain believers, and I played tennis with equally fervent blockchain skeptics. I read more scholarly articles than I ever thought could possibly have been written on a single topic, let alone on as esoteric a field as the blockchain.

Throughout the course of my research, it was hard not to be impressed by the devotion of the blockchain community. It permeates every part of the blockchain ecosystem, from virtual currencies to utility tokens to decentralized applications. It is on ample display in blog posts and twitter rants and message rooms. And it is demonstrated quite viscerally by the people who have put their life savings into virtual currencies, moved into vans and traveled the world as blockchain evangelists. It is even discernible in the expansive investments in time and money that major companies have poured into the industry. This combination of passion and incentive, of morality and greed, has led observers to remark that the technology might become the world's greatest invention since the internet.

But time and again, in conversations and emails and posts and articles, a theme emerged. To enthusiasts, blockchain represents more than just a new technology. It is more than just the next Facebook or Google or Apple. It is even more than the code that Satoshi Nakamoto wrote. For believers, the blockchain represents a cure for the most pressing problems of our time, from the pervasive power of Big Tech to the paralysis and division of modern politics. The blockchain is what democracy looks like in the Age of Technology.

Introduction

May I consider the wise man rich, and may my pile of gold be of a size that a moderate man could bear and carry with him.

Socrates, *Phaedrus*

On the morning of February 7, 2014, the world woke up to discover that history's greatest bank robbery had taken place while it was sleeping. But the target was not Fort Knox or Goldman Sachs. The robbers did not use guns or sticks of dynamite. And the stolen assets were not gold ingots or dollar bills.

Instead, the target was an obscure company called Mt. Gox – an acronym for Magic: The Gathering Online Exchange – operating out of a small office in Tokyo. The robbers used sophisticated hacking tools to exploit a flaw in the company's software. And the stolen assets were a recently created virtual currency called bitcoin.

Bitcoin was the brainchild of a man named Satoshi Nakamoto, a shadowy figure active in cryptography circles on the internet who has yet to be identified in real life. Nakamoto viewed his creation as a kind of anti-money, a "peer-to-peer" virtual currency that would exist only on computers and would zip around the world at the speed of light. At the heart of the currency was a set of features that made it uniquely and, to some, radically democratic. Bitcoins, unlike dollars or euros, would be created and controlled by everyone. Anyone with a computer would have access to the network and could start creating new currency. People could send and receive the virtual money over the internet without ever going to a bank. Users would operate the network by consensus. Importantly, all of this would take place anonymously; the only identifying information in the system would be long strings of numbers and letters that could not be traced back to real-world individuals. For those who feared the growing power of the state and the corporation in modern society, bitcoin was the perfect antidote. It provided a way for regular people to take back control of their financial lives.

But an undertaking with the radical aspirations of bitcoin, operating on the fringes of the internet (and the law) as bitcoin did, was bound to run into trouble at some point. It was not a question of whether. It was a question of when.

It was 2011 when Mark Karpeles became the chief executive officer of Mt. Gox. He had acquired the company from its founder, a man named Jed McCaleb who originally created the site as a way to trade Magic: The Gathering cards over the internet. Eventually, McCaleb gave up on a future in Magic and transformed the site into a bitcoin exchange. Soon after, Karpeles came calling.

Karpeles, like many of the early adopters of bitcoin, was an unlikely CEO. He was a baby-faced, twenty-six-year-old Frenchman who had a penchant for wearing graphic t-shirts and went by the name of Magical Tux. He had previously worked for a small online gaming company in Paris but was fired after being accused of stealing customer usernames and passwords. His great passion was baking – apple pie was his favorite – and he was always on the lookout for the best croissants in Tokyo, where he had relocated after acquiring Mt. Gox.[1]

Despite his apparent lack of qualifications, Karpeles oversaw a rapid expansion of Mt. Gox's business. By 2012, the company was the world's largest bitcoin exchange. At its height, it handled 80 percent of global transactions in the currency. If you owned bitcoin in 2014, you almost certainly dealt with Mt. Gox.[2]

But Karpeles struggled under the burdens of running his new corporate empire. It didn't help that he was hopelessly devoted to his cat, Tibanne, which, he claimed, required daily shots of medicine, a fact that prevented him from traveling outside the country. And as bitcoin started to gain wider notice in the investment community, and the value of bitcoin spiked, Mt. Gox became an obvious target for hackers looking for vulnerabilities in the cryptocurrency.[3]

By 2014, Karpeles was responding to "daily hacking attempts." At one point, a hacker briefly took control of the site and caused the value of bitcoin to plummet below one cent. It took Karpeles weeks to fix the problem. In another incident, Karpeles reassured users that delays they were experiencing on the site were due to overwhelming demand, not hackers. Hackers, apparently taking Karpeles' statement as a challenge, immediately launched a cyberattack on the site and forced it to shut down entirely. Eventually, Karpeles had to bring in outside help to strengthen Mt. Gox's cybersecurity systems.[4]

In January 2014, however, users of Mt. Gox again began to experience delays on the site. The delays were sporadic – some transactions went through without a glitch – but frequent. Complaints started to mount. Some investors reported that they paid for bitcoins but never received them. For an exchange, this was a definite problem. Mt. Gox marketed itself as a platform that made the process of buying and selling virtual currencies easy. If it could not deliver on that promise, its service was useless. Panicked messages to Mt. Gox's customer service account went unanswered. Bitcoin message boards lit up with angry investors asking what was happening.

"Where are my Bitcoins MTGOX?"[5]

"WTF GOX!"[6]

"Get your popcorn ready as the fireworks show is just beginning . . . ."[7]

"MtGox always finds a way to continue f**king everyone into oblivion, indefinitely."[8]

Karpeles, who had lately been spending much of his time designing a "Bitcoin Café" that would sell bitcoins and pastries to Tokyo patrons, finally decided to look into the complaints. Doing so was harder than it might sound. This was because Karpeles had instituted a security mechanism known as "cold storage" for keeping client accounts safe. Instead of keeping users' private keys – essentially passwords that allowed bitcoin owners to buy and sell their coins – on his company's computers, Karpeles had stored them on paper slips stashed all around Tokyo. Cold storage was thought to protect client assets from theft because hackers could not access the passwords even if they managed to break into the company's systems. Instead, they would need to physically access the paper slips. But, ironically, the very system that was designed to prevent theft now made it very hard to determine whether a theft had actually occurred. In order to find out what was wrong, Karpeles had to race around the city manually retrieving the slips of paper and then scanning them into his computer.[9]

It is remarkable that Karpeles had not thought to do this before. After all, it would have been natural for users to assume that the world's largest bitcoin exchange would perform regular audits of its accounts. If it had handled physical currency, as a normal bank does, it would have been obligated to do so by numerous laws and regulations. But bitcoin operated in a legal nether-world, where it was unclear which rules, if any, applied to it. Plus, Karpeles had another reason for not checking his clients' accounts. As he explained it, "each time you want to check the balance of a cold wallet, you're making it less cold." In other words, by storing his clients' private keys offline, he protected them from cybertheft. But every time he typed those keys into his computer to check their accounts, the chances that a hacker might be able to discover the keys increased. In other words, in order for Mt. Gox's security system to work, it was paramount that no one check that it was working.[10]

When Karpeles finally decided to check, he was in for a surprise. Wallet after wallet came back empty. Hundreds of thousands of bitcoins that were supposed to be in his accounts were gone. And despite furious efforts to locate the missing coins, he could not track them down. They had disappeared into thin air.

Karpeles had no choice. He swiftly halted all withdrawals from the Mt. Gox exchange. He took his website offline. He filed for bankruptcy. The world's largest bitcoin exchange had just gone under.

Karpeles would eventually announce the full extent of his losses: a staggering 850,000 bitcoins had disappeared from Mt. Gox's accounts.[11] At bitcoin's height, these coins would have been worth $17 billion.[12]

***

Blockchain Democracy tells the story of the blockchain. This remarkable new technology stormed onto the stage in the last decade and quickly captured the public's imagination, as well as much of its money. Strange forms of virtual currency, entirely divorced from traditional monetary systems such as the American dollar or the Japanese yen, seemingly appeared out of nowhere to challenge existing hierarchies and power structures. Some see them as a powerful tool for good, a way of protecting individual freedom and privacy. Others see them as the greatest scam ever perpetrated, a Ponzi scheme that is doomed to collapse under its own weight. This book aims to help sort out these claims.

As such, *Blockchain Democracy* is a story about technology. Where it comes from. How it is created. And what happens when it meets the messy facts of the real world. Each Chapter of the book explores a different facet of the blockchain technology, from the underlying code and the miners that implement it to the businesses and governments that seek to control it. It is hoped that these bite-sized views of the blockchain, when put together, provide a comprehensive view into the role of this important technology in society today.

Blockchain Democracy is also a story about money. Proponents of the block-chain, after all, hoped to ignite a revolution in the way that money worked in the world. Despite the fact that people spend a great deal of time thinking about dollars and cents, it is surprisingly difficult to define precisely what money is and what purpose it serves in society. Until we know these things, it is hard to assess how we can improve on it. It turns out that the founders of bitcoin and other cryptocurrencies thought deeply about these questions and had well-worked-out answers. It is hoped that by studying money and its role in the economy, we can get a better handle on what cryptocurrencies are. But it is also hoped that by studying cryptocurrencies, we can begin to sort out our ideas about what money is and how we might change it.

Finally, *Blockchain Democracy* is a story about democracy. How it works. How it doesn't. And whether it can withstand the powerful forces unleashed by those other great mechanisms: money and technology. The blockchain was founded on the idea of wresting control of our lives back from the government. Giving power to the people sounds a lot like democracy. But it is not necessarily so. Modern democracies have struggled for centuries to find a proper balance between popular sovereignty and individual rights, between freedom and equality, between government regulation and self-determination. The blockchain has been around for only a decade and, in many ways, rejects many of the precepts of modern democracy. Can a democratic system of government coexist with a technology of the likes of the blockchain? Can governments harness the power of decentralized networks without losing control over those they govern? These are the questions that this book seeks to answer.

At the root of all of these grand themes lies a central question: Where should power reside in modern society? Should it be centralized and concentrated? Or should it be decentralized and dispersed? The blockchain was founded on the concept of decentralization; it was purposely designed so that everyone could have a say in its future. For its founders and original programmers, decentralized networks offered a set of benefits to the community that no other form of organization could offer. They were secure and stable and democratic. But decentralized networks also have a set of costs that are hard-wired into them and that are difficult to avoid. And, just as importantly, the invisible hand of the market may lead to centralization even when the system itself begins in a decentralized state. The internet, after all, bred Facebook, Google and Amazon. People like one-stop shops, coherent ecosystems and easy-to-use interfaces. Companies like monopolies. All of which suggests that market forces may end up pushing even the most decentralized and democratic technologies in a centralized, antidemocratic direction.

Technology. Money. Democracy. These ideas are the great challenges facing our world today. They permeate our lives in ways that are hard to overstate, but they are also the source of much anxiety and controversy. Tech companies like Apple, Google and Facebook have come under criticism for their addictive effects and their hoarding of private data. Soaring levels of debt, from mortgages to student loans, have been blamed for a variety of ills, and the gap between the rich and the poor grows wider every day. Democracy itself is under attack by nationalists and populists around the globe. It is hard not to think that somehow these troubling trends are linked.

At the same time, technology, money and democracy seem more important than they have ever been. We need democracy to define our common values and our common goals. We need technology to pursue those values and to reach those goals. And we need money to make this all possible. Resolving society's ills requires us to confront these great challenges.

The blockchain lies squarely at the intersection of these great leitmotifs of modern society. It has led to advances in technology by pioneering new uses of encryption and peer-to-peer networks. It has harnessed these tools to create new forms of money. And it uses lessons from democracy to inform its decision-making processes. In many ways, its achievements warrant celebration. They have shown how decentralized networks can be used to replace a wide variety of outdated systems, from financial recordkeeping to the tracking of election results. They have also shone a light on the many flaws of our current monetary system. The founders of bitcoin and other cryptocurrencies saw the contradictions and failings of the modern economy and decided to fashion a new one, using technology to refine and improve on old models. What they created was revolutionary and new. It challenged powerful incumbents. And it broke all the rules.

But if the blockchain has ushered in a revolution in finance and politics, it has also created opportunities for the unprincipled and the immoral to flourish. Criminals and terrorists have rushed into the industry, and their actions have threatened to undermine the accomplishments, and indeed the continued existence, of cryptocurrencies. Governments have watched these developments with a wary eye and, in some cases, have gone further, stepping in to limit or even ban the currencies. The life of the blockchain, thus, in many ways resembles Plato's description of life in a democracy: "It will be an agreeable kind of regime – anarchic, colourful, and granting equality of a sort to equals and unequals alike."[3]

***

The story of Mt. Gox is meant to be a cautionary tale. It highlights the challenges of democratizing technologies, particularly in an area as fundamental to our economy as money is. Mistakes will be made. Unintended consequences are to be expected. Technology magnifies these consequences by making them instantaneous and infinitely repeatable.

But the failure of Mt. Gox also shows something else. It shows that millions of people were willing to put their trust in an algorithm. That this algorithm had become the repository for billions of dollars of real-world money. And that, somehow, through this algorithm, people across the globe were able to communicate and make decisions as if they were a single community.

This book will tell the story of what made that possible.

PART I

THE BLOCKCHAIN

1

The Origins of the Blockchain

The life of money-making is one undertaken under compulsion, and wealth is evidently not the good we are seeking; for it is merely useful and for the sake of something else.

Aristotle, *Nichomachean Ethics*

At 2:10 PM on October 31, 2008, a message popped up on an obscure cryptology mailing list. The message was written by a man going by the name of Satoshi Nakamoto. Nakamoto had never posted to the site before, and he was entirely unknown to its participants. But in his message, he made a bold claim. "I've been working on a new electronic cash system that's fully peer-to-peer, with no trusted third party," he wrote. It was now ready to be unveiled to the world. He included a link to a nine-page white paper bearing the title *Bitcoin: A Peer-to-Peer Electronic Cash System*.[1] In the paper, Nakamoto outlined in crisp and uncluttered English his idea for a new kind of digital money. This money, or bitcoin as Nakamoto called it, would allow people to send money directly to each other over the internet. Banks would have no control over the system, and neither would governments. It would be run, instead, by everyone. Bitcoins would be a kind of pure money, completely democratic, with minimal transaction costs, no middlemen and completely digital.[2]

Looking back, we know that this message was the start of something big. But at the time, it did not seem like much. In fact, most of the initial responses on the mailing list were negative.

"We very, very much need such a system, but the way I understand your proposal, it does not seem to scale to the required size," wrote one participant.[3]

"The real issue with this system is the market for bitcoins," wrote another. "They have no intrinsic value."[4]

Bitcoin would be overwhelmed by hackers and frauds, concluded yet another, because "the good guys have vastly less computational firepower than the bad guys."[5]

One commentator, noting that the country was in the throes of the deepest financial crisis since the Great Depression, feared that governments would never allow a cryptocurrency like bitcoin to thrive.

"The government regularly attacks financial networks," he wrote, "with the financial collapse ensuing from the most recent attack still under way as I write this."[6]

Not all the responses were so negative. One of the few messages of support came from Hal Finney, a computer programmer who had been active in cryptography circles for some time. Finney had studied engineering at the California Institute of Technology before going to work in the nascent video game industry for Mattel. There, he programmed a number of games, from *Adventures of Tron* to *Astroblast* to *Dark Cavern*. An avid reader of science fiction novels like Neal Stephenson's *Cryptonomicon* and Larry Niven's *Ringworld*, Finney had become convinced that corporations and governments were exercising pervasive and oppressive control over their citizens, Big Brother-style. Encryption and cryptography, he believed, provided a way for ordinary citizens to regain their rights. As early as 1992, he had written:

> It seemed so obvious to me. Here we are faced with the problems of loss of privacy, creeping computerization, massive databases, more centralization – and [cryptography pioneer David Chaum] offers a completely different direction to go in, one which puts power into the hands of individuals rather than governments and corporations. The computer can be used as a tool to liberate and protect people, rather than to control them.[7]

In his own work, Finney had developed an encrypted email system called "Pretty Good Privacy" that sought to shield personal communications from government snooping. When he saw Nakamoto's proposal for a system of digital cash that was both democratic and anonymous, he was intrigued.[8]

"Bitcoin seems to be a very promising idea," Finney wrote back. "I'd be satisfied [if] the bitcoin system turns out to be socially useful and valuable, so that [participants] feel that they are making a beneficial contribution to the world by their efforts . . . . In this case it seems to me that simple altruism can suffice to keep the network running properly."[9]

Nakamoto, encouraged by the response, grew bolder.

If his new cryptocurrency were successful, Nakamoto argued, we could "win a major battle in the arms race and gain a new territory of freedom for several years. Governments are good at cutting off the heads of a centrally controlled networks [sic] like Napster, but pure [peer-to-peer] networks like Gnutella and Tor seem to be holding their own."[10]

"It's very attractive to the libertarian viewpoint if we can explain it properly," he added. "I'm better with code than with words though."[11]

Nakamoto's code would indeed prove attractive, and not just to the obscure corners of the internet. It would prove to be the basis of the blockchain.

***

Digital cash is an odd way to start a political revolution. The clarion calls of revolution tend to be more, well, revolutionary – the oppression of the colonies; the rights of man; the class struggle. These are grand ideas that hearken to something greater than the individual; that promise a better, more virtuous world for all. Distributed ledger systems, on the other hand, do not on their face lend themselves to the same stirring of passions and raising of spirits. In fact, most people's eyes glaze over before you even finish the phrase "hash-based proof-of-work," the central idea behind Nakamoto's virtual currency. So why, precisely, did Nakamoto, Finney and other libertarian theorists coalesce around a digital cash system as their route to social and political change? What, precisely, is the philosophy of the blockchain?

The roots of the blockchain lie in a long-standing debate in political philosophy about power and where it should lie. On one side of this debate stand the centralizers, those who believe we should concentrate power in the hands of the few. On the other side stand the decentralizers, those who believe we should spread power across the hands of the many. Ultimately, the question of centralization versus decentralization turns on understandings about the proper relationship between the state and the individual. It is often posed as a clash of opposing values: the power of the state versus the rights of the individual; the knowledge of the elite versus the wisdom of the masses; the decisiveness of a king versus the deliberation of the parliament. This clash is played out in any number of hot-button issues today, from gun control (should the government have the power to restrict gun ownership or should individuals have an unconditional right to own guns?) to abortion (should the government have the power to ban abortions or should individuals have the right to make decisions about their bodies?) to discrimination (should the government have the power to force shops to serve all customers regardless of sexual orientation, or should individuals have the right to refuse service to certain groups based on their religious beliefs?). These sorts of questions get to the very root of our ideas about how government and society should work.

The questions are not new; indeed, one can find them animating one of the great philosophical disputes in the history of the Western world. Thomas Hobbes and John Locke lived through one of the most tumultuous centuries in English history. During the course of the seventeenth century, England witnessed a civil war, a revolution, a counterrevolution and the beheading of a king. The country was riven by dissension and factionalism, and the resulting rivalries often proved deadly for whichever side happened to be out of favor. Both Hobbes and Locke were forced to flee the country at various times in fear of their lives, with Hobbes leaving for Paris and Locke for Amsterdam. One might have predicted that these shared experiences would lead to shared worldviews. Indeed, a mere thirty-eight years separates the publication of their defining works, Hobbes' *Leviathan* and Locke's *Two Treatises on Government*. But the exact opposite happened.[12]

Thomas Hobbes was born in 1588 in Malmesbury, England, the son of a vicar of Westport. In that year, the Spanish Armada was readying to attack England, and he later blamed his mother's fear of the impending invasion for instilling him with a healthy dose of cowardliness. After his father abandoned the family, Hobbes was raised by a wealthy uncle, a local glover and alderman. He eventually ended up at Magdalen Hall in Oxford, where he studied logic and physics, graduating in 1608. Afterwards, and upon the recommendation of the president of Magdalen Hall, Hobbes took a position as a tutor for the son of William Cavendish, the Baron of Hardwick. Over the next forty years, he would write a number of scholarly works, from scientific treatises on optics and psychology to essays on political philosophy. His political writings established him as a staunch Royalist against the cause of the Parliamentarians in the coming Civil War. One of his more notable publications of this time was a translation of Thucydides' *History of the Peloponnesian War*, which he claimed provided a lesson to the English people about the dangers of democracy. Another was *The Elements of Law*, in which he extolled the virtues of absolutism to such a degree that its circulation made him fear for his life during the resurgence of the parliamentary cause during the Long Parliament of 1940. That year, he fled to Paris. But all of these works pale in comparison with his magnum opus, *Leviathan*, published in 1651.[13]

In *Leviathan*, Hobbes famously argued that the life of man in the state of nature was "nasty, brutish, and short."[14] By this, he meant that when there was no government to enforce the law, individuals necessarily lived in a constant state of fear, of theft, of violence, of depredation. His belief about the natural condition of man led Hobbes to clear conclusions about the rightful powers of the state. "Sovereign power ought in all commonwealths to be absolute," he wrote.[15] "The condition of man [under an absolute sovereign] shall never be without inconveniences, but there happeneth in no commonwealth any great inconvenience, but what proceeds from the subjects' disobedience and breach of those covenants from which the commonwealth had its being."[16] Individual rights had to give way, in other words, to the rights of the state. After all, individuals had decided to associate with one another under a government precisely to avoid the perilous and fraught condition of life in a state of nature. They could not then argue that the state was mistreating them, given that the alternative was a perpetual state of omnipresent war. Absolute government was by far the lesser of two evils.

Going further, Hobbes argued that one of the most common "diseases" of a nation was the tendency to reserve rights for its citizens. According to Hobbes, what the state did was by definition good, and what was good was by definition what the state did. "It is manifest," he wrote, "that the measure of good and evil actions is the civil law; and the judge the legislator."[17] If it were otherwise, men would be "disposed to debate with themselves, and dispute the commands of the commonwealth; and afterwards to obey, or disobey them, as in their private judgements they shall think fit. Whereby the commonwealth is distracted and weakened."[18] For Hobbes, then, the power of the state was paramount, and the rights of the individual were subordinate. Any other arrangement would lead to the erosion of the sovereign and a return to the state of nature. While "men may fancy many evil consequences" of granting "so unlimited a power" to government, Hobbes wrote, "the consequences of the want of it, which is perpetual war of every man against his neighbour, are much worse."[19]

John Locke, on the other hand, came to very different conclusions about the wisdom of centralization. Locke was born in 1632 in Somerset, England, and, like Hobbes, was born into a time of tumult. "I no sooner perceived myself in the world, but I found myself in a storm which has lasted almost hitherto," he wrote of his childhood. His father, a country attorney, set aside his profession in 1642 to fight on behalf of the parliamentary army in the English Civil War as the captain of a cavalry troop. Locke himself studied at Christ Church in Oxford, where he struggled academically, a fact that he blamed on his "not being fitted or capacitated to be a scholar." Overcoming these early struggles, he afterwards became a physician and wrote widely on medicine, economics, natural philosophy and government. In 1683, he fled England for the Netherlands after coming under suspicion for involvement in the Rye House Plot to assassinate King Charles II. He only returned to England in 1688 after the Glorious Revolution. A year later, he finished his *Two Treatises of Government*, a book that contained such dangerous political ideas that he decided to publish it anonymously.[20]

In the *Treatises*, Locke articulated a view of government that contrasted starkly with that of Hobbes. According to Locke, men created government in order to preserve their "lives, liberties and fortunes."[21] "The great and chief end, therefore, of men's uniting into commonwealths, and putting themselves under government, is the preservation of their property," he wrote.[22] But if they created government to protect these things, Locke asked, how could they possibly be presumed to consent when government threatened to destroy them? Locke concluded that they could not. "Whenever the legislators endeavour to take away, and destroy the property of the people, or to reduce them to slavery under arbitrary power," Locke wrote, "they put themselves into a state of war with the people, who are thereupon absolved from any farther obedience."[23] In other words, if governments overstep their societal role, individuals are justified in refusing to obey them.

Locke believed that this same logic could be used to justify revolution. If a government attempted to take away its citizens' lives, liberty or property, then citizens had a right to replace it.

> Whensoever, therefore, the legislative shall transgress this fundamental rule of society; and either by ambition, fear, folly, or corruption, endeavour to grasp themselves, or put into the hands of any other an absolute power over the lives, liberties, and estates of the people; by this breach of trust they forfeit the power the people had put into their hands for quite contrary ends, and it devolves to the people, who have a right to resume their original liberty, and, by the establishment of a new legislative (such as they shall think fit), provide for their own safety and security, which is the end for which they are in society.[24]

Locke recognized that his defense of revolution would be viewed as radical, and that critics would label it a recipe for chaos and anarchy and frequent rebellion. But he did not share these concerns. In his view, after all, "revolutions happen not upon every little mismanagement in public affairs." Only the most egregious cases, where "a long train of abuses, prevarications and artifices, all tending the same way" occur, would lead a people to overthrow its government. What is more, decentralized control would provide a strong disincentive to government abuse in the first place. "This doctrine of a power in the people of providing for their safety a-new, by a new legislative, when their legislators have acted contrary to their trust, by invading their property, is the best fence against rebellion, and the probablest means to hinder it."[25]

Hobbes and Locke thus arrived at two very different perspectives on the proper relationship between the state and the individual. Hobbes saw the state as a "leviathan," a body of immense power and authority to whom the individual must, in the final analysis, submit. Locke, on the other hand, saw the state as a tool: ultimate authority rested with the people, and if the state violated their rights, then they might ignore or, in extreme cases, even overthrow it. Importantly, however, both Hobbes and Locke grounded their ideas about government power in assertions about how humans act when government is absent. Discussions of the "state of nature" abound in their writings. Hobbes thought that the state of nature was an abhorrent state, one in which humans were in perpetual fear of one another. This was so, Hobbes believed, because, without a government empowered to create binding laws, humans possessed complete freedom. This freedom included the freedom to make use of anything that one desired, meaning that "every man has a right to everything, even to another's body."[26] This was a recipe for chaos and violence.

Locke, on the other hand, had a rosier view of life in the absence of government. He agreed with Hobbes that the state of nature was a state of "perfect freedom," but he believed that liberty was not tantamount to license. The state of nature, instead, was governed by a counterpart "law of nature." This law of nature forbids individuals to harm others, whether in their "life, health, liberty or possessions."[27] Even in the absence of government, humans could understand basic rules of conduct simply through the use of their reason. Of course, even in a state of nature, problems arose, problems which were sufficiently serious as to give rise to demands for some degree of centralization. In particular, Locke concluded that a completely decentralized society, with no central authority, lacked three fundamental goods.

First, there wants an established, settled, known law, received and allowed by common consent to be the standard of right and wrong, and the common measure to decide all controversies between them: for though the law of nature be plain and intelligible to all rational creatures; yet men being biased by their interest, as well as ignorant for want of study of it, are not apt to allow of it as a law binding to them in the application of it to their particular cases. Secondly, in the state of nature there wants a known and indifferent judge, with authority to determine all differences according to the established law: for every one in that state being both judge and executioner of the law of nature, men being partial to themselves, passion and revenge is very apt to carry them too far, and with too much heat, in their own cases; as well as negligence, and unconcernedness, to make them too remiss in other men's. Thirdly, in the state of nature there often wants power to back and support the sentence when right, and to give it due execution, they who by any injustice offended, will seldom fail, where they are able, by force to make good their injustice; such resistance many times makes the punishment dangerous, and frequently destructive, to those who attempt it.[28]

Thus, the debate between Hobbes and Locke ultimately came down to a debate about the benefits of centralization. To Hobbes, centralization was an unalloyed good: citizens must surrender their individual rights to an all-powerful central government, or else condemn themselves to a world of depredation and violence. But to Locke, centralized government was a flawed and corruptible thing, one that had to be tempered with an overlay of decentralization, the right of the many to object to the power of the few.

In the field of public opinion, Locke won this argument hands down. Today, it is nearly universally accepted that democratic governments have limited powers and that individuals retain certain fundamental rights. The United States Constitution enshrines these principles in its Bill of Rights, recognizing such fundamental rights as the right to freely exercise one's religion, the right to free speech and the right to a fair trial. The U.S. Supreme Court has steadily expanded the breadth and scope of these rights to include such matters as the right to an abortion, the right to same-sex marriage and the right to spend money on political campaigns. The Hobbesian argument for absolutist government is a nonstarter in most circles today, and it is entirely rejected under the law. Indeed, Locke's perspective has become so pervasive in Western political philosophy that Frederick Mundell Watkins, in his survey of political theory, wrote that "the object of most Western thinkers has been to establish a society in which every individual, with a minimum of dependence on the discretionary authority of his rulers, would enjoy the privileges and responsibility of determining his own conduct within a previously defined framework of legal rights and duties."[29]

But to a small online community of cryptographers, computer scientists and anarchists who came together in the early 1990s, this debate between Hobbes and Locke about the costs and benefits of centralization was alive and well. And they thought it required a more radical solution than even Locke was prepared to defend: a return to the radical decentralization of the state of nature.

***

In the early 1990s, the internet was just beginning to take shape. The backbone infrastructure of the internet – such as the worldwide web, domain names, and URLs – had been created, growing out of research conducted by the Department of Defense's Advanced Research Projects Agency beginning in the 1960s. But many of the tools for accessing the internet were still nonexistent or underdeveloped. The first internet service providers had been founded in 1989. American Online launched its Windows-based program in 1992. The first widely used web browsers were yet to be released (Netscape would be launched in 1994, while Microsoft's Internet Explorer would launch in 1995). The internet was still primarily the stomping ground of government officials, academic researchers and a few tech-centric companies.

It was clear, however, that the internet was poised to become something much more. "The digital revolution is whipping through our lives like a Bengali typhoon, [causing] social changes so profound their only parallel is probably the discovery of fire," wrote *Wired* magazine in its first issue, published in 1993.[30] The internet's promise of spreading information and knowledge across the world to anyone with a computer, without regard to national borders or geographical barriers, seemed revolutionary. New websites and services were sprouting up every day. Usage rates were increasing rapidly – one study found that internet traffic doubled annually from 1991 to 1994, with rates as high as 400 percent for the years preceding that. Companies poured money into any technology vaguely related to the internet. It was a heady time.[31]

But not everyone was enthusiastic about the direction the internet was taking. Some believed that the spread of the internet was just as much a cause for concern as it was for jubilation.

"Governments derive their just powers from the consent of the governed," wrote John Perry Barlow, a prominent early thinker on internet privacy, in *A Declaration of the Independence of Cyberspace*. "You have neither solicited nor received ours. . . . Cyberspace does not lie within your borders. . . . We are forming our own Social Contract. This governance will arise according to the conditions of our world, not yours. Our world is different."[32] If the internet allowed information to spread to the furthest ends of the earth, a group of nascent "cyberlibertarians" worried, it also allowed governments to do the same. An enterprising government might use the internet to suddenly have access to the most intimate details of every living person on earth. Privacy would be a thing of the past. Lives, liberties, fortunes, they would all be accessible, and thus vulnerable, to government power. Just as the internet had the power to create, it also had the power to destroy.

Timothy May, John Gilmore and Eric Hughes, the founders of a movement that would soon come to be known as the "cypherpunks," came to their beliefs about the oppressive power of the internet by separate but parallel paths. They had all spent their lives studying computers, and they all shared a particular interest in cryptography – the study of securing communications against eaves-droppers. May had worked at Intel, where he became famous for solving a notoriously difficult problem involving alpha particles that created software glitches on Intel's chips. His stock options at Intel had appreciated so much that he was able to retire at thirty-four years old. In his free time he took care of his cat, Nietzsche, and read an eclectic mix of libertarian-minded novels and science fiction adventure stories, from Ayn Rand's *Atlas Shrugged* to Orson Scott Card's *Ender's Game* (which, appropriately, featured a character named Locke). Gilmore, on the other hand, had been the fifth employee at Sun Microsystems and, like May, had quickly struck it rich, giving him the freedom to "retire" and pursue his interests in the internet and online privacy. Among other ventures, he founded the Electronic Frontier Foundation, a nonprofit devoted to promoting internet freedom. Hughes, the final member of the trio, had studied mathematics at Berkeley and had hit it off with May after crashing at his house when he could not find a place to live in San Francisco. They all met at a party thrown by Gilmore and quickly realized the depth of their shared interests. In 1992, they decided to form a group to meet monthly to discuss their ideas on the internet, computers and cryptography. They named it the cypherpunks.[33]

The first few meetings of the cypherpunks were small, intimate affairs. The trio invited forty friends to their first meeting, hosted at Hughes' house in Oakland, but only twenty showed up. Hughes had recently purchased the house and had not had time to buy furniture for the living room, so everyone sat on the floor. May handed out a packet of reading materials to everyone present, and they all proceeded to play "Crypto Anarchy," a game May and Hughes had invented to illustrate simple concepts of encryption and secure communication. The highlight of the meeting, however, came when May read an essay he had been working on called *The Crypto Anarchist Manifesto*.[34]

"A specter is haunting the modern world," May read to the group, "the specter of crypto anarchy. Computer technology is on the verge of providing the ability for individuals and groups to communicate and interact with each other in a totally anonymous manner. Two persons may exchange messages, conduct business, and negotiate electronic contracts without ever knowing the True Name, or legal identity, of the other. Interactions over networks will be untraceable . . . .. Reputations will be of central importance, far more important in dealings than even the credit ratings of today. These developments will alter completely the nature of government regulation, the ability to tax and control economic interactions, the ability to keep information secret, and will even alter the nature of trust and reputation."

"The State will of course try to slow or halt the spread of this technology," May continued, "citing national security concerns, use of the technology by drug dealers and tax evaders, and fears of societal disintegration. Many of these concerns will be valid; crypto anarchy will allow national secrets to be trade

[sic] freely and will allow illicit and stolen materials to be traded. An anonymous computerized market will even make possible abhorrent markets for assassinations and extortion. Various criminal and foreign elements will be active users of CryptoNet. But this will not halt the spread of crypto anarchy. Just as the technology of printing altered and reduced the power of medieval guilds and the social power structure, so too will cryptologic methods fundamentally alter the nature of corporations and of government interference in economic transactions."[35]

May's message to the group was clear: governments and corporations had grown too powerful in the modern world, and the internet threatened to tilt the balance even further in their favor. But May believed that the path to restoring the balance lay in embracing, not rejecting, the internet. Computers, networks and encryption could be used to promote liberty and remove government control. While this crypto-revolution might lead to some undesirable repercussions (such as drug dealing, extortion and assassination), these repercussions were minor compared to the benefits of securing individual privacy from rapacious governments and corporations. Encryption would give people the means of throwing off the shackles of government oversight.

The cypherpunks greeted May's speech with widespread acclamation, and the trio of May, Hughes and Gilmore soon set their sights on grander achievements. One of their first goals was to spread their ideas beyond their immediate community of friends and colleagues to the wider world. It would be difficult to launch a revolution with just twenty programmers based in San Francisco, and if the cypherpunks wanted to make progress on their real goals, they would need to find ways to reach people around the world. May and Hughes eventually struck on the idea of forming an email mailing list, where interested individuals could share their thoughts about encryption, computers and the internet. Gilmore agreed to host the mailing list on his personal website, Toad.com. And thus was born the Cypherpunk Mailing List.

With the creation of a mailing list, the cypherpunk movement quickly took off. Subscriptions to the list jumped from seven hundred subscribers in 1994 to two thousand in 1997.[36] Subscribers exchanged hundreds of messages daily. Topics ranged from new encryption techniques, to government efforts to crack down on anonymous messaging systems, to constitutional law. Cypherpunks used the mailing list to organize meetings, trade ideas and improve their skills. Local chapters of the cypherpunk community opened up in London, Boston and Washington. It was a remarkable bazaar of diverse voices and viewpoints, seemingly united only by their interest in cryptography. But over time, and through their voluminous daily communications, a distinct cypherpunk culture started to emerge. Cypherpunks were starkly antigovernment, often to the point of anarchism. They were optimistic about the possibility of computer-driven change. And they were paranoid about government snooping.[37]

With increased size came increased attention. Soon the media started paying attention to the cypherpunks. *Wired* magazine ran a cover story on the group in May 1993, with a photo of May, Hughes and Gilmore in masks holding an American flag before them on the cover. In the photo, Gilmore's white t-shirt peaks above the flag and you can just make out the words "Electronic Frontier Foundation" and, perhaps just as importantly, its website address. The story described the "swelling movement" of civil libertarians and hackers who were taking back privacy in the era of cyberspace. "There is a war going on," the article said, "between those who would liberate crypto and those who would suppress it. The seemingly innocuous bunch [of cypherpunks] represents the vanguard of the pro-crypto forces. Though the battleground seems remote, the stakes are not: the outcome of this struggle may determine the amount of freedom our society will grant us in the 21st century." May, Hughes and Gilmore had found an outlet for their work, and the cypherpunk movement picked up speed.[38]

In the meantime, Hughes, concluding that the cypherpunks needed to unify their message, decided to write a statement of purpose for the group. Inspired by May's *The Crypto Anarchist Manifesto*, he titled the essay *A Cypherpunk's Manifesto*. Hughes' manifesto was a remarkable collection of all the ideas about technology, government and decentralization that had been circulating in meetings, mailing lists and chat rooms. "Privacy is necessary for an open society in the electronic age," Hughes began the manifesto. "We cannot expect governments, corporations, or other large, faceless organizations to grant us privacy out of their beneficence." Instead, the cypherpunks had to take matters into their own hands. "We the Cypherpunks are dedicated to building anonymous systems. We are defending our privacy with cryptography, with anonymous mail forwarding systems, with digital signatures, and with electronic money." And Hughes was optimistic about the cypherpunks' chance of success: "We know that software can't be destroyed and that a widely dispersed system can't be shut down. ... Cryptography will ineluctably spread over the whole globe, and with it the anonymous transactions systems that it makes possible."[39]

A Cypherpunk's Manifesto would prove to be an inspiration to many would-be cryptographers and hackers. Word of its existence quickly spread, and soon people were writing in to the mailing list asking for copies. Some members started signing their messages with quotations from the manifesto. Others debated key tenets of the charter in long back-and-forth exchanges on the mailing list. The document would serve as both an introductory text for new members of the group and an organizing principle for the community's diverse set of followers.

A CYPHERPUNK'S MANIFESTO
by Eric Hughes

Privacy is necessary for an open society in the electronic age. Privacy is not secrecy. A private matter is something one doesn't want the whole world to know, but a secret matter is something one doesn't want anybody to know. Privacy is the power to selectively reveal oneself to the world.

If two parties have some sort of dealings, then each has a memory of their interaction. Each party can speak about their own memory of this; how could anyone prevent it? One could pass laws against it, but the freedom of speech, even more than privacy, is fundamental to an open society; we seek not to restrict any speech at all. If many parties speak together in the same forum, each can speak to all the others and aggregate together knowledge about individuals and other parties. The power of electronic communications has enabled such group speech, and it will not go away merely because we might want it to.

Since we desire privacy, we must ensure that each party to a transaction have knowledge only of that which is directly necessary for that transaction. Since any information can be spoken of, we must ensure that we reveal as little as possible. In most cases personal identity is not salient. When I purchase a magazine at a store and hand cash to the clerk, there is no need to know who I am. When I ask my electronic mail provider to send and receive messages, my provider need not know to whom I am speaking or what I am saying or what others are saying to me; my provider only need know how to get the message there and how much I owe them in fees. When my identity is revealed by the underlying mechanism of the transaction, I have no privacy. I cannot here selectively reveal myself; I must *always* reveal myself.

Therefore, privacy in an open society requires anonymous transaction systems. Until now, cash has been the primary such system. An anonymous transaction system is not a secret transaction system. An anonymous system empowers individuals to reveal their identity when desired and only when desired; this is the essence of privacy.

Privacy in an open society also requires cryptography. If I say something, I want it heard only by those for whom I intend it. If the content of my speech is available to the world, I have no privacy. To encrypt is to indicate the desire for privacy, and to encrypt with weak cryptography is to indicate not too much desire for privacy. Furthermore, to reveal one's

(cont.)

identity with assurance when the default is anonymity requires the cryptographic signature.

We cannot expect governments, corporations, or other large, faceless organizations to grant us privacy out of their beneficence. It is to their advantage to speak of us, and we should expect that they will speak. To try to prevent their speech is to fight against the realities of information. Information does not just want to be free, it longs to be free. Information expands to fill the available storage space. Information is Rumor's younger, stronger cousin; Information is fleeter of foot, has more eyes, knows more, and understands less than Rumor.

We must defend our own privacy if we expect to have any. We must come together and create systems which allow anonymous transactions to take place. People have been defending their own privacy for centuries with whispers, darkness, envelopes, closed doors, secret handshakes, and couriers. The technologies of the past did not allow for strong privacy, but electronic technologies do.

We the Cypherpunks are dedicated to building anonymous systems. We are defending our privacy with cryptography, with anonymous mail forwarding systems, with digital signatures, and with electronic money.

Cypherpunks write code. We know that someone has to write software to defend privacy, and since we can't get privacy unless we all do, we're going to write it. We publish our code so that our fellow Cypherpunks may practice and play with it. Our code is free for all to use, worldwide. We don't much care if you don't approve of the software we write. We know that software can't be destroyed and that a widely dispersed system can't be shut down.

Cypherpunks deplore regulations on cryptography, for encryption is fundamentally a private act. The act of encryption, in fact, removes information from the public realm. Even laws against cryptography reach only so far as a nation's border and the arm of its violence. Cryptography will ineluctably spread over the whole globe, and with it the anonymous transactions systems that it makes possible.

For privacy to be widespread it must be part of a social contract. People must come and together deploy these systems for the common good. Privacy only extends so far as the cooperation of one's fellows in society. We the Cypherpunks seek your questions and your concerns and hope we may engage you so that we do not deceive ourselves. We will not,

(cont.)

however, be moved out of our course because some may disagree with our goals.
The Cypherpunks are actively engaged in making the networks safer for privacy. Let us proceed together apace.

Onward.

Eric Hughes <hughes@soda.berkeley.edu>

9 March 1993

One early member of the cypherpunk community was Julian Assange. Assange would eventually gain notoriety for founding WikiLeaks, the website devoted to publishing leaked documents from governments and corporations around the globe, famously publishing thousands of secret U.S. government files documenting the wars in Afghanistan and Iraq. But before rising to worldwide prominence, he was just another frequent poster on the cypherpunk mailing list. His first message to the list dates back to 1995, when he was only twenty-four years old, and his last dates from 2002, just before he enrolled at the "University of Melbourne. In his messages, he comes off as alternately curious ("Does anyone have any pointers to cryptanalysis papers on the Zip encryption scheme?"), whimsical (noting at one point that National Security Agency is an anagram for National Gay Secrecy Unit) and caustic ("boy are you a dummy," he wrote in response to one commenter). But one can also detect hints of the ideology that eventually led to his founding of WikiLeaks. After mentioning economist Joseph Stiglitz's Nobel Prize work on asymmetric information markets, he wrote that "you don't need a Nobel to realize that the relationship between a large employer and employee is brutally asymmetric." "To counter this sort of assymetry [sic] . . . employees naturally start trying to collectivise to increase their information processing and bargaining power."[40] Assange would refine these ideas, and expand on them, when he founded WikiLeaks as an outlet for dissatisfied employees to share their employers' most prized information. Recognizing the debt he owed the cypherpunks, and his ideological affiliation with the group, Assange titled his 2012 book on internet security *Cypherpunks: Freedom and the Future of the Internet*. In the introduction he wrote that "the cypherpunks always saw that . . . combined with [the internet's power to expand communications] was also the power to surveil all the communications occurring."[41]

One of the more troubling elements of the cypherpunk movement was its enduring fascination with what it called "assassination markets." An assassination market was a place, typically envisioned as a website or sometimes even a company, where people could go to put bounties on the heads of their enemies. With the rise of anonymous transaction systems, some cypherpunks believed, these markets could operate more or less in the open – the placer of the bounty would anonymously send money to an online account, and the assassin would collect it without ever revealing his identity to the outside world. The government would have no way of identifying any of the participants in the market, and thus the market could develop without fear of law enforcement. May had written about the possibility of assassination markets as early as 1988 in *The Crypto Anarchist Manifesto*, but at the time he had condemned the idea as "abhorrent." A number of cypherpunks, however, thought that the idea of an assassination market was a good one and started writing to the mailing list about how it might be implemented. One member, Jim Bell, went so far as to write a ten-part essay, entitled *Assassination Politics*, actively promoting the idea. Bell sketched out the basic structure of the market and the technical requirements for its development. He then went on to argue that assassination markets were just what the cypherpunks needed, the means that would allow them to achieve their ends.[42]

An assassination market, Bell argued, would allow citizens to kill off leaders that violated their rights (he cited as examples the government agents responsible for the Waco and Ruby Ridge sieges). Government leaders, fearful of retribution, would stop "taxing us to death, regulating us to death, or for that matter sending hired thugs to kill us when we oppose their wishes." "Consider how history might have changed," he wrote, "if we'd been able to bump off Lenin, Stalin, Hitler, Mussolini, Tojo, Kim Il Sung, Ho Chi Minh, Ayatollah Khomeini, Saddam Hussein, Moammar Khadafi, and various others, along with all of their replacements if necessary, all for a measly few million dollars." Once assassination markets were in place, militaries would become unnecessary because "any threatening or abusive foreign leader would be subject to the same contribution/assassination/reward system, and it would operate just as effectively over borders as it does domestically." And even if a government wanted to shut down the market, it would be powerless to do so because "no prosecutor would dare file charges against any participant, and no judge would hear the case, because no matter how long the existing list of 'targets,' there would always be room for one or two more." Assassination markets, Bell concluded in his final analysis, would topple governments around the world and restore power to individuals. To critics who argued that this would lead to anarchy, he responded that they misunderstood the concept: "People presumably will continue to live their lives in a calm, ordered manner. Or, at least as calm and ordered as they WANT to. It won't be 'wild in the streets,' and they won't bring cannibalism back as a national sport, or anything like that." Assassination markets would not be out of control, Bell argued. To the contrary, they would be subject to a different kind of control: "not a centralized control, decidable by a single individual, but a decentralized system in which everyone gets an implicit 'vote.'" Assassination markets would be democratic.[43]

Bell's essay on assassination markets stirred up the cypherpunk community. Some condemned it as immoral – "nothing more than a plan to commit murder for political purposes, i.e. racketeering."[44] Others argued that it was unrealistic: noting that the U.S. Internal Revenue Service (IRS) has more than 110,000 employees, one commentator wrote that "if you tackle the whole tax system, you get into problems of scale" and that "you have to successfully kill about 10% to have enough effect to shut off the government's money supply."[45] Others worried that its publication would draw unwanted government scrutiny. As one commentator wrote to Bell, "if I were you, I'd watch my back . . . because the spooks are probably already trying to figure out a way out of it."[46] Others defended Bell as a visionary, arguing that "such an important innovation in political theory should certainly be shared with the world."[47] In any case, Bell's activity in the cypherpunk community would soon come to an ignominious end. In 1997, he was arrested and convicted of using a false Social Security number, exploding a stink bomb outside an IRS office and collecting the names and home addresses of IRS employees and FBI agents. Law enforcement agents who searched his car found instructions for making bombs and Molotov cocktails.[48] After serving two years in prison, Bell was released in 2000, but was rearrested a few months later after stalking and harassing an IRS agent. This time, he was sentenced to ten years in prison.[49]

The cypherpunks, on the other hand, would survive and, indeed, thrive. It was clear that May, Hughes and Gilmore had tapped into something deep and powerful, and even the debacle over assassination markets could not slow them down. As May wrote in his essay *The Cyphernomicon*, the cypherpunks had hit on a fundamental feature of the new world: harnessing the new tools of cryptography and the internet, individuals could suddenly use their computers to "change the nature of the balance of power between individuals and larger entities."[50] This was a powerful message for aspiring young hackers and programmers, and it swept more and more of them into its fold.

But the holy grail of the cypherpunks was money. As with any social movement, the cypherpunks quickly realized that, if they were to succeed, they needed it. But it was not just any kind of money they wanted. They wanted virtual money. "We want to use digital payments so that we can transact business over the net," Hal Finney explained to his fellow cypherpunks in 1992.[51] The rationale was simple. Many of the core beliefs of the cypherpunks – from desiring privacy, to distrusting government, to despising corporations and big banks – drove them to question the role of money in the modern world. Money was issued by governments. It was held in banks. And it was earned, largely, by corporations. But what was worse, from the perspective of the cypherpunk community, was that the monetary system was not set up to protect users' anonymity. (Cash, which does offer substantial anonymity to users, was viewed as inconvenient, cumbersome and still, ultimately, controlled by governments.) Even the most secure computer network would fail if, at the end of the day, participants had to go to the bank to send money to the other side. So the cypherpunks set out to create, in their words, "anonymous transaction systems." This holy grail for the cypherpunks would simultaneously imbue their system with perfect anonymity and take it entirely outside the control of the state.[52]

***

The cypherpunks' interest in virtual money dates back to their very beginnings. Soon after their first meeting in Hughes' living room in the fall of 1992, May wrote a message to the cypherpunks list, making the connection between privacy and virtual currency:

> And then there is digital money. You all know about this, or should. . . . IMHO, we should be spending more of our time at our meeting discussing this, and less in playing more iterations of the Game. . . . In conclusion, we are in at the beginning of Something Big. While I'm somewhat skeptical about the claims for things like nanotech, I see this whole cyberspace/cryptology/digital money/ transnationalism ball of wax being _much_ easier to implement. Networks are multiplying beyond any hope of government control, bandwidths are skyrocketing, CPUs are putting awesome power on our desktops, PGP [Pretty Good Privacy, a secure email system] is generating incredible interest, and social trends are making the time right for crypto anarchy.[53]

May thought that virtual currency was important because, without it, any virtual interactions, no matter how well encrypted, would eventually have to pass through a bank, where the government had tools for monitoring and sanctioning individuals. And he thought that a virtual currency was eminently achievable with existing technologies.[54] The leap from private information to private money was not a long one. "Information _is_ money," he wrote. "Information is liquid, flows across borders, and is generally convertible into real money."[55]

The idea of virtual money was not entirely new when the cypherpunks started discussing it in the early 1990s. Indeed, in its purest form, it predates even the electronic age. Virtual currency, at its most basic, is just money that is intangible. This, of course, excludes much of what we typically think of as money: dollar bills and pennies are out. So are gold and silver, or, for that matter, those other exotic objects that have at one time or other served as units of exchange in certain cultures, such as cowrie shells in West Africa[56] and cacao among the Aztecs.[57] But virtual currency includes much that we typically think of as falling squarely within the bounds of traditional money. For example, when the Medici Bank discovered that it could take deposits from one person and loan them out to another just by recording these transactions on its ledger, it had in a sense created virtual currency – additional money was now magically circulating in the economy. This astonishing, and profitable, discovery led the economist John Kenneth Galbraith to remark that "[t]he process by which banks create money is so simple that the mind is repelled."[58] It truly took just a stroke of a pen.

But the dawn of the electronic era greatly expanded virtual money's reach. In the 1950s and 1960s, the first credit cards began to circulate widely, with American Express, Visa and Mastercard quickly becoming a preferred payment method for much of the country.[59] In 1975, the U.S. Social Security Administration began offering recipients the option to receive their deposits directly into their bank accounts through an electronic funds transfer, rather than mailing them a check, making it simpler and faster for retirees to receive money.[60] And in the 1990s, PayPal started offering online money transfers to make it easier for consumers to pay for goods they bought on the internet.[61] All of these developments came from efforts to make currency more flexible and adaptable to the demands of consumers, and all, in one way or another, represented new forms of virtual money. But they also had one thing in common: they all ultimately linked back to a traditional, nonvirtual currency, such as dollars, euros or yen.

The virtual currency that the cypherpunks were interested in was something different, and something significantly more radical. The virtual currency that they were trying to create would be purely intangible, one that existed solely on computers. It would have no corresponding bills or coins circulating in the real world. It would have no physical existence at all. Instead, it would be created, stored and maintained on the internet. And, perhaps most importantly, it would not be issued by a government. A *pure* virtual currency, thus, would be controlled by the people who used it. It would be democratic.

One of the early pioneers in the world of these "pure" virtual currencies was a man named David Chaum. Chaum, like many of the cypherpunks, was a computer scientist with an abiding interest in cryptography and anonymous transaction systems. He had a bushy beard, a long ponytail and a deep paranoia about the erosion of privacy in the age of the internet. In 1992, in an article for the *Scientific American*, he argued that privacy was the internet's Achilles' heel. In a strikingly prescient description of what the world would look like in thirty years, he wrote:

Every time you make a telephone call, purchase goods using a credit card, subscribe to a magazine or pay your taxes, that information goes into a data base somewhere. Furthermore, all these records can be linked so that they constitute in effect a single dossier on your life – not only your medical and financial history but also what you buy, where you travel and whom you communicate with. It is almost impossible to learn the full extent of the files that various organizations keep on you, much less to assure their accuracy or to control who may gain access to them.[62]

This, to Chaum, was a problem. And he thought he had a way to solve it.

There were few people in the world in the 1980s and 1990s who could rival Chaum in his understanding of the internet and its vulnerabilities. He studied computer science at Berkeley and afterwards ended up at a cryptography research group in Amsterdam. He had devoted his life to restoring a measure of security on the internet, and he developed a number of foundational principles for internet cryptography that would continue to be used in the sector for decades. In 1983, he wrote a paper, entitled *Blind Signatures for Untraceable Payments*, that proposed a form of virtual currency that would be untraceable by governments or banks. In it, he wrote that "the ultimate structure of the new electronic payments system may have a substantial impact on personal privacy as well as on the nature and extent of criminal use of payments. Ideally a new payments system should address both of these seemingly conflicting sets of concerns." The paper proposed a solution to the problem: an anonymous payments system that would ensure the privacy of its participants while simultaneously protecting against theft.[63]

A few years later, he put his idea into practice, creating a company, DigiCash, along with a corresponding virtual currency called ECash. The currency was launched to much fanfare in 1990. Breathless newspaper articles at the time announced that "cash is dying,"[64] "the bulging leather wallet has had its day"[65] and "the age of cybercash" was here.[66] Backing this hype up, ECash quickly notched up a number of major successes. Deutsche Bank signed a deal to use it on a pilot basis.[67] So did Credit Suisse.[68] The wonderfully named Mark Twain Bank in St. Louis launched the currency in the United States.[69]

ECash, however, was not long for the world. Just three years after being launched in the United States, the virtual currency went under, with DigiCash filing for bankruptcy in 1998.[70] Its failure was a testament to the difficulties of creating a currency detached from sovereign government. Chaum himself was convinced that the idea for ECash was solid but that his timing had been bad: in his mind, people simply weren't ready for a virtual currency in the early 1990s. E-commerce had not taken hold in the way it would just a few years later. Consumers were just starting to get comfortable with the idea of the internet. The concept of storing money on the internet was pushing the edges of consumer confidence in the internet. Others argued that ECash failed because of the classic chicken-and-egg problem: merchants did not want to go to the trouble of accepting ECash unless consumers were using it, and consumers did not want to use it unless merchants were accepting it. (The fact that Mark Twain Bank convinced a mere 300 merchants to accept it and just 5,000 people to use it, certainly gives credence to this theory.[71])

A final theory holds that the real problem behind ECash was Chaum himself. Chaum was a notoriously prickly character with a strong antiauthoritarian streak. While these traits might have helped him in developing his theories of encryption, they were not so great for business. He is reported to have rejected offers from Netscape, Visa and the Dutch banks ING and ABN Amro, all major players in the industry that might have given his currency the initial user base it desperately needed. He rejected them all. But even those missed opportunities pale in comparison to the biggest: Bill Gates offered to integrate ECash into Windows 95 and was willing to pay $100 million to do so. The deal might have taken virtual currency into the houses of millions of daily users. But Chaum refused again. Participants in the deals constantly complained about Chaum's distrust of others' motives. Chaum asked for nondisclosure agreements from the other side even before beginning negotiations. As one of his own employees put it, "He was so paranoid that he always thought something was wrong."[72]

But while ECash withered away, the ideas behind it did not. The cypherpunks were fascinated by ECash as a step on the way towards truly anonymous transaction systems. References to Chaum and his writings pop up frequently on their mailing list, often in reverent tone. "When I found Chaum's stuff, it just blew me away," Hal Finney wrote to the cypherpunks in 1992. "Chaum's ACM paper is titled, provocatively, 'Security Without Identification – Transaction Systems to Make Big Brother Obsolete.' The work we are doing here, broadly speaking, is dedicated to this goal of making Big Brother obsolete. It's important work. If things work out well, we may be able to look back and see that it was the most important work we have ever done."[73] Other virtual currencies, many of them explicitly modeled on ECash, soon arrived to replace Chaum's defunct currency. There was hashcash and B-Money and Bit Gold. All of them represented efforts to create a virtual currency for the internet age, but they all took different approaches. Hashcash, for example, aimed to solve a new problem that users of email were discovering: their email boxes were filling up with unwanted messages from unknown people. This "spam" was a nuisance and difficult to stop, due to the fact that sending email to large numbers of people was easy and free. The hashcash system would require people to spend a nominal amount of the virtual currency each time they sent an email and would, it was thought, eliminate spam. Bit Gold used some of the concepts from the hashcash infrastructure but made the resulting currency decentralized and transferable. B-Money claimed to be both anonymous and distributed.[74]

All of these virtual currencies, like Ecash, failed. Some failed because of technological issues. Hashcash's problem was that there was no way to reuse the currency, greatly reducing its value as a method for buying and selling goods. Others failed because of a lack of interest. Bit Gold, for example, was never even launched after it was initially proposed by Nick Szabo in 1998.[75] The cypherpunks never managed to sort these problems out. They were intractable for any number of reasons, some of which had nothing to do with technology. But regardless of their inability to create a form of digital money that lived up to their dreams of a cashless world, the cypherpunks had accomplished much in their decade of existence. They developed an analytical framework for assessing the trade-offs of the internet. They identified many of the core vulnerabilities of the internet's protocols. And they proposed a number of nifty technical solutions to them. But perhaps their greatest impact was inspirational: they energized a generation of cryptographers and programmers to continue to think and code and tinker away at finding new solutions to old problems.

***

By the late 1990s, virtual currencies had run into a brick wall. Merchants refused to accept them. Consumers did not trust them. And most of the commercial efforts crashed and burned. At the root of these problems was a more basic one: virtual currencies just did not seem to be an improvement over traditional ones. If they wanted to gain widespread acceptance, they needed to prove not just that they worked but that they worked *better*, that they offered something qualitatively different than cash and credit cards and bank accounts. These other, more accepted forms of money had much to recommend them, including convenience, speed and the backing of a sovereign government. What did virtual currencies offer?

In order to understand this problem, it is worthwhile to begin by examining the purposes of money more broadly. Monetary theorists generally agree that money serves three main purposes in an economy: to buy, to save and to value. First, and perhaps most obviously, money provides a great way to buy things.

This is what economists call the "medium of exchange" function of money: it facilitates exchanges between people. When you walk into Whole Foods on Sunday to go grocery shopping, you know that when you get to the end of the checkout line with your cart brimming with groceries, you will be able to pay with the dollar bills you have in your wallet. The cashier will not inform you that, no, today, unfortunately, they are only accepting payment in the form of, say, gallons of almond milk. You know that the cashier will take the cash in your pocket. Money makes transactions simpler, and it does so for both sides: you hand the cashier the money, and the cashier hands you the groceries. There is no need to barter back and forth about what products Whole Foods happens to need at that time, or how many gallons of almond milk are exchangeable for that jug of cold brew coffee. Money smooths the gears of commerce and makes these kinds of interactions less onerous for both sides.[76]

Second, money allows people to save. This is what economists call money's "store of value" function. When an investment banker receives his bonus at the end of the year, he does not need to rush out to Whole Foods and spend it all at once. He can, instead, hold onto it until, say, he finds that new apartment that he has been looking for. What's more, if he puts the money in a bank, he may even earn some interest on it. Imagine a world in which money did not exist: even assuming that the investment banker would still have a job, he would have to be paid for his labor in some other way. Perhaps he would receive food, perhaps he would receive land or perhaps he would receive some free services from his employer. But food eventually goes bad, land must be maintained and services are only as valuable as the person offering them. And perhaps most importantly, the investment banker may not want these assets in the future. If he wants to get rid of them for the nice apartment he has finally found, he will need to find someone else willing to take them. Money solves this short-term/long-term divide. It allows individuals to store value for later periods and, when needed, convert that value into valuable goods. It is, in other words, a highly liquid investment. It allows people to turn the fruits of their labor into future consumption, while imposing no hard-and-fast deadline by which that future consumption must occur.

Finally, money helps people to value things. Of all money's purposes, this is perhaps the least well understood. Economists refer to this function as money's "unit of account" function. What this means is that people not only use money to buy and to save, they also use it to measure things. Whole Foods posts its prices in dollars. Investment banks set salaries in dollars. And home sellers list their apartments in dollars. The fact that all these different features of life are conveniently tracked using the same measure (dollars) makes it much simpler for everyone to measure, to compare and to judge. The investment banker knows how many cans of cold brew he can buy with his salary, and he can compare that price with the price of the apartment he is thinking about buying. If, instead, everyone chose different units of account, the process of measuring value would become dramatically more complicated. It would be preposterous for Whole Foods to post its prices in gallons of almond milk (one six-pack of cold brew coffee costs two gallons of almond milk, while one dozen free-range eggs cost one gallon of almond milk), or for investment banks to set salaries in hectares of land. Comparing prices would become nearly impossible, and tracking expenditures and profits would as well. Money, again, smooths these processes – it allows individuals to compare the values of different products by looking at their respective prices. Now, of course, some would argue that this process has gone too far: people have started to take the price of something as not just an indication of its economic value but also as a judgment on its moral worth. And, indeed, there is even evidence that the listed price of a good affects how consumers value it; home buyers, for example, tend to overvalue overpriced homes, and undervalue underpriced homes.[77] As Oscar Wilde put it, a cynic knows "the price of everything and the value of nothing."[78] But setting aside the psychological effects of currency, we can see how useful it is to have a single unit of account for such a wide variety of goods.

Ideally, a currency would serve all three of these purposes perfectly. And indeed, the United States dollar has been remarkably good at doing so. Dollars are a great medium of exchange – they are so great, in fact, that they transcend national borders, with merchants in many developing countries preferring to be paid in dollars than in their own national currencies, a testament to the global reach of the United States' currency. Dollars are also a historically safe store of value; inflation rates have tended to be low and relatively predictable, particularly in comparison with other national currencies. And dollars are also an excellent unit of account; we take it for granted that prices are listed in dollars, and we comparison shop with that fact in mind.

But of course, in reality, currencies often fail to serve all of their functions perfectly and, in some cases, they may cease to fulfill any of them at all. History is littered with examples of national currencies experiencing destructive bouts of hyperinflation. The results are generally catastrophic. After World War I, for example, when Weimar Germany was saddled with crippling war debts and punitive reparations payments, the German government decided to simply print more money to pay off all its debts. But the large increase in the number of marks in circulation led to a sharp rise in inflation in the country, forcing the Weimar Republic to print even more marks to pay off their (now even greater) debts (which typically needed to be paid in gold or foreign currency and thus could not be gamed by printing valueless marks). The vicious cycle quickly spiraled out of control. Prices rose to astronomical heights, on average

1.26 trillion times higher in 1922 than they were in 1913.[79] Inflation reached 182 billion percent per year. And despite the fact that the German government started printing billion mark notes, people still did not have enough cash to pay for even basic necessities: tales of Germans transporting wheelbarrows full of paper marks to the store to buy groceries became commonplace. In fact, wheelbarrows became so important to the economy that even their price spiraled out of control. One German had a wheelbarrow full of marks stolen and, to his surprise, discovered that the thief left the marks behind and took only the wheelbarrow.[80] Germany's subsequent economic collapse is often viewed as a contributing factor in the rise of the Nazis and World War II.[81]

Zimbabwe experienced similarly catastrophic currency volatility in the late 1990s and 2000s. During this period, President Robert Mugabe instituted a set of radical economic reforms, including the widespread expropriation of land owned by white Zimbabweans, that devastated the economy. With the domestic economy in ruins, and trust in the Zimbabwean government quickly disappearing, inflation ran rampant. At one point, the government began printing 100 trillion Zimbabwean dollar notes. By 2008, inflation had reached 79.6 billion percent on a monthly basis.[82] In response to the monetary chaos, much of the economy shifted to the black market, where American dollars became the primary medium of exchange. After decades of stagnation and government disorder, Zimbabwe eventually decided in 2015 to "demonetize," valuing the Zimbabwean currency at zero and turning foreign currencies (again, primarily American dollars) into the de facto and de jure national currency. An effort to create a new currency linked to the dollar, called a "zollar," has failed spectacularly. The country continues to struggle with the consequences as currency shortages plague the economy and hamper businesses and consumers alike.[83]

As both these cases show, money, the fundamental building block of modern-day economies, is not a perfect instrument. It has flaws. In both Weimar Germany and Zimbabwe, national currencies ceased to fulfill their intended functions in society. They made it harder, not easier, for people to buy things, to save for the future, and to value different goods. The resulting economic hardship, in both Weimar Germany and Zimbabwe, was extreme and shows how essential the money function is in our lives. Without money, countries fall apart. But the cases of Germany and Zimbabwe also demonstrate some of the flaws of current money systems, based as they are on centralized government control. Reckless, incompetent or self-interested governments can mint new currency at irresponsible or dangerous rates. Without a check on central banks' authority, the sky's the limit. Excess money supply can lead to rapid inflation and, more broadly, the dissolution of trust within economic communities.

This insight about money's fundamental weakness – that it is wholly controlled by central authorities, and yet depends on a fragile social belief that it will continue to be valuable in the future – gave Satoshi Nakamoto's soon-to-be-launched virtual currency, bitcoin, a key advantage. Because bitcoin, and the blockchain technology that underlay it, was decentralized, it promised to offer a hedge against reckless government, a way of preventing the excesses and corruptions of elite bankers and self-interested politicians. And when Nakamoto's white paper was released, it provided step-by-step instructions on how exactly this could be accomplished.

***

We will discuss the technical workings of the blockchain in more depth in the following Chapter, but it is important to note for now that Nakamoto designed his virtual currency to be a decentralized, democratic form of money. As Nakamoto put it in his first email on the subject, "I've been working on a new electronic cash system that's *fully peer-to-peer, with no trusted third party.*"[84] Thus, he viewed his core contribution as being the creation of a virtual currency that was run and maintained by its users. Governments and corporations would have little or no say over the operation of the currency. They would not create it. They would not maintain it. And they would not monitor it. It would be a fully decentralized system run by peers.[85]

Nakamoto's writings make it clear that he was keenly aware of the ignominious history of virtual currencies. In a post from February 2009, soon after the launch of bitcoin, Nakamoto mentioned Chaum's work and then went on to distinguish bitcoin from that effort.

> A lot of people automatically dismiss e-currency as a lost cause because of all the companies that failed since the 1990's. I hope it's obvious it was only the centrally controlled nature of those systems that doomed them. I think this is the first time we're trying a decentralized, non-trust-based system.[86]

Nakamoto worried that bitcoin would be viewed as just another promising but unrealistic effort to introduce a form of digital money. He thought that bitcoin's true innovation, and the one that would lead it to succeed where others had failed, was that his currency had no center. There was no final decision-maker or authoritative body that would decide disputes or determine the direction of the currency. Users would decide their own fate as a collective body.

From the cypherpunks' point of view, a decentralized virtual currency made perfect sense. The main problem in the age of the internet was that governments and corporations had become too powerful, to the point that they posed an existential threat to the privacy rights of individuals. In addition, governments and corporations were abusing their positions at the center of government and society, charging consumers with excessive fees and citizens with burdensome taxes. The answer to these kinds of problems was not more centralization, or centralization in the hands of someone else. That would just recreate the pathologies of abuse and rent-seeking in a different place. Instead, the answer lay in decentralization – the diffusion of power and decision-making from the few to the many. But until bitcoin came around, it was unclear how this could be done. Nakamoto provided the solution.

But what does it mean for a system to be decentralized? It is an awkward term, and one that is often rushed over without careful thinking. It does not mean that a system is imbalanced or top-heavy or prone to falling. It also does not mean that its center has been removed, donut-style. Instead, it is a system in which power is held by a large number of separate parties. Many different actors have a say in its workings. Power may take different forms, depending on the system. It might mean a formal right to vote on a body's actions, such as a shareholder's right to vote on whether a corporation will merge with another. It might also mean less formal influence over a decision-making process, such as a large family's discussion of where to go for vacation next year. It might also mean, simply, the inability of a single actor to dictate the policies of others, such as world order under a system of sovereign nation states. This is all rather abstract, so perhaps a few examples can be given, one in the realm of politics and one in the realm of economics.

Political regimes are, in a way, defined by how centralized or decentralized they are. In the *Republic*, for example, Plato identified five types of governments: tyranny (rule by one), democracy (rule by all), and three middle regimes of aristocracy (rule by the best), oligarchy (rule by the wealthy) and timocracy (rule by property holders). In the *Politics*, Aristotle divides the types of government into kingships (rule by one), aristocracies (rule by the few) and polities (rule by the many).[87] In the *Discourses*, Machiavelli identified four types of government: monarchy (rule by one), aristocracy (rule by the few), democracy (rule by all) and a republic (which balances elements of all the other three types).[88] All of these thinkers believed that the level of centralization within a political regime had important consequences for the nature of government. Plato, for example, argued that centralization determined not just a government's structure but also its substantive policies and, perhaps most importantly, the very character of its citizens. Democracies, he believed, were typified by an excess of freedom, where "a man may say and do what he likes," leading to a "life has neither law nor order; and [a] distracted existence he terms joy and bliss and freedom."[89] Tyrannies, on the other hand, were warlike, oppressive and prone to excessive taxation.[90] Aristotle was more circumspect, arguing that any of the three types of government (kingship, aristocracy and polity) could become corrupted into "perversions" of their ideal types, in which case they would devolve into tyrannies, oligarchies or democracies, respectively.[91] He did, however, recognize the possibility that decentralized democracies might reach better policies by allowing all to have a say in government. Even if the masses are flawed and have limited knowledge, Aristotle argued, "if the people are not utterly degraded, although individually they may be worse judges than those who have special knowledge, as a body they are as good or better."[92] Machiavelli, ever the cynic, believed that democracies inevitably decayed into anarchy, just as monarchies inevitably decayed into tyranny, because of the "close resemblance which the virtue [of each regime] bears to the vice," and that the only way to resolve these conflicts was to blend elements of both centralized and decentralized structures into the fabric of government.[93] But, regardless of the conclusions that these political philosophers reached about the desirability of particular levels of centralization, centralization itself was the key to understanding their arguments. In order to know how a government works, they believed, one must know where power lies.

Economies, too, can be defined by their levels of centralization. Today, we largely take for granted that capitalism is the way that economies work. Private companies buy and sell goods free of government dictates, and individuals are free to do the same. To be sure, they must abide by relevant rules and regulations, but the basic premise that they are free to pursue their own economic self-interest to the exclusion of others is unchallenged. Capitalism is a paradigmatic system of decentralization: instead of having a single government or entity decide how much corn to produce or how many cars to manufacture, we allow individual actors to make those decisions for themselves. In *The Wealth of Nations*, Adam Smith famously argued that capitalism acts as an "invisible hand" that guides people to efficient results. "By pursuing his own interest," Smith wrote, "he frequently promotes that of the society more effectually than when he really intends to promote it."[94] However, it is worth recognizing that, despite capitalism's seeming inevitability today, for much of the twentieth century it seemed anything but. The Soviet Union deployed a system of state controls and centralized decision-making that provided a rival to capitalism, and many thought that its method of centralized economic planning would soon overtake capitalism as the dominant structure for organizing economic affairs. The Soviet government's ability to intentionally direct productive resources towards important state goals (such as ramping up production of steel or heavy machinery) seemed like a competitive advantage over the disordered and haphazard system that prevailed in the West. Of course, these predictions turned out to be wrong; the Soviet system of state ownership and central planning was rife with inefficiencies and corruption, and it eventually crumbled. But today, China's system of close state oversight of the economy again has people questioning the effectiveness of a purely decentralized system of capitalism that rules so many economies around the globe. But again, the key question in these competing types of economy is where power lies. Is it in the hands of the few, or is it in the hands of the many?

But as may be clear from the examples above, it is rare to see a system that is fully centralized or fully decentralized. Instead, most systems combine elements of centralization with elements of decentralization. Even the most centralized governments nowadays tend to have a large absolute number of people involved in decision-making. Even the most decentralized ones give citizens a final say on only a small portion of the workings of government, with the rest being delegated to representatives and administrative bodies. The same goes for economies; even in Soviet Russia, where the government handed down decrees about production targets and resource priorities, many people were involved in the decision-making process, from the committees that set the priorities, to the factory managers that decided how to meet them. Similarly, in capitalist economies, individuals have some influence over the direction of markets, but large corporations ultimately make many of the most meaningful decisions about what products will be available and how much they cost. Thus, it is most useful to distinguish systems by the degree of decentralization that they exhibit, not the simple presence of centralization or decentralization. It is not an on-off switch.

Another complication is that what it means to have the final say on something is not always clear. In the United States, for example, we have a democratic system in which all citizens can vote in elections. In this sense, "We the People" have the final say over the direction of government. At the same time, however, once the citizens have exercised their power by voting in elections, they then suddenly cease to have control, handing over their powers and responsibilities to their representatives. As Seymour Lipset observed, "the distinctive and most valuable element of democracy is the formation of a political elite in the competitive struggle for the votes of a mainly passive electorate."[95] Presidents are elected to four-year terms, which means that once they have been sworn into office, they have forty-eight months to wield their powers and have the final say on any matters falling within the executive branch's realm without citizen input. Senators and Congressmen, similarly, have the final say on the matters within their power for the length of their term as well. Neither the executive nor the legislature has any obligation to go back to the citizens for approval on the decisions they take. Of course, eventually citizens will be able to judge their representatives and decide whether to reelect them, but this is a very indirect way of exercising power. And even if voters strongly disapprove of a president's or senator's decisions, they cannot directly force them to implement particular policies. Even if they elect a president that promises on the campaign trail to reverse the previous president's policies, there is no requirement that he live up to that promise once he is in office. Thus, the question of where power lies in the U.S. political system is a complicated one, and simply asserting that it is a centralized or a decentralized or a hybrid system does not end the discussion.

There are many potential advantages to creating a system that is decentralized. For one, political philosophers have argued that decentralization promotes freedom and equality. In democracies, citizens are free to vote how they like, and their votes all count equally. In capitalist economies, consumers are free to buy what they like, and their purchases in turn will influence what producers make in the future. Of course, the reality is more complex than this; even in a well-functioning democracy, powerful or wealthy citizens may exert a disproportionate influence over politicians and their policies, and even in capitalist societies powerful corporations may influence what consumers come to see and desire. But the basic principle – that decentralized systems promise to grant participants a greater degree of freedom and equality – is a plausible one. Decentralized systems also benefit from being able to aggregate the knowledge and ideas of the many. What better way to find out what policies a citizenry prefers than to ask them? What better way to determine the value of a good than to sell it in a free marketplace? Instead of relying on a central decision-maker to determine in his or her wisdom how a system should be run, decentralized systems rely on the collected wisdom of the masses. To the extent that these masses have better knowledge about relevant information, they should be able to come to more informed decisions than a single authority figure.

The disadvantages of decentralization are, in many ways, the flipside of its advantages. Because decentralized systems are dependent on the actions of many participants, they can be slow and indecisive in times of crisis. Where the decentralized decision-makers are unsophisticated or gullible, they may be prone to miscalculation. Populist leaders may make promises on the campaign trail that they could never fulfill in office. Advertisements might paint unrealistic portraits of the value of their products. In many ways, the drawbacks of decentralization track those that Plato ascribed to democracies. The system is anarchic and unruly, and rules are hard to enact and enforce:

> There is no compulsion to hold office in [a democratic] city, even if you're well qualified to hold office, nor to obey those who do hold office, if you don't feel like it, nor to go to war when the city is at war, nor to be at peace when everyone else is, unless peace is what you want. Then again, even if there's a law stopping

you holding office or being a member of a jury, there's nothing to stop you holding office and being a member of a jury anyway, if that's how the mood takes you. Isn't this, in the short term, a delightful and heaven-sent way of life?[96]

It is perhaps worth noting the response of Glaucon, Socrates' companion, to this: "It probably is, in the short term."[97] Another related problem is that, while decentralized systems have the advantage of reducing the risk that a few actors will oppress the many, it gives rise to another risk: that the many will oppress the few. This is a problem often referred to as the tyranny of the majority. If a majority of the populace or the economy or the network prefers an outcome that a small minority does not, they may be able to impose their preference over the objections of the minority. The fear of minority oppression in decentralized systems may be mitigated by, for example, restricting the kinds of actions the majority can take, or guaranteeing constitutional rights or subsidizing minority actors. But these mechanisms are imperfect and can never fully eliminate the threat of abuse from the majority.

We will return to the advantages and disadvantages of decentralization later, but for now, it is enough to point out that decentralization is not, on its own, an inherent good. There are benefits from decentralizing power, but there are also costs. Economists, philosophers and lawyers tend to justify arguments about decentralization by reference to other values, such as freedom, equality and efficiency, and these other values are often ambiguous and contestable. As long as we disagree about these other values, we will likely find it difficult to reach agreement about the relative merits of decentralization in any given system.

***

The blockchain, radical as it may be, thus has its roots in long-standing debates about the relative merits of centralization and decentralization. From Hobbes and Locke to the cypherpunks of Silicon Valley, this debate has raged for centuries. But new technologies and advancements have made the debate more relevant than ever. The internet provided new tools for governments and corporations to monitor their constituents, enabling intrusive forms of surveillance over ever-growing portions of people's lives. The cypherpunks, wary of these threats, sought to reduce the surveillance power of governments and corporations by creating a set of programs and methods for ensuring privacy, including strong cryptography, secure emails and virtual currencies. Their ultimate goal was to decentralize decision-making on the internet. Instead of concentrating power in the hands of a few giant entities, the cypherpunks sought to distribute authority to the masses, with individuals determining for themselves how the system should be run. But, despite their impressive achievements in the 1990s, the cypherpunks never managed to crack the puzzle of virtual money, where decentralization seemed, to put it mildly, difficult to achieve. This is where blockchain enters the picture. The technology was designed to decentralize currency, handing power over the monetary system to the individuals who used it. Just how Satoshi Nakamoto, the inventor of the system, accomplished this is the subject of the next Chapter.

2

The Technology of the Blockchain

But I believe that the practical principle in which safety resides, the ideal to be
kept in view, the standard by which to test all arrangements intended for overcoming the difficulty, may be conveyed in these words: the greatest dissemination
of power consistent with efficiency; but the greatest possible centralisation of
information, and diffusion of it from the centre.

John Stuart Mill, *On Liberty*

In March 2013, a bitcoin user noticed a strange occurrence on the network.
While his computer showed that the next update to bitcoin's ledger should
count as block 225,430, other computers were telling him that it should count
as block 225,431. When he pointed this out to other users, they too noticed the
discrepancy, with some computers showing block 225,430 as the next block,
and others 225,431. To an outsider, this might not have looked like much. Out
of two hundred thousand blocks, just a single one was out of place. But this
small difference was in fact a major problem. It was so major, in fact, that some
believed that it threatened the very existence of bitcoin. In order to understand
why, we need to begin to look at how the blockchain actually works.[1]

The blockchain, somewhat intuitively, is made up of blocks. Blocks are
effectively entries on bitcoin's ledger, tracing where bitcoins have been sent
and who owns them now. Bitcoin relies on this publicly available ledger, the
blockchain, as the true source of its value; in a very real sense, it *is* the
currency. The blockchain is a single document that records the entire history
of the currency, a chain of separate blocks linking entries together all the way
back to the first block ever created, a block that Nakamoto added when he first
ran the software and which has come to be known as the "genesis block." But
the key to the blockchain is that it is supposed to be immutable. If it is working
correctly, there should only be one version of it. If, on the other hand, the
blockchain could become confused, if the record of where bitcoins reside
could fail, then bitcoin would be worthless. The system was only as valuable as
the blockchain was trustworthy. A discrepancy in the network of the sort that

had just been discovered – what is referred to as a "fork" – was the community's worst nightmare. Somehow, the network had lost track of who owned what bitcoins.

"so??? yay accidental hardfork? :x," one user wrote on a bitcoin-developer chat site.

"Holy crap," wrote another.

"This seems bad?" asked one user.

"Seems is putting it lightly," concluded another.[2]

The blockchain community quickly descended into turmoil. Thousands of messages flooded the developer chat room. Some worried that a hacker had secretly added an extra block of transactions and gifted themselves free bitcoin. Others worried that someone was launching an all-out attack on the block-chain in order to gain control over it. Still others worried that the problem could permanently undermine bitcoin as a currency and blockchain as a technology.

After several hours of back and forth on chat sites, the developers soon identified the source of the problem. It was not, as many had feared, an intentional attack on the blockchain. There was no hacker out there inten-tionally creating splits in the chain. Instead, the problem stemmed from a mistake in the source code. Or, to be more precise, a conflict in the source code.

All participants in the blockchain must use special software to access the network. This software is regularly updated, much as Microsoft issues regular updates to its Word and PowerPoint programs. What the community quickly recognized was that the latest update to the software, version 0.8, introduced a set of rules that were not consistent with the rules contained in the previous version, version 0.7. Version 0.8 recognized certain blocks as valid that version 0.7 did not. Users running the latest bitcoin version would thus see different transactions than users running the older version.

This explained why some users were seeing one record of the blockchain, and other users were seeing another. Their bitcoin software disagreed about how the system should work. But now that the problem had been identified, a more difficult question arose. How could they solve it?

Gavin Andresen, the lead developer for bitcoin, had an idea. He recognized that this small irregularity had the potential to grow into a permanent split in the blockchain, and he knew that it was paramount that the problem be fixed as soon as possible. Every minute that passed without a fix meant another minute in which discrepancy would pile onto discrepancy, leading to more and more divergence between the two competing records. At the same time, he also recognized that there was only one true fix: the community had to agree on which version was better. He could not force it down their throats. And so he wrote to the community with a proposed solution.

"First rule of bitcoin: majority hashpower wins," Andresen wrote, referring to the computing power – or hashpower – that underlay the network.[3]

What Andresen meant by this was that all users should mutually agree to follow the direction that the majority of users decided upon, regardless of what that direction might be. If the community concluded that upgrading to the newest version 0.8 was preferable, then everyone (even the ones who preferred version 0.7) should do so. If, instead, the community decided that downgrading to the older version 0.7 was preferable, then everyone should do that, instead. It was not particularly important which version won out. What mattered was that all users agree on a single one. To Andresen, it was paramount that the majority position win the day and that the minority agree to accept it. If it did not, and instead users continued to use different versions based on their personal preferences, the split could become permanent. Andresen originally believed that version 0.8 had the support of the community, but when others started weighing in, a different position emerged. It soon became clear that the consensus opinion among participants was that everyone should downgrade to the older version, version 0.7.

This decision did not come without costs. Several of the largest companies in the sector had already upgraded to the latest version. Reverting back to the earlier version would mean that some of their profits from recent transactions – and that they had recorded on their version of the blockchain but that had not been recorded on competing versions – would simply disappear. This meant that they would lose real money. One estimate put the cost to them of reverting to version 0.7 at around six hundred coins, then worth approximately $26,000. Despite this, the companies agreed to revert back to the earlier version for the sake of the bitcoin network. They were willing to sacrifice for the greater good of the currency. And of course, even though they lost some money by agreeing to do so, it was not entirely selfless. They too had a financial interest in maintaining a single, stable bitcoin network, as they were earning profits from the growth of the virtual currency. They believed that it was much better to take a short-term loss than witness the destruction of bitcoin itself, a real possibility at the time.[4]

And so the blockchain technology weathered its first major test in the market. After being confronted with a problem, the community had come together to identify the source, propose solutions to it, and ultimately take timely action. The decentralized decision-making structure had functioned more or less as it was meant to. This was an important moment in the history of the blockchain and, for some, a cause for celebration.

But some thought otherwise.

The day after the crisis was resolved, one user wrote to the chat list with a question. "What would happen if Eleuthria wasn't available yesterday?" he asked, referring to one of the major miners who had agreed to revert back to the older version.

"We will never know," another user responded.

***

It is now time to talk about the inner workings of the blockchain. While a description of all the applications of the blockchain is beyond the scope of this Chapter, it is important to understand the fundamentals before we can analyze its unique system of decentralized decision-making. Because the blockchain was originally devised for the specific purpose of launching bitcoin, much of this discussion will focus on bitcoin itself. But it should be recognized that the blockchain technology itself is an inherently malleable tool, one that can be used for a vast array of purposes. And it has, in fact, been adapted by numerous industries to address their own particular purposes and needs, in areas as diverse as finance, shipping and consumer products.

Let us begin by providing a definition of what bitcoin is. Bitcoin, at its simplest, is a decentralized virtual currency that is maintained by its network of users. It is designed to be unhackable, anonymous and decentralized. It has no physical coin or bill associated with it; instead, it is represented entirely by entries on a public, digital document known as the blockchain. The blockchain itself is an immutable record of where bitcoins reside. When new transactions in the currency take place, they are recorded in blocks that are added to the blockchain, thereby updating the official record. Anyone can access and view this blockchain and, thus, verify that transactions have been accurately recorded. The blockchain maintains privacy by assigning users "addresses" that do not have names or identities attached to them.

What do we mean when we say that bitcoin, and the blockchain, are decentralized? In a technical sense, it is that the blockchain does not have a single, authoritative administrator. There is no bank or a government that is tasked with maintaining the official record of where bitcoins reside. Instead, all users maintain the records on their own computers and have the ability to make changes to them. As a result, a large number of actors have influence over important decisions regarding the blockchain. For example, anyone can download the software and start participating in the day-to-day running of the network, validating transactions and communicating with other nodes. They do not need to register with a central administrator, set up an account at a bank or even identify themselves. They can just participate, no strings attached.

But, just as with democracy or capitalism, the degree of decentralization within the blockchain can be overstated. For starters, not all participants have an equal say in how the blockchain is run. While it is true that any computer can become a node and even start mining for new blocks in the system, the influence of a node is heavily dependent on its computing power. As will be described further in the next Chapter, the only way to add information to the blockchain is by getting your computer to solve difficult mathematical problems. Over time, these problems have become more difficult, to the point that today only computers with specialized hardware can have a realistic shot at solving them. Your average MacBook will have little to no chance of ever creating a new block, and thus most people, most of the time, will have little or no say in the actual governance of the blockchain. In effect, some votes count more than others. The problem has become so acute that, at one point in 2018, one company controlled 42 percent of all computing power on the bitcoin network, meaning that a single miner was dangerously close to taking majority control over the virtual currency.[5] Thus, bitcoin's system of decentralization is not written in stone. There is nothing in the code that requires computing power to be distributed equally among users, or even among computers. It is very much dependent on facts in the real world.

Another important source of centralization with the blockchain is the software itself. In order to be able to communicate with others in the network, users must download bitcoin software, known as Bitcoin Core. This software is freely available through the website bitcoin.org and is open-source, meaning that it can be modified by users. The open-source nature of the software lends a degree of decentralization to the system, as anyone can access or modify the software. But the software itself, the one that is available at bitcoin.org, is maintained and revised by a small group of developers. These developers are the only people who have "commit" authority to make changes to the software found on bitcoin.org. Outside programmers can request changes to the bitcoin software through something known as a Bitcoin Improvement Proposal, but the developers retain full discretion about whether these changes are made. To be sure, there is nothing to prevent people from creating variants of the Bitcoin Core software and trying to convince others that their version is better. But, as a practical matter, most users run the basic software provided by bitcoin.org. Thus, the developer team is a key source of centralization within the bitcoin ecosystem.[6]

So bitcoin was designed to provide an unhackable, anonymous and decentralized currency that could be used in lieu of money. In order to do this, though, bitcoin had three basic problems it had to solve. First, it had to ensure that its system of digital money was secure. We would not want hackers to be able to come in, steal people's money and get away with it. If a virtual currency is to succeed, its users must be confident that it is reasonably safe and secure to use. Second, it had to ensure that people who used it could remain anonymous. If bitcoin users could be readily identified by others, then its promise of privacy would fail. Third, bitcoin had to achieve all of these goals in a way that did not require a central authority. Instead, it had to rely on a decentralized system that allowed a large number of actors to participate in governance. Its core benefit, after all, was that it would take power out of the hands of central authorities, such as governments and banks, and place it in the hands of the many.

Even a cursory glance at these three requirements – security, anonymity and decentralization – should alert readers to the fact that there are serious tensions within the bitcoin system itself. If we want a system that is anonymous, it may be difficult to ensure that it is also fully secure. If all transactions in the currency occur entirely over the computer, and everyone using the currency is anonymous, it may be easier for fraudsters and criminals to infiltrate the system and steal money. One reason why it is so hard to rob a bank in the real world is that robbers have lots of identifiable features – their faces may be caught on camera, their fingerprints may be left on counters and their license plates may be registered with the state. A system that promises complete anonymity aims to hide this kind of information, and thus may as a result make it easier for thieves to hide. There is also a tension between decentralization and anonymity. It is relatively simple to keep people's identities secret when there is just one central authority that has to know their identities. A bank has to know the identity of the owner of a bank account – in order to know where to deposit funds, who can withdraw money, who can make changes to the account, etc. – but no one else does. The rest of the world can remain blissfully ignorant of how much money resides in everyone else's bank account. But if we want a decentralized system, where many people are cooperating in maintaining the money system, it is much harder to keep people's identities secret. More people have to be involved, and thus more people may be able to identify who owns what bank accounts. Bitcoin has devised a number of strategies to address these concerns, but scholars and policy-makers disagree about its success in doing so.

In order to understand how these various elements work together, it may be easiest to walk through a hypothetical transaction and see the various steps involved.[7] The blockchain is an intricately designed puzzle, with each puzzle piece fitting into and interacting with multiple other pieces. Understanding one piece of the puzzle requires us to understand other pieces as well. By looking at a hypothetical transaction in which all of the pieces come into play, we can examine the wider mosaic of the system.

***

For our hypothetical, we will use two characters, Hobbes and Locke (cryptographers, it should be noted, prefer to use Alice and Bob as their characters, but we don't need to be so bland here). Let us imagine that Hobbes and Locke are students at Oxford. One day, they meet up for a cup of coffee. Hobbes happens to bring with him a copy of a new book he is writing on political philosophy, which he has tentatively titled *Leviathan*. Locke, after perusing the first few chapters, decides that he would like to buy the book from Hobbes. Locke does not have cash on him, so he offers to pay for the book using bitcoin. Hobbes agrees, and they settle on a price of one bitcoin. How does Locke go about making the payment?

The first step to know is that bitcoin, instead of using people's real names, assigns people addresses. These addresses are, for most intents and purposes, anonymous. They consist of long strings of numbers and letters that have no connection to a person's real-life identity. For example, one real address is 18BUZZSmW1yZ6g88CYn6wmuUdGnTpjY6aT. Anyone who wants to use bitcoin can generate an address themselves simply by downloading the bitcoin software for free on the internet and then running it on their computer. In fact, a person can generate as many addresses for themselves as they like, if they so wish. There is no need to stop at one. The addresses are public. Everyone can see them. And not only can they see them, they can also see what is inside them. In other words, if Hobbes wants to check how many bitcoins are owned by address 18BUZZSmW1yZ6g88CYn6wmuUdGnTpjY6aT, he can do so. This is why it is tremendously important that the public addresses are random. If they were not random, and if instead information about their real owners were available (such as at what time they were created or where), someone might be able to identify the true, real-life owner of a bitcoin address and then, perhaps, exploit that knowledge to their advantage. Thus, the fact that public addresses are anonymous is an essential part of bitcoin's method for maintaining privacy on the network. Individuals are known to others on the network only through their anonymous public addresses.

So Locke needs to send bitcoin from his public address to Hobbes' public address. In order to do this, he must know Hobbes' address (Hobbes can simply tell him this, or perhaps write it down on a sheet of paper), but he also needs to prove that he really is the true owner of his own address. After all, his public address is completely anonymous; we can see the string of numbers and letters, but we can't know from that string alone whether Locke is the person who owns it. Locke can of course tell Hobbes that he owns a particular address, but Hobbes will have no way of knowing, simply by looking at the address, whether Locke is telling the truth. Thus, the fact that public addresses are not identifiably linked to real-life individuals is a potential problem from the perspective of security. A robber might try to impersonate someone else in order to spend their money. And since public addresses are public – everyone can see them, and everyone can see what is in them – there is a real incentive for people to find wealthy addresses and try to use those addresses to send money to themselves. If Locke were unscrupulous, he might simply look up the public address that has the most bitcoin in it and then tell Hobbes that he owns all those bitcoins. The bitcoin system, needless to say, cannot allow for this kind of end around. Instead, Locke needs to prove that he owns the bitcoins in the public address.

Of course, not just any means of authentication will work. Bitcoin, recall, also needs to protect people's privacy, so it needs to let Locke prove that he owns the bitcoins in his address without somehow giving up his real-life identity to the rest of the world. It would not be great, from a privacy stand-point, if every time that Locke wanted to spend his bitcoin, he had to announce to the world, "Hey everybody, I own public address 18BUZZSmW1yZ6g88CYn6wmuUdGnTpjY6aT and here is my driver's license to prove it." Rather, Locke needs a way to assure the bitcoin community that the account really belongs to him without revealing who he in fact is.

This is where things get tricky. When Locke first generated his public address using the bitcoin software, he also generated something called a private key. This key, unlike the address associated with it, is private – it is not known by anyone else on the network. It is a bit like a password. It can be used to gain access to, and thus spend, bitcoins contained in the associated public address. But again, Locke cannot simply send his private key to the rest of the network – that would expose his account to theft. It would be like saying, "Hey everybody, I own public address 18BUZZSmW1yZ6g88CYn6wmuUdGnTpjY6aT and here is the password to prove it." Instead, Locke has to find a way to prove to the network that he owns the coins without also allowing the network to figure out what his password is. Or, in the terminology of the industry, Locke needs to find a way to "sign" his transaction in such a way as to allow others to recognize the signature as legitimate while not simultaneously exposing his private key.

Locke does so using something called a hash function. Hash functions are a fundamental concept in computer science, and they pop up in lots of places within the blockchain ecosystem, so it is worthwhile to take some time familiarizing ourselves with them. A hash function is a method for turning inputs of varying length and size into outputs of a single size. In other words, it transforms complex information into standardized, simple information. This is useful for any number of reasons, from storing information to finding information to, more importantly for our purposes, encrypting information. I could, for example, have a hash function that changed English language sentences into a short numerical format. The function might have the rule that any sentence with an even number of letters becomes 0 and any sentence with an odd number of letters becomes 1. Using this function, I could hash the sentence, "The life of man is solitary poor nasty brutish and short" into 0. This hash function would be very good at obscuring the original information that was contained in the sentence: if I knew the hash of the sentence was 0, I would have a very difficult time reverse engineering the original sentence itself. This property of cryptographic hash functions is referred to as "hiding": the hash, or output of the hash function, effectively hides the original input from being found by observers of the hash.

But my rudimentary 0 or 1 hash function would not be particularly good at distinguishing sentences from one another. Lots of different sentences have an even number of letters, and lots of different sentences have an odd number of letters. Thus, if I hash two sentences, there is a high likelihood that their outputs will be the same (in fact, the probability is likely close to 50 percent since there are only two possible outputs, 0 or 1). If an impartial observer knows that the hash of a sentence is 0, but does not know the sentence itself, it would be impossible for that person to determine which sentence had been used to create the hash. If somebody came along and said that, instead of "The life of man is solitary poor nasty brutish and short," I had actually hashed the sentence "The life of man is social rich pleasant noble and long," there would be no way of knowing who was correct. Both of these sentences have the same hash of 0, and both are equally plausible inputs (but don't tell that to Hobbes!). This feature of my 0 or 1 hash function is a problem from a cryptographic standpoint. It makes it trivially easy for bad actors to take advantage of ambiguity in the hash output to wreak havoc; they might try to impersonate others, or falsify documents or engage in any number of other malicious activities. A good cryptographic hash function, thus, must make it very difficult to find two inputs that have the same hash.[8] This is a property of hash functions that is referred to as "collision resistance": the hashes for different inputs must coincide, or collide, very rarely.

One hash function that is good at both hiding and collision resistance is a function known as SHA-256 (SHA stands for secure hash algorithm), and it also happens to be the hash function that bitcoin uses. The National Security

Agency designed SHA-256 in 2001 to serve as a secure hash function for government use, but it was later published publicly by the National Institute of Standards and Technology. It is thus available to the private sector and has become widely used in the information security world.[9] (As a side note, the NSA's involvement in the creation of this popular cryptographic standard has led to some suspicion about its security, with some suggesting that the NSA might have inserted a back door that would allow it to break the encryption, but this view has not been widely accepted.) The hash function SHA-256 converts inputs of any length into outputs of a set string of sixty-four letters and numbers, anything from 0 to 9 and A to Z. It is designed to make it simple for anyone to check that a given hash output really was generated from a purported input. In fact, any of a number of online hash generators will do this for you, for free, in a matter of milliseconds. But – and this is important – it is nearly impossible to reverse engineer the original input from the hash, or output, if the only thing you know is the hash itself. For example, using SHA-256, I can convert my message "The life of man is solitary poor nasty brutish and short" into:

774F25C760FBC93DD398064F38FF0F729F978B4E30303BDE864B124A3-F411C72

Looking at this hash, I would have no way of knowing what the original input was. There is no apparent connection between the hash and the original message. In fact, not only is there no apparent connection, it is practically impossible for even the most powerful computers on earth to reverse engineer the original message from just the hash itself.

One important consequence of this property of the SHA-256 hash function is that it is tremendously sensitive to even small changes in the underlying data. If, for example, I change the sentence "The life of man is solitary poor nasty brutish and short" to "The life of man is solitary poore nasty brutish and short," adding an "e" to the end of "poor," as it was spelled in Hobbes' original *Leviathan*, the resulting hash changes dramatically. Instead of receiving the hash:

774F25C760FBC93DD398064F38FF0F729F978B4E30303BDE864B124A3-F411C72,

I receive the hash:

6580C437CE6C23F06EB09D3D90CFA6099E90A9AA6611FA47526CAC599-CDB5306.

Again, these two outputs have no perceivable connection, even though the two sentences used to generate them are so similar that their only difference is one letter. This is attractive from a cryptologist's standpoint because it makes it very hard for outside observers to determine the contents of a message just by looking at its hash. But, just as importantly, once an outside observer knows the original message, they can very easily check that it really was used to create the hash.

Returning to the hypothetical, Locke can use these features of hashes to create a digital signature that proves he owns the bitcoins he wants to spend. He does so by taking his message (that is, "send 1 bitcoin from my public address to Hobbes' public address"), combining it with his private key and running it through a hash function (along with another complicated algorithm called an Elliptic Curve Digital Signature Algorithm, or ECDSA). The result of these calculations is known as a digital signature. Locke takes this digital signature and signs his message with it as proof that he owns the bitcoins in question and really does want to send them to Hobbes. Anyone receiving the digital signature can see that he owns the bitcoins, but they cannot work backwards from the digital signature to figure out what his private key is.

You might be asking yourself how someone can check that the digital signature was generated from Locke's private key without also knowing what the private key actually is. After all, in order to check that a hash was generated from a sentence, normally a third party has to know what the sentence was. The answer to this question involves a cryptographic concept known as public key cryptography. Public key cryptography is a kind of asymmetric cryptography, but in order to understand what asymmetric cryptography means, it is probably easiest to start with symmetric cryptography. Symmetric cryptography is a system in which a single key encrypts and decrypts information. This is how most real-world security measures work: we have a safe filled with valuable documents or money, and we can lock it and unlock it with one and only one key.

But suppose you had a safe with two different keys: when one was used to lock the safe, the other was needed to unlock it, and vice versa? In the 1970s, the community of Cold War codebreakers at academic and government institutions showed that this was not just an odd thought experiment but an idea that would create invaluable capabilities in an untrustworthy world. Specifically, it would enable a mechanism for both (1) an unforgeable signature and (2) an "envelope" that was impossible to peer into. To see how the unforgeable signature works, assume that the owner of the safe puts something in it, locks it with his private key, and then stores the other key on a rack that is available to the public. The act of locking the safe with his private key is taken as the owner's signature, unique and doable only by him. Later, should someone want to check what the owner had put into the safe, they need only retrieve the public key from the rack and use it to unlock the safe. If the new safe opens with the public key, then we know that the owner put it in there. If not, then the safe was not secured with the private key, and thus the contents should be considered suspect. But this system also works in reverse. Suppose that someone wants to send something (say, valuable documents) to the owner of the safe and wants to make sure that no one else can see what the documents contain. The sender can simply retrieve the public key from the rack, put the documents in the safe, and then use the public key to lock the safe. In an asymmetric cryptosystem, the safe can then be opened only with the owner's private key.

Beyond being an interesting thought experiment, and even a promising idea, a digital form of this asymmetric lock-and-key system was developed using some of the most advanced mathematics known to computer scientists. Many of its developers (including Whitfield Diffie, Martin Hellman, Michael Rabin, Ronald Rivest, Adi Shamir and Leonard Adleman) would win Turing Awards for their work in this field. Multibillion-dollar companies operate today that forge the digital keys and provide the digital rack on which to hang public keys. Public key cryptography is still considered one of the most important tools for protecting information and identity in the modern world.[10]

Public key cryptography, thus, gives Locke the ability to prove to the world that he owns the public address in question (and thus the bitcoins that reside in it) without exposing his real-world identity (he simply signs his message with his private key, and the community can confirm this using his public key or address). The next step is for Locke to broadcast his message, along with his digital signature, to the rest of the system. Remember that bitcoin is a decentralized system, one that is maintained by users' computers around the world. In order for other users to know that Locke wants to send a bitcoin to Hobbes, they first have to hear about it somehow. Thus, Locke needs to broadcast the information in a message to other "nodes" on the network. Nodes are simply computers that are running the bitcoin software, and they serve as connections to the rest of the network – they send and receive information about bitcoin transactions to and from other nodes. Not all nodes are connected, though, and so the nodes that receive Locke's message must then transmit it along to other nodes. The method by which these messages are transmitted from one node to another is called a "gossip proto-col," with the message zipping around the globe like supersonic gossip.[11]

In addition to spreading word of Locke's transaction to other parts of the network, nodes also perform another important function: they check to make sure that the transaction is a valid one. "Valid" here has a very specific mean-ing. The nodes are not plumbing the intent of the parties to determine whether the transaction accords with some real-world agreement. They are not calling Locke to ask if he really meant to send bitcoin to Hobbes or if he meant to send a different amount. Instead, they are checking to make sure the transaction meets the formal requirements of the bitcoin code. To do this, they take Locke's public address and confirm that the digital signature that accompanied Locke's message really was generated by Locke from the private key that belongs to the public address. If it does, then they know that Locke owns the public address from which he wants to send coins. They do not, after all, want someone else to fool them into believing that the message is from Locke, when it is really coming from someone seeking to steal Locke's money. The nodes also check to make sure that Locke's public address really does have the bitcoins that he wants to spend. Just as they do not want someone else to spend Locke's coins, they also would not want Locke to be able to spend coins that he does not own, or that he has already spent (something called a "double spend" attempt, a notoriously tricky problem in virtual currencies). Once the nodes have performed both these checks and the results come back fine, they know that the transaction is valid. If, instead, the calculations do not match up (that is, the private key that Locke used to generate his signature is not connected with the public address he claimed to own, or if the public address does not contain the bitcoins he claimed it contained), then the transaction is considered invalid and the nodes reject it. In fact, the "gossip protocol" mentioned earlier prevents nodes from forwarding along transactions that are invalid. Thus, if a node receives a message from Locke that tries to spend bitcoins that he does not own, it will simply ignore it and not broadcast it to other nodes in the system.[12]

One might imagine a system that stopped here: Locke has sent out his message to the rest of the bitcoin ecosystem, they know that he owns the bitcoins in question, and they know that he wants to send them to Hobbes. The nodes could simply keep track of all these transactions as they take place, and this might work as a currency. But bitcoin adds one last step in the process. Just as it is important for everyone to hear about transactions, it is also important that everyone has a single definitive version of all these transactions. The bitcoin system, after all, is decentralized. This means that there is no single authoritative body to decide who owns what. But if everyone can decide for themselves where bitcoins reside, there might be disagreement between various nodes about the state of the system. So bitcoin adds one last piece to the puzzle. This piece is the blockchain.

The next step for Locke's transaction is for it to be recorded on the block-chain. As mentioned earlier, all transactions in bitcoin are recorded on a publicly available ledger known as the blockchain. The blockchain is effectively a long list of addresses and transactions. It records every time that bitcoins are transferred from one address to another. This list is publicly available, but also anonymous, with individuals owning bitcoin through public addresses that look like long strings of random letters and numbers. But the transactions on the blockchain are in fact not listed individually – this would be long and cumbersome. Instead, they are sorted into groups, or "blocks," each of which contains multiple transactions.[13] Grouping the blockchain into blocks makes the entire ledger shorter and thus easier to store – an important feature given that every node has to download the entire blockchain for the system to work.[14]

Each block on the blockchain contains two things: first, a reference to the previous block in the chain, showing how the blockchain looked before new transactions were added; and second, a reference to the new transactions themselves, showing how the blockchain will look after the new transactions have been added. Each of these is done using, you guessed it, a hash function. The reference to the previous block in the chain is a hash of the previous block, and the reference to the new transactions is a hash of all the information contained in the new transactions. This first hash is what makes the blockchain a chain: it connects each block to the previous block, all the way back to the first block ever created (the "genesis block," mined by Satoshi Nakamoto on January 3, 2009).[15]

This is a nifty feature of hash functions: because they can be used to transform *any* input into a hash of fixed length, they can also be used to transform hashes themselves into new hashes. So, I could hash "The life of man is solitary poor nasty brutish and short" into:

774F25C760FBC93DD398064F38FF0F729F978B4E30303BDE864B124A3-F411C72,

and I could hash "The life of man is social rich pleasant noble and long" into:

A09AF95CA63F8A5F9D39FE8D5A1D621162A84CB5099A909E-C4235112685C1154,

and then I could take both those hashes and hash them into the combined:

B041EA2274B61C1BC3CBFA2F865928DA5968F42D68DE7E98693D28E3-F1E3D4FA.

I would then have a single hash that incorporated all the information from both of the previous hashes, which in turn incorporated all the information from the original sentences. I would have a chain that linked every step to every step before it.

Why would I want to do this? The answer is simple: it makes the chain remarkably tamper-proof. If someone wanted to go back into the blockchain to, say, make it look like they had more bitcoins than they really had, not only would they have to change the hash of the block where this fictional transaction supposedly took place, they would also have to change the hash of every other block that came afterwards. After all, each block contains the hash of the previous block, and thus any change, even of the smallest amount, has a waterfall effect on all the other blocks. The bad actor would, thus, have to calculate a new hash for every single block that had ever been added to the blockchain.

A determined thief might still be able to do all this if it were not for one last feature of the blockchain system called proof of work. Recognizing that it was essential to make it prohibitively expensive to launch these types of attacks on bitcoin, Nakamoto added a feature that intentionally introduced a certain amount of difficulty into the process of creating blocks. Rather than simply allowing any node to create a new block by gathering new transactions and hashing them all together, he created a rule that nodes would have to solve difficult mathematical problems before their proposed blocks could be accepted. In other words, nodes would have to prove that they performed a certain amount of work (or at least that their computers did) before their proposed blocks would be added. By making it difficult to create new blocks, this proof-of-work system renders the blockchain resistant to manipulation.

With our knowledge of hash functions, we can now understand how this proof-of-work system works. In order to create a block, nodes must find a number (referred to as a nonce) that, when combined with the hash of the previous block and the new transactions, hashes to a very specific output. In particular, the node must find an input that hashes to an output that is lower than a certain target value. The target value might, for example, be a hash that is equal to or lower than:

OOOOOOOOOOOOOOOOOOO1OOOOOOOOOOOOOOOOOOOOOOOOOOOOOOOOOOOOOOOOOOOOOOOOO.

This is very difficult to do. Remember that the SHA-256 hash function is infeasible to reverse engineer: one cannot determine the original message from looking at the hash. One consequence of this is that one also cannot know ahead of time what input will generate a given hash, or even a hash that falls within a range. So how do nodes go about finding an input that has a hash value equal to or lower than:

OOOOOOOOOOOOOOOOOOO1OOOOOOOOOOOOOOOOOOOOOOOOOOOOOOOOOOOOOOOOOOOOOOOOO?

They have to guess! Over and over and over again. Eventually, given enough time and enough guesses, they should randomly look into finding an input that works.

The process of finding a valid block is thus quite difficult and, what is more, the difficulty increases over time. Recognizing that computers would likely get better at solving proof-of-work problems as their processing speed improved and new nodes entered the network, Nakamoto hard-coded into the bitcoin software a method for increasing the difficulty of the calculations over time. The goal was to ensure that new blocks would be added at roughly the same rate over time, regardless of how much computing power (or "hash" power) is used to find new blocks. In order to accomplish this, the bitcoin software periodically adjusts the difficulty of the hash function depending on how quickly miners are finding new blocks. So, if new computing power is added to the network, and blocks are suddenly being added twice as fast, the software will change the difficulty of the hash function so that block creation will slow down to the preferred rate. The preferred rate for bitcoin is ten minutes per block, meaning that the difficulty of the hash problem is constantly being adjusted to ensure that, regardless of how much computer power is being thrown at it, computers will only find new blocks every ten minutes.

Thus, the process of finding (or "mining") new blocks is hard. It is also expensive. In order to create new blocks, miners must run powerful computing systems at high speeds for long periods of time. At the end of 2015, in order to find a valid block, a computer would have had to make, on average, 2^{68} – or around 300,000,000,000,000,000,000 – guesses.[16] That is a mind-bogglingly large number of guesses. If it took a human one second to make a guess, and you took the entire population of the world and tasked them with doing nothing but making guesses, it would take them more than 1,000 years to make that many guesses. As one can imagine, performing these calculations on a computer is much faster, but it is still hard. It also requires significant amounts of electricity. One study found that bitcoin mining was consuming around the amount of electricity needed to power the entire country of Ireland.[17] Another concluded that executing a single bitcoin transaction required the same amount of energy as a typical household in the Netherlands uses in a month.[18] In order to perform these hashing operations more quickly, bitcoin miners have invented specialized computer chips that are optimized for making these kinds of guesses. These application-specific integrated circuit chips, or ASICs, are costly to buy and also to maintain. And with the constantly increasing level of difficulty, ASICs quickly become outdated and must be traded in for newer, faster ones. All of this means that being a miner is expensive.

Let's take a step back here for a moment. On a certain level, all of this work and effort seems quite pointless. Locke just wants to send some money to Hobbes so that he can have his book. Why should this require the world's fastest computers to run on overdrive for days on end just to solve a pointless math equation? This critique is even more pointed if one compares the use of bitcoin in the real world with the amount of computing power applied to bitcoin in the mining world. In March of 2018, the bitcoin network was handling between two and three transactions per second. This is a small number, particularly compared with the number of transactions that credit card companies handle per second, but it still adds up to a sizable number of annual transactions, approximately seventy-three million per year. At the same time, however, miners were performing approximately twenty-six quintillion hashing operations every second. The proportion is shocking. In order to handle three transactions, the bitcoin network was running hashing equations twenty-six quintillion times.[19] To put it mildly, this seems odd.

Why would a miner go through the expensive process of mining new blocks, and performing all these calculations, just to process a few transactions? The answer is simple: they get paid to do so, through something called the coinbase transaction. Any miner that creates a new block is rewarded for their work with newly created bitcoins. In addition to all the pending transactions that the miner needs to include in the block, the miner can also add one additional transaction, called the coinbase transaction. Whereas all the other transactions in a block must specify where the bitcoins that are being sent came from, the coinbase transaction has no source transaction. It simply appears out of thin air. This is because the bitcoins awarded to the miner are newly created – they have no history, they have never been spent and they do not reside in anyone's public address. In fact, the coinbase transaction is the only way that new bitcoins can be created. Initially, the reward for creating a new block was fifty bitcoins, but the reward automatically decreases over time, halving every four years or so. At the time of the writing of this book, 12.5 bitcoins were being issued for each new block. Eventually, once the total number of bitcoins in circulation has reached twenty-one million, the issuance of new bitcoins will cease entirely.[20] Thus, there is a hard cap on the amount of bitcoin that will ever be issued. Once twenty-one million bitcoins have been created, no new bitcoins will be issued. This provides users with some certainty that the value of their bitcoins will not be inflated away, as they know the expected rate of growth in the currency, as well as the maximum amount of currency that can ever exist. No meddling central government can decide to print new bitcoin in order to pay off debts, or fund wars or enrich itself. Bitcoin is capped.

So Locke has agreed to buy Hobbes' book using bitcoin, he has broadcast this transaction to the bitcoin network, he has signed this message with his cryptographically secure digital signature, participating nodes have verified the validity of this transaction and spread it through the rest of the network, and a miner has grouped his transaction into a block to be added to the blockchain. Does Locke now know that the transaction is complete? Not quite. The final step is for the miner that found the block to broadcast this block to the rest of the network. Much as Locke had to broadcast word of his transaction to the bitcoin ecosystem, so too does the miner have to broadcast word of his block to the ecosystem. And just as nodes check to make sure that Locke's transaction was valid under the rules of the system, so too do nodes check to make sure that the block is valid under the rules of the system. Once they have done that, they will then add it to their copies of the blockchain.

One potential wrinkle here is that many miners are competing to find new blocks. There is thus a chance that two miners will find valid blocks at the same time and simultaneously send their blocks out to the network. These two blocks might, in fact, contain different transactions; there are often a number of pending transactions that miners can choose to include in their blocks, and blocks have a limited size.[21] Both of the blocks could still be valid under the rules of the system. The question then becomes which one wins. This question is particularly important because the blocks could potentially contain conflicting transactions. For example, Locke might send out one transaction telling the network to send his bitcoin to Hobbes, but he might then try to send out a different transaction telling the network to instead send the same bitcoin to a different bookseller to buy a different book. This is known as a double-spend attack – Locke is trying to spend his bitcoins twice. Because the network does not know in the abstract which one of these transactions is the true one, but it does know that Locke owns only one bitcoin, if Hobbes hands over his book, and so does the other bookseller, only one of them can receive payment.

Nodes have two protocols to help resolve this problem. The first is that they always extend the longest valid blockchain. This means that the blockchain that has the longest history will win, even if a miner finds an otherwise perfectly valid block for a slightly shorter copy of the blockchain. This policy helps ensure that the blockchain is effectively immutable; if someone tries to go back and reverse a transaction that occurred in the previous block by mining a different block, they will not be able to convince other nodes that their version of the blockchain is correct. The second protocol that nodes follow when confronted with two valid blocks is to accept the block that they heard about first.[22] This protocol does not perfectly resolve the problem, because some nodes might have heard about Block A first, while other nodes might have heard about Block B first (it takes some time for messages to propagate through the network). Thus, there is some uncertainty about which block is the true block in the blockchain. But this uncertainty will be reduced when the next block comes around. Some miners heard about Block A first, and started trying to find a block that would extend Block A. Some miners heard about Block B first, and started trying to find a block that would extend Block B. One of these groups will find a block first, and then send out their proposed block to the network. *Their* version of the blockchain will now be longer than the version being mined by the other group, and so nodes will switch to start mining on top of the longer version. The block that lost out is known as an "orphaned block" and will not be included in the blockchain. Over time, consensus should develop about the state of the blockchain, and this consensus will become stronger and stronger as blocks are continually added on top of previous blocks. Thus, once Hobbes has seen that Locke's transaction has been added to the blockchain and sufficient time has passed for additional blocks to be added on top of that block, he can be reasonably sure that the payment is irreversible. Locke cannot now go back and double-spend the coins. Hobbes can hand over his copy of *Leviathan* to Locke, and they can both go on with their day.

* * *

So that is how bitcoin works. As one can see, it is an intricate process, one in which each step is closely linked with the others. It is impossible to understand how bitcoins are created without also understanding how bitcoins are used. It is impossible to understand how bitcoins are used without also understanding how bitcoins are stored. And it is impossible to understand how bitcoins are stored without also understanding how bitcoins are created.

But now that we have walked through how a bitcoin transaction takes place, we can step back and survey the system as a whole. New bitcoins are created by miners who perform the hard work of verifying transactions and maintaining the blockchain. Bitcoins are used by broadcasting secure messages to the network about the details of the transaction and its place in the blockchain. And bitcoins are stored in public addresses listed on the blockchain.

All of these features are driven by blockchain's unique system of decentralization. If there were a single authoritative decision-maker in the structure, we would not need to incentivize miners to maintain the system, or broadcast transactions to other nodes or even mask identities. The central authority, whether it be a bank or a corporation or a government, would handle these things. But with the blockchain there is no single entity that creates new currency (the software simply has a rule that new bitcoins are awarded to miners that add blocks to the blockchain); there is no single entity that maintains the system (the nodes and miners that observe and record transactions perform the hard work of executing transactions); and there is no single entity that has authority over the blockchain's ledger itself (the nodes that maintain copies of the blockchain perform this service through consensus).

Perhaps the most startling feature of this decentralized system is that even the number of bitcoins that a person owns is subject to the consensus of the community. If one day the bitcoin network decides that Locke does not own the bitcoins in his address, then he will cease owning them. If the network decides that a different version of the blockchain, in which a different address owns the bitcoins in question, is preferable, then that different version becomes the definitive record. As may be clear by now, the blockchain has a very different concept of ownership than most people have in mind when they think about owning a bank account.

At the center of all this intricate system is the blockchain. The blockchain, at its heart, is a method for disseminating knowledge. It is a public record of information, stored and maintained through a decentralized system of peers, and secured by sophisticated cryptographical algorithms. It is thus open to all, democratically run and protected from intrusion. It is in many ways the culmination of what the cypherpunks sought for so many years to accomplish.

It turns out that these features of the blockchain are useful in any number of other areas, and not just for use as a virtual currency. The technology of blockchain can be used to store any kind of information, from shipping records to financial instruments to contracts. The technology is flexible enough to handle these sorts of applications, and its promise of immutable, secure records that can be viewed by all has drawn heavy interest, and investment, from banks, corporations and governments. The blockchain, like other technologies, is a tool. Its uses are limited only by the decisions of its users. For that reason, if we are to understand the blockchain, we must examine not just how it is designed but also how it is being used. It is to that question that we turn in the next Chapter.

3

Blockchain in the World

The problem is to find a form of association which will defend and protect with the whole common force the person and goods of each associate, and in which each, while uniting himself with all, may still obey himself alone, and remain as free as before.

Jean Jacques Rousseau, *The Social Contract*

In 2016, Christoph Jentzsch had a radical idea. If bitcoin could revolutionize money, why couldn't it do the same for business? If it were possible to decentralize the creation of currency, certainly it would be possible to decentralize corporations as well. Instead of putting corporate decision-making in the hands of wealthy executives and boards of directors, who too often used their power to enrich themselves at the expense of shareholders, a decentralized corporation could be run immediately and directly by its true stakeholders, the owners themselves. The blockchain could introduce the biggest change in the gears of capitalism since the invention of the joint-stock company.[1]

Jentzsch, a thirty-four-year-old German with a background in theoretical physics, quickly went to work fleshing out the details. The key, he realized, was to find a way to program corporate governance rules into the blockchain. In other words, just as bitcoin has certain rules about how and when owners have the right to send bitcoins to others, a decentralized corporation might have rules about how and when the corporation would take action, such as purchasing assets, distributing dividends or investing in research. Holders of digital tokens in a decentralized corporation might, for example, have the right to vote on actions the corporation took, much as shareholders have the right to vote on some (but not all) corporate decisions. But unlike with real corporations, which are subject to extensive bodies of corporate law that place hard limits on the powers of shareholders, a blockchain corporation would have infinite flexibility to structure itself as its holders desired.[2]

The bitcoin software itself did not have the flexibility required to introduce these kinds of complex rules, but another blockchain-based program called

Ethereum did. Ethereum, which had been created by the nineteen-year-old Russian wunderkind Vitalik Buterin in 2013, had been built specifically to allow for any sort of scripting program to be included on a blockchain. Jentzsch, familiar with Ethereum, became convinced that he could use it, and in particular its smart contract features, to create a corporation that had no executives, no boards and no employees. It would be the world's first virtual corporation.

Jentzsch made rapid progress. In March 2016, he published a white paper containing the details of what he called a Decentralized Autonomous Organization (DAO).[3] In April, he opened the DAO to investment, promising to investors that if they bought shares, or tokens, in the DAO, they would have a say in how the DAO was run. The DAO's website set forth its mission: the DAO would "blaze a new path in business organization for the betterment of its members, existing simultaneously nowhere and everywhere and operating solely with the steadfast iron will of unstoppable code."[4] Investments poured in. By May, the DAO had received more than $150 million, a remarkable sum for a company whose very form had been thought up just two months before.[5]

Jentzsch himself was shocked by the success of the DAO. Even in his most optimistic projections he never thought that the DAO would raise more than a few million dollars, let alone $150 million.[6] "This was an order of magnitude larger than we or anyone could have expected," he said. While the extraordinary success of the venture could have been a cause for celebration, Jentzsch greeted it, instead, with trepidation. "The code of the DAO had been purposely kept very simple, and more complex governance models . . . had not been included for the sake of simplicity," he wrote afterwards. But, "with so many ethers inside of its contract, the DAO's government model was now *too* simple."[7]

In other words, the DAO had been so successful that now, flush with cash, it presented a ripe target for hackers. Worse still, it was a leaderless, decentralized, digital organization, with its rules written into immutable code and no blueprints for handling a potential crisis. It was a sitting duck.

It did not take long for people to start spotting vulnerabilities in the DAO's code. On May 26, before the DAO had even completed its fundraising, Emin Gün Sirer, a computer scientist at Cornell University and one of the world's leading experts in blockchain technology, published an article calling for the DAO to cease operations. He had spotted serious flaws in the DAO's structure (nine of them, to be precise), and he believed they were sufficiently problematic that the DAO should institute a "moratorium" until security upgrades could be made to fix them.[8] Then, on June 5, an Ethereum developer discovered a flaw that would allow users to endlessly siphon off funds from the DAO.[9] Jentzsch and the rest of the DAO team rushed to deploy patches to fix the problems, but the fixes would be slow. And they were already too late.

On June 17, just three weeks after the DAO opened for business, a hacker launched an attack on the entity. The hacker had identified a vulnerability in the code that none of the patches had yet fixed. And it was a major one: it effectively turned the DAO into the hacker's personal debit card, allowing the hacker to make withdrawals over and over until the DAO's entire bank account had been drained. The hacker swiftly exploited this flaw, creating a contract with the DAO that forced the company to send him ether at a rate of approximately $4,000 every three minutes. And so in the early morning hours of June 17, the DAO's money started disappearing.

One of the first alerts that the DAO was losing money came from a post to the online discussion site Reddit (a popular place for blockchain followers to gather and discuss the news of the day).

"I think the DAO is getting drained right now," a user going by the name of ledgerwatch wrote on June 17. "Unfortunately I am on a train to work, so cannot investigate."[10]

Within an hour, Buterin (Ethereum's creator) wrote back, asking for additional details and requesting help from other users. The race was on to stop the hacker, and every second counted, given the DAO's rapidly depleting bank account.

The flaw that allowed this remarkable breach would have been nearly impossible for anyone but the most knowledgeable insiders to spot. The problem lay in line 666 of the DAO's code. This section of the code was part of the "splitDAO function," a feature of the DAO that allowed investors to withdraw their funds from the organization. This was an essential part of the DAO, as it ensured that people would not be forced to stay in the enterprise if they wanted to leave it. Among other things, it was believed that the splitDAO function would prevent majority investors from exploiting minority investors: if the majority did something that the minority did not like, the minority could leave the organization. By giving everyone a right to exit the enterprise, the splitDAO function would not just give tokenholders an ability to protect themselves in the event that a group of tokenholders took control of the enterprise, it would also create incentives for controlling tokenholders to take into account the interests of others. This concern about the protection of minority investors is an integral part of corporate law, and the splitDAO function was, in a way, an attempt to enshrine these legal concepts into the language of code.

But code is an unforgiving master. And in the DAO case, the splitDAO code was implemented poorly. Because of the order in which the function was written, an investor could ask the DAO to send him his funds and then, before the DAO's records were updated to show that the investor's account was now empty, he could ask it to send him his funds again. It was as if a customer could go to the ATM, cash out the entirety of his bank account, and then, before the ATM had sent the transaction for processing, he could cash out again. What is more, this exploit was "recursive": he could do it over and over again.[11]

This existential threat to the DAO had been created by the simplest of errors. "If the capital 'T' in line 666 had been a small 't,' that would also have prevented the hack," Jentzsch would explain later.[12] "The main problem was that reviewers did not know what to look for. Both our team and the community did know about things such as the Call Stack Depth attack, the problems with unbound loops, and many other specific vectors, but the reentry exploit was simply something no one was aware of at the time the DAO Framework was written."[13]

By the time that Jentzsch had discovered the problem with the code, it was too late to fix it; the hack had already begun. Now, the community had to find another way to stop the attack. Doing so would be considerably more involved than just changing a capital "T" to a lower case "t."

Transactions in the blockchain are supposed to be immutable. This means that once a record has been added to the blockchain, it should not be possible to go back later and tamper with it. That is a good thing when your primary concern is thwarting opportunistic hackers; the blockchain cannot be changed, and thus we can be reasonably sure that cyberthieves cannot go into previous blocks and steal money from them. But immutability can be a bad thing when your primary concern is punishing past behavior. Just as the blockchain cannot be changed by hackers to steal money from people, the blockchain also cannot be changed by monitors to punish someone for stealing money from people. Except that, in very limited circumstances, it can.

The response of the community to the DAO hack was twofold. The first response was to attempt to salvage what was left of the DAO's funds. Interestingly enough, doing so required the good guys to do precisely what the bad guy was doing: they set about draining the DAO as quickly as possible. After all, if they could remove the DAO's funds before the hacker could remove them, then it would not matter if the hacker could continue his attack; his seemingly bottomless ATM would suddenly dry up. Thus, step one of the response was for a group of Robin Hood programmers to set about transferring the DAO's funds to a separate, and safe, address.[14]

Step two of the response was more drastic. Given that the hacker had already stolen a significant portion of the DAO's funds – funds that could not be taken back as long as its record on the blockchain remained valid – the Ethereum community pondered whether it was time to revisit the immutability of the blockchain. What if, instead of accepting the theft as a *fait accompli*, they went back and rejected the improper transactions? Everyone could see where the money had gone, since all records in the blockchain are publicly available. Why not just go back to the state of things before the hack had occurred?

This was a radical strategy. As we have seen before, altering the blockchain requires a "hard fork," in which two versions of the blockchain exist. The blockchain community generally views hard forks as problematic because they undermine the core assumption that the blockchain presents a consensus view. If there is no definitive version of the blockchain, then users cannot be sure that their transactions are valid or that their records are secure. As Bruce Fenton, a member of the Bitcoin Foundation, said at the time in an article entitled *It is Better to Lose Your Investment Than Lose Your Blockchain*: "The strength of blockchain tech is that it is a ledger, a statement of truth. That ledger is only as good as its resistance to censorship, change, demands or attack."[15] To some observers, changing the core principles of the blockchain in order to stop a single theft was throwing the baby out with the bathwater: it would permanently harm the blockchain for the sake of a short-term gain.

But this was a moment of crisis for the Ethereum blockchain. It had been launched just a year before. If the first large-scale use of Ethereum resulted in a theft of this magnitude (the hacker made away with around four million ether, approximately a third of the DAO's funds, an amount worth $55 million at the time), it could potentially cause irreversible damage to the fledgling virtual currency.[16] Indeed, the DAO contained around 16 percent of all ether in circulation. The Ethereum blockchain might never recover. On the day that news of the attack broke, the value of Ethereum currency dropped by 33 percent.[17] If there was ever a time to let pragmatism triumph over principle, many believed, it was now.

Vitalik Buterin, the creator of the currency, led the charge in favor of a hard fork. He set up a website to allow all holders of ether to vote on whether to initiate a hard fork back to the prehack state. The principle was "one ether, one vote," not "one person, one vote," so wealthy holders of ether had more weight than small holders. The result, however, was overwhelmingly in favor of restoring the DAO's funds: 87 percent voted for the hard fork and only 13 percent voted against.[18] So, on July 20, just three days after the hack had begun, the Ethereum blockchain was modified to allow DAO investors to get their money back. Ethereum miners began mining on top of the new block 1,920,000, thus locking the change in place.

Not all the community accepted the hard fork. Around 15 percent of Ethereum miners continued to view the old blockchain as the valid one, and thus continued to build on top of it.[19] This meant that there now existed two versions of the Ethereum blockchain – one in which the theft occurred, and one in which it did not. This is a very strange situation, and one with no real parallel in real-world currency. It would be as if a robber robbed a bank and the government, in response and in order to prevent the robber from profiting from his ill-gotten gains, declared all currently circulating currency invalid and issued an entirely new currency. And what is more, it would be as if, after this occurred, a portion of society continued to use the old currency while another portion adopted the new one. In the real world of fiat currency, a functioning government would never let a competing currency grow and flourish under its nose. But in the blockchain, with no central government capable of punishing law-breakers, or even one that is capable of establishing what counts as lawbreaking, this strange scenario is perfectly possible. Indeed, some commentators went so far as to suggest that the DAO hack itself was legitimate; since it was permitted under the rules established in the DAO's code, there was nothing wrong with a user taking advantage of it. Even if the programmers did not intend for the code to work in this way, it isn't a hack if the code allows it. The code was a complete statement of what was and was not legitimate. The code simply was the law.[20]

To these hardliners, the hard fork that restored the DAO funds that had been taken was the real problem, and so they simply refused to accept the fork. Instead, they continued to accept only the original blockchain – the one in which the hacker got away with the money – as the true record. Over time, these originalists came up with a name for their version of the Ethereum blockchain: Ethereum Classic. The Ethereum blockchain is the most widely used version, with a market cap of around $26 billion in June 2019, as opposed to a market cap of $909 million for Ethereum Classic.[21] But Ethereum Classic continues to draw a large cadre of vocal supporters for its purportedly "pure" version of the blockchain.

What do we know of the hacker himself? Not much. He has never been identified in the real world, although investigators have found one public address that he used. It is 0xF35e2cC8E6523d683eD44870f5B7cC785051a77D.[22] Look familiar? This is a public address used on the blockchain, but instead of being located on the bitcoin blockchain, it is located on the Ethereum blockchain. And while the efforts of the Ethereum community to reverse his theft might have reduced the value of the theft, he still managed to get away with assets of substantial value. The Ethereum that he stole from the DAO was still his in the alternative version of the blockchain, Ethereum Classic. As of June 11, 2019, a single unit of Ethereum Classic was worth $8.18, making his loot worth approximately $30 million.

***

Moses Finley, the classicist, once wrote that "the history of ideas is never just the history of ideas; it is also the history of institutions, of society itself."[23] In much the same way, the history of the blockchain is not just about how the code itself spread around the world; it is also about the individuals, the companies, and the communities that sprang up around it. Blockchain, at its heart, is a tool that allows us to decentralize things that we have always thought of as requiring centralization. But simply inventing a tool is not enough to ensure that it is used, or that it is used in the way it was intended. And what is more, even if a technology is designed to be decentralized, as the blockchain is, it can only be as decentralized as the number of people who decide to use it. It does not matter if we have code that allows for collective decision-making if only one person is running it. Thus, the history of the blockchain is in a very tangible sense a history of the efforts, by investors, programmers, businessmen and others, to convince the wider world of its worth.

When Satoshi Nakamoto first announced his plan for a decentralized virtual currency he called bitcoin, the world was in the midst of the worst financial crisis since the Great Depression.[24] His white paper on bitcoin was published on October 31, 2008. At that time, the financial crisis was at its feverish peak. Just over a month before, the Wall Street bank Lehman Brothers had filed for bankruptcy. Fannie Mae and Freddie Mac, the mortgage finance companies, had just been placed into conservatorship by the U.S. Treasury. The federal government's bailout program, the Troubled Asset Relief Program, was in full force. Currency crises around the world were heating up.[25]

This could have gone either way for the fledgling virtual currency. On the one hand, the fear and tumult in the markets could easily have caused people to retreat from risky new ventures, which bitcoin certainly was. On the other hand, the crisis itself also seemed to vindicate one of the core rationales behind blockchain. The crisis, after all, had been caused by large banks playing fast and loose with other people's money, and national governments were using taxpayers' wallets to bail the banks out. Bitcoin promised to give people a way out of this seemingly rigged system.

But bitcoin couldn't do this unless people started using it, and so Satoshi Nakamoto and other early adopters spent much of their time in those early days convincing others that the venture was worthwhile. Partly, this was a matter of talking up the potential profits that could be made from it. Hal Finney, the computer programmer who had shown an interest in Nakamoto's white paper, was the first person other than Nakamoto to actually download the software and start mining new bitcoin. In a message to the cryptography mailing list (a successor to the original cypherpunk mailing list, which had by then disbanded), he wrote:

As an amusing thought experiment, imagine that Bitcoin is successful and becomes the dominant payment system in use throughout the world. Then the total value of the currency should be equal to the total value of all the wealth in the world. Current estimates of total worldwide household wealth that I have found range from $100 trillion to $300 trillion. With 20 million coins, that gives each coin a value of about $10 million. So the possibility of generating coins today with a few cents of compute time may be quite a good bet, with a payoff of something like 100 million to 1! Even if the odds of Bitcoin succeeding to this degree are slim, are they really 100 million to one against? Something to think about ... [26]

These kinds of thought experiments, about how much bitcoin could conceivably be worth one day, were common at the time, as people began to think through its systemic implications.

Reading through the initial posts on the bitcoin forum hosted on Bitcointalk.org feels a bit like a time machine, as though we are getting a front-row view of the original thinking of its founders. The conversation is at times mundane, at times quite enlightening. Sometimes Nakamoto acts like a cheerleader. Responding to a post that questioned whether people would find any use for bitcoins, for example, Nakamoto wrote:

> It might make sense just to get some in case it catches on. If enough people think the same way, that becomes a self fulfilling prophecy. Once it gets bootstrapped, there are so many applications if you could effortlessly pay a few cents to a website as easily as dropping coins in a vending machine.[27]

At other times, he explains at great length the technical workings of the blockchain and its historical background. He responds to random questions from posters. He interacts with the community. He is engaged. It is clear that he wants others to believe in the future of bitcoin as fervently as he himself does.

It did not take long for people to recognize the novelty of the blockchain and its decentralized system of security and consensus. To many, it made intuitive sense that removing central authorities from the system would provide greater protection from overbearing governments or greedy corporations. James Donald, one of the original cypherpunks, wrote: "Recall Nero's wish that Rome had a single throat that he could cut. If we provide them with such a throat, it will be cut."[28] The basic message – that decentralization provided an answer to the problems that had bedeviled virtual currencies in the past – had a kind of magnetic effect on the community. In 2009, new users flocked to the forums that hosted bitcoin discussions, with every month seeing dozens of new members. The number of people downloading bitcoin software to their computers similarly grew by leaps and bounds.[29] To a certain extent, however, this was to be expected. The kinds of people who frequented the cryptography mailing lists and online forums that hosted bitcoin discussions were also the kinds of people who were most likely to buy into its message. If not cypherpunks themselves, they shared a direct lineage with those hackers, libertarians, anarchists and cyberspace utopians who first started exploring the implications of the internet for privacy. The real test for bitcoin would be whether it could gain traction in the real world.

Getting people to use bitcoin in the real world was much harder than simply getting people to download free bitcoin software, or mine free bitcoin currency. All of that was free, and so there was little downside to doing it. But getting people to use bitcoin to trade goods and services in the physical world was something entirely different. It meant convincing people to sacrifice real money for virtual money. Laszlo Hanyecz, a software programmer from Jacksonville, Florida, who was one of the first bitcoin miners, and thus the owner of a substantial horde of bitcoins, made it his own personal mission to bridge this gap. On May 18, 2010, he wrote to the Bitcoin Forum with a proposal: "I'll pay 10,000 bitcoins for a couple of pizzas. . [sic] like maybe 2 large ones so I have some left over for the next day."[30] Several commenters wrote back asking where he lived and how they could buy pizza for him if they lived abroad, but no one went so far as actually buying the pizza. Three days later, he wrote again. "So nobody wants to buy me pizza? Is the bitcoin amount I'm offering too low?"[31] The question, about bitcoin's value, was a complicated one. No one had ever yet used bitcoin to buy real things, so it was hard to peg its value in the abstract. And anyone who was willing to buy a real-world pizza and get bitcoin in return was taking the risk that the bitcoin they received would turn out to be worthless. Despite this, and after more prodding from Hanyecz, a willing transactor stepped forward. Jeremy Sturdivant, a nineteen-year-old student from England who went by the name of "jercos," offered to buy Hanyecz two pizzas from Papa John's, placing the order online and paying with his credit card.[32] Hanyecz proudly announced to the forum: "I just want to report that I successfully traded 10,000 bitcoins for pizza."[33] He even posted a photo of the pizzas for all to see. It was the first real-world transaction in bitcoin, and it would go down in history as the most expensive pizza ever. Those two pizzas cost Hanyecz $70 million at bitcoin's exchange rate as of August 2018.[34]

The pizza stunt was an attention grabber, but two other developments were even more important in cementing bitcoin's spot in the public's attention. The first was the creation of bitcoin exchanges, where people could buy bitcoin using their credit cards and bank accounts. Nakamoto's software, as brilliant as it may have been, was not particularly user friendly. If you wanted to get bitcoin, you had to mine for new blocks using your computer, a process that was quickly becoming more expensive as new entrants added computing power to the network. You could also try to find someone willing to send you new bitcoin, but this required you to lurk on message boards or chat forums to identify a willing seller. Perhaps even more dauntingly, bitcoin users had to store and keep track of their public address, their private key and their holdings. If they lost this information, any bitcoin they owned would become worthless; they would have no way to prove that they owned the bitcoin, and thus they would have no way to spend it. Stories abound of users losing their laptops or misplacing their slips of paper storing their private key, and then forever losing their bitcoin. One poor user in Wales accidentally threw away a laptop containing the private keys to wallets containing 7,500 bitcoin, worth approximately $150 million at bitcoin's height (leading him to try, unsuccessfully, to dredge the landfill where he believed the laptop could be found).[35] All of this meant that there were significant barriers to entry for people who were interested in the virtual currency. Bitcoin exchanges promised to eliminate all this hassle. They aimed to provide a central place where interested investors could come to buy and sell bitcoin for real-world currencies such as dollars and euros. They would provide a liquid marketplace that would show the current value of bitcoin quoted in real time. And they would help manage user accounts and private keys. One of the first exchanges was Mt. Gox, which was launched in July 2010.[36] Although it is now famous for going down in flames after just four years of operations, it was also responsible for helping usher in a period of extended growth for the virtual currency. The Bitcoin Forum, which had been growing at the rate of tens of members a month, all of a sudden starting adding members by the thousands. In February 2011, when Mt. Gox had added Mark Karpeles as its CEO, the forum added more than 14,000 new members.[37]

The second major development that helped spur bitcoin's growth was the opening of online bitcoin stores. Just as it was important to make it easy for users to *acquire* bitcoin, it was also important to make it easy for users to *spend* bitcoin. Bitcoin would not be a very useful currency if every time someone wanted to use it they had to post a proposed transaction online and then wait for a willing seller to arrive, like Laszlo Hanyecz had done with his pizza. Online stores, it was hoped, would provide the stability needed for sellers to list their goods and services with publicly available prices and receive payment in bitcoin. Just like exchanges, they promised to smooth the process of using bitcoin. One of the first, and most important, of these sites was a website called the Silk Road.[38]

Launched in February 2011, the Silk Road promoted itself as an anonymous marketplace, operating on the dark web and accessible only through an encrypted browser known as Tor. The site was run by a man who called himself the "Dread Pirate Roberts," named after the character in the movie *The Princess Bride*. The Silk Road quickly gained attention both inside and outside the bitcoin world because of its unique merchandise: unlike Amazon, which was significantly easier to use and had a much wider selection of goods, but did not provide its users with anonymity, the Silk Road specialized in illegal goods, primarily drugs. As the site boasted:

> The Silk Road is an anonymous online market. Current offerings include Marijuana, Hash, Shrooms, LSD, Ecstasy, DMT, Mescaline, and more. The site uses the Tor anonymity network, which anonymizes all traffic to and from the site, so no one can find out who you are or who runs Silk Road. For money, we use Bitcoin, an anonymous digital currency.[39]

One journalist who visited the Silk Road in 2013 categorized the items he found there: the site had 2 items of fireworks, 54 items of jewelry and 8,670 items of drugs, including separate subcategories for cannabis, dissociatives, ecstasy, opioids, psychedelics and the ominous "other." Seventy dollars could buy you ten hits of LSD. Three hundred and forty dollars could buy you ten grams of ketamine crystals.[40] While the site was largely devoted to drugs, other listings included counterfeit bills, firearms, ammunition and hitmen.

The Silk Road garnered wide-eyed attention from the mainstream media. The website Gawker published an article in June 2011 titled *The Underground Website Where You Can Buy Any Drug Imaginable*.[41] The article even instructed readers about how to start using the site:

> To purchase something on Silk Road, you need first to buy some Bitcoins using a service like Mt. Gox Bitcoin Exchange. Then, create an account on Silk Road, deposit some bitcoins, and start buying drugs. One bitcoin is worth about $8.67, though the exchange rate fluctuates wildly every day. Right now you can buy an 1/8th of pot on Silk Road for 7.63 Bitcoins. That's probably more than you would pay on the street, but most Silk Road users seem happy to pay a premium for convenience.[42]

The story went viral, and quickly other newspapers were reporting on the Wild West of the dark web, as well as the virtual currency bitcoin that made it all possible. Politicians and law enforcement were swift to condemn the service, as well as the currency. Just four days after the Gawker article was published, Senator Charles Schumer held a press conference where he called for federal authorities to shut the site down. Referring to the use of bitcoin on the site, he said: "It's an online form of money laundering used to disguise the source of money, and to disguise who's both selling and buying the drug."[43] Soon, the FBI had launched an investigation into the site and started looking closely at the use of bitcoin. It would take them more than two years, but eventually they managed to shut the site down and arrest the Dread Pirate Roberts, who, it turned out, was an Eagle Scout from Austin, Texas (we will return to him later).

In the meantime, the Silk Road was driving bitcoin usage through the roof. It is estimated that more than one million people had accounts on the site. Over the course of its existence, the site generated sales revenue of around 9.5 million bitcoins, or $58 billion at bitcoin's price in August 2018, making annual revenue of approximately $29 billion, more than the average Fortune 500 company at the time. From February 2011 to July 2013, the site handled approximately 1.2 million transactions.[44]

Satoshi Nakamoto was well aware that bitcoin could be used to skirt the law and, although he never outright condemned it, he did seem to view the possibility with concern. In 2010, after banks had cut off donations to WikiLeaks in response to its dissemination of classified documents, some members of the bitcoin community argued that people should start making donations in bitcoin instead. Bitcoin, after all, allowed individuals around the world to donate to the website with complete anonymity, and no bank or government could stop them. One user wrote to the bitcoin forum: "Basically, bring it on. Let's encourage WikiLeaks to use Bitcoins and I'm willing to face any risk or fallout from that act." Nakamoto quickly responded with a warning:

> No, don't "bring it on." The project needs to grow gradually so the software can be strengthened along the way. I make this appeal to WikiLeaks not to try to use Bitcoin. Bitcoin is a small beta community in its infancy. You would not stand to get more than pocket change, and the heat you would bring would likely destroy us at this stage.[45]

Soon after, the magazine *PCWorld* wrote an article about bitcoin and argued that the WikiLeaks scandal could increase the popularity of the anonymous virtual currency.[46] Nakamoto again pooh-poohed the suggestion: "It would have been nice to get this attention in any other context. WikiLeaks has kicked the hornet's nest, and the swarm is headed towards us."[47]

These less savory aspects of bitcoin caused many mainstream institutions to shy away from entering the fledgling market. Jamie Dimon, the CEO of J. P. Morgan, told a conference of bankers that bitcoin was a "fraud" that was "worse than tulip bulbs."[48] Goldman Sachs issued a report calling bitcoin a "mania" that "garner[s] far more traditional media and social media attention than is warranted."[49] The skepticism of banks towards bitcoin also created a problem for companies seeking to enter the cryptocurrency industry. Bitcoin-focused companies in the early years of the currency struggled to convince banks to allow them to open accounts with them. There was no easy fix for this. Banks in most well-developed countries have strict know-your-customer and anti-money-laundering rules that require banks to research the identities and backgrounds of users and to keep track of where their money is coming from and going to. These are difficult things to do with bitcoin, where transactions are designed to be anonymous. So many banks simply refused to do business with bitcoin companies. It didn't help when, in 2014, the CEO of one of the more prominent bitcoin exchanges, BitInstant, was arrested in New York and charged with money laundering.[50]

Despite these ominous signs, a few intrepid investors started wading into the field with the hopes of cleaning it up. Cameron and Tyler Winklevoss, twin brothers who had studied at Harvard and later made millions from a lawsuit against Facebook, were early investors. In April 2013, they announced that they had invested $11 million in bitcoin and soon started putting together a plan for a bitcoin exchange-traded fund, a kind of mutual fund that would track the price of bitcoin and that would be open to retail (i.e., regular, Joe Shmoe) investors.[51] Silicon Valley investors similarly poured money into the currency. Marc Andreesen, a prominent venture capitalist, invested millions of dollars in bitcoin starting in 2013.[52] In an influential op-ed in the *New York Times*, he compared the invention of bitcoin to the invention of the internet and personal computers: like these other technologies, bitcoin's "effects will become profound; and later, many people will wonder why its powerful promise wasn't more obvious from the start."[53] For Andreessen, bitcoin's great value was that it could introduce a welcome degree of innovation and efficiency to a number of cumbersome businesses, from international remittances, to serving the "unbanked," to micropayments for content distribution and spam fighting. "The more people who use bitcoin, the more valuable bitcoin is for everyone who uses it, and the higher the incentive for the next user to start using the technology."[54]

Another early proselytizer was Wences Casares. Born in 1974 in Argentina, Casares had been raised on a sheep ranch in Patagonia. He would later tell interviewers that he had vibrant memories of the hyperinflation that wreaked havoc on Argentina's economy during his youth. He went on to become a serial tech entrepreneur, starting up and selling multiple companies by his thirties, including an online financial services company that he sold for $750 million in 2000. During all this time, however, he never opened an Argentinian bank account – he was too wary of the country's precarious financial system. "I think I understand economics better than most people because I grew up in Argentina," he said. "This is the street-smart economics. Not the complex Ph.D. economics."[55] So when he first heard about bitcoin in 2011, he was intrigued. For Casares, bitcoin represented a haven for people who lived under unstable regimes and suffered the financial and personal consequences of volatile currencies. "A world in which bitcoin is successful is a world in which bitcoin has become two things: it's a global nonpolitical standard of value, and it's a global nonpolitical standard of settlement," he said.[56] But before investing, he wanted to know one thing: Was it really safe? In order to find this out, he paid a group of hackers in Eastern Europe to see if they could find any vulnerabilities in bitcoin's underlying code. When they couldn't, he went all in and started holding regular gatherings of Silicon Valley investors and influential people, trying to convince them that bitcoin was for real.[57]

One of the primary consequences of all this attention, both in the media and in investment circles, was that bitcoin's price steadily began to rise. When Laszlo Hanyecz bought two pizzas for 10,000 bitcoins in May 2010, a single bitcoin was worth slightly less than half of a penny.[58] When the Silk Road opened for business in February 2011, it was worth approximately a dollar. By April 2012, it was worth $100. By November 2013, it was more than $1,000.[59] Of course, this rise was not without its tumbles. The value of bitcoin experienced substantial volatility throughout this period – it was not uncommon for the virtual currency to drop 10 or 20 percent, or more, in a single day – but the direction was clear. Bitcoin was becoming valuable.[60]

The increasing value of bitcoin in turn introduced another important change in the blockchain ecosystem, one that in many ways would come to define the bitcoin industry. This was the beginning of the arms race in bitcoin mining. The only way to create bitcoins, remember, is to mine for new blocks – a process that requires computers to solve complicated hashing equations. At the outset, this process was relatively easy; it could be done by a regular person using a reasonably capable personal computer. Hal Finney mined some of the first blocks in 2009 using a basic IBM ThinkCentre.[61] But as more people came online and started mining for bitcoin, the difficulty of the hashing equations increased. Nakamoto had recognized that it was important for bitcoins to be released at a consistent rate, both to avoid inflation and, perhaps more importantly, to ensure that individuals would still have an incentive to do the intensive work of maintaining the blockchain ecosystem. In order to keep the rate at which new bitcoins were issued consistent, Nakamoto had hard-wired into the bitcoin software a regular revision of the difficulty of the hashing equations. As a result, as new computing power came online and accelerated the rate at which new blocks were being mined, the difficulty of the equations they had to solve increased proportionally, periodically resetting the issuance rate to the desired one.

This created a bit of a catch-22 for miners. As the price of bitcoin rose, the value of the reward for mining new blocks increased. This incentivized miners to buy faster computers in order to win a greater share of the block rewards. But every time they brought new computing power online, the difficulty of winning blocks rose, thus setting everyone back to where they started. The only way out was to have a comparative advantage over others; if one miner could get faster at solving the hashing equations, while everyone else remained the same, they could reap the rewards of mining new blocks while not fully resetting the hash difficulty to negate their advantage. But, of course, every miner wanted to do this, so there was fierce competition to build, buy or invent new and faster processors.

The first step in the arms race was a switch from personal computers to graphics processing units or GPUs. Laszlo Hanyecz, the programmer who had bought pizzas using bitcoin, recognized that GPUs, which specialize in running videos and computer games that require rapid processing of large data blocks, were much better at solving hash functions than the central processing units found in most computers. So, in early 2010, he rigged his GPU to start mining bitcoin and set it to work. His switch led to a massive improvement in his mining capacity. Whereas he had previously been finding a block a day, he now found significantly more, with his GPU mining twenty-eight blocks on May 17 alone, a haul that earned him 1,400 newly minted bitcoins.[62] His GPU was now processing hash equations roughly eight hundred times faster than his CPU.[63] But it wasn't long before others heard of Hanyecz's breakthrough with GPUs, and soon many other people were rigging up their own GPUs to mine for new blocks. This negated Hanyecz's advantage, and also significantly increased the hash difficulty of bitcoin mining due to bitcoin's built-in recalibration mechanisms. This, in turn, led miners to search for newer and even faster processing units.

Nakamoto had worried about an arms race nearly from the time he launched bitcoin. In December 2009, he wrote:

> We should have a gentleman's agreement to postpone the GPU arms race as long as we can for the good of the network. It's much easier to get new users up to speed if they don't have to worry about GPU drivers and compatibility. It's nice how anyone with just a CPU can compete fairly equally right now.[64]

But, despite Nakamoto's warnings, the arms race in computing power contin-ued and, indeed, accelerated. The next leap forward came when miners started building chips specifically designed to perform bitcoin's hash equations. These processors, known as application-specific integrated circuit chips, or ASICs, significantly outperformed GPUs, which, despite their power, were still at heart general-purpose chips. The first commercial ASICs came on the market in January 2013 and they marked a giant leap in the bitcoin ecosystem's computing power.[65] A cutting-edge ASIC in 2018, for example, could perform 13 tera-hashes (i.e., 13 trillion hash equations) per second.[66] The speed and power of these ASICs led to a sharp increase in the bitcoin network's overall computing power as well. On January 1, 2013, the total hash power of the bitcoin network was 23 terahashes per second, meaning that all miners combined were per-forming 23 trillion hash equations a second. Just six months later, the rate had risen tenfold: the bitcoin network was performing 250 terahashes per second. By the end of the year, the hash rate had soared to 11,389 terahashes per - second.[67] ASICs had revolutionized the speed and power of bitcoin's network.

The arms race in mining power turned mining into a big business. Gone were the days when an interested programmer could simply download the bitcoin software and start mining on his home computer. The cost of new ASIC chips was rising, and even the fastest ASICs were not enough to guarantee miners that they would win bitcoins. Companies started setting up mining "farms" – giant factories filled to the brim with ASICs, all of which would be wired together and cooled by enormous fans. The farms sucked up massive amounts of energy, too. One large mining farm in Inner Mongolia was estimated to be spending $39,000 per day just in electricity costs.[68] Companies began locating their mining farms in places with low electricity costs to gain a competitive advantage, and so increasingly large operations moved to places like Mongolia, Iceland (with its geothermal power plants) and Siberia (with its frigid weather and energy surpluses).

It did not take long for a few mining giants to acquire a dominant position in the field. With the ability to design and build the latest and fastest chips, and the resources to employ engineers to constantly maintain them, companies like BitMain and BitFury controlled massive amounts of the network's resources. At one point in 2018, BitMain controlled around 42 percent of all hash power on the bitcoin network, generating enormous profits as a result.[69] It is estimated that BitMain earned $4 billion in 2017.[70] This would make it just slightly less profitable than Goldman Sachs (which turned a profit of $4.3 billion in 2017)[71] and quite a bit more profitable than Amazon (which made $3 billion in 2017).[72]

By the time that the professional mining companies arrived on the scene, the days of regular people mining bitcoin on their computers were over (at least, if they were in it to make a profit). They simply could not afford to compete with the enormous computing power held by these companies. Instead, many started joining "pools" that aggregated together the computing power of many different computers to ensure that users could still win the race for new bitcoins. They would then share any resulting bitcoin rewards. These pools, of course, were run by centralized administrators that doled out the rewards as they came due. The bitcoin ecosystem was starting to centralize.[73]

***

At the same time, bitcoin's success, or, perhaps more importantly, the success of investors in bitcoin, led to imitation. Other people wanted in to the cryptocurrency game. A variety of programmers, seeing the price of bitcoin soaring and believing that they could do better, used insights from bitcoin's structure to create virtual currencies of their own. Many of these currencies promised to improve on some aspect of bitcoin that had received criticism in the community. For example, the cryptocurrency Monero (named after the word for "coin" in Esperanto) aimed to provide a fully anonymous cryptocurrency, something that bitcoin failed to do given its system of public addresses that could potentially be traced back to an individual. Dash, another cryptocurrency, aimed to improve on bitcoin's notoriously slow transaction speed. Whereas bitcoin blocks are added at a rate of one every ten minutes, providing a hard limit on the maximum number of transactions per second the system can handle, dash blocks would be added at a rate of one every two and a half minutes, thereby increasing the overall speed of the network.[74] Litecoin aimed to combat the centralization of power in the hands of large miners that had been criticized by many in the community. It did so by adopting a new hashing algorithm that was thought to make it easier for regular computers to win the hunt for new blocks, and thus draw in a greater variety of regular users. The "ASIC-resistant" cryptocurrency appealed to more democratically minded investors who sought to maintain a truly decentralized virtual currency. Tether, on the other hand, aimed to reduce price volatility by promising to back each unit of currency with a dollar held in reserve.

One of the earliest imitators was Dogecoin, a virtual currency based on an internet meme of a grammatically challenged Shiba Inu dog. Despite its transparently unserious motivations, or perhaps because of them, the virtual currency gained a significant following in the emerging cryptocurrency world. At one point, it had a market capitalization of more than $2 billion. Its creator,

Jackson Palmer, was so shocked by its success that he penned an article in *Motherboard* entitled *My Joke Cryptocurrency Hit $2 Billion and Something is Very Wrong*. In the article, he explained that he had conceived of the currency as a way to further awareness of the possibilities of blockchain, but, as he learned to his great regret, "a passionate community of people throwing around money is like blood in the water to ... shark-like scammers and opportunists."[75]

Over time, as competing virtual currencies launched and met with success, more and more programmers were encouraged to enter the market with their own products. The sheer growth in the number of virtual currencies was indicative of investor appetite for the sector. In April 2013, when the website CoinMarketCap first launched, the site tracked seven virtual currencies.[76] By January 2014, it had risen to sixty-seven.[77] By January 2015, the number of virtual currencies had surpassed the total number of national currencies in the world: the site was tracking 491 currencies.[78] Growth then slowed down for a bit (in January 2016, it was tracking 551 currencies;[79] in January 2017, 617),[80] before sharply spiking upwards in 2018 (by January 2018, CoinMarketCap was tracking 1,355 virtual currencies).[81]

The rapid growth in the world of virtual currencies gave rise to a new term: "initial coin offering." An initial coin offering (ICO) referred to the first sale of a virtual currency to the public. The name evokes the better-known process of an initial public offering (IPO), where companies issue their stock to the public, but it in fact differs in important ways. Among other things, many of the companies offering virtual currencies to the public took the position that the currencies were not truly "securities," and thus were not subject to the extensive disclosure and liability obligations governing the sale of stock in IPOs. Initial coin offerings, instead, were often accompanied by not much more than a short white paper outlining the coin's features, followed by an intense social media campaign to drive investor interest. Often, the founder of the coin offered "discounts" to early buyers as a way to drum up urgency in the minds of investors. Not infrequently, celebrities were called in to promote the virtual currency. For example, when LydianCoin, a virtual token that promised to provide the "first marketing cloud for blockchain," launched in 2017, Paris Hilton, the wealthy hotel heiress and socialite, took to Twitter to announce that she was looking forward to "participating in the new @LydianCoinLtd Token!" The actor Steven Seagal backed a bitcoin competitor called "Bitcoiin" (that is not a typo: the virtual currency was called bitcoiin, or bitcoin with an extra "i" thrown in). Floyd Mayweather, the boxer, promoted several ICOs, including Centra, which the SEC later charged with fraud.[82]

Initial coin offerings exploded in 2017 and 2018. In 2017, companies raised $5.5 billion through initial coin offerings. By May of 2018, initial coin offerings had more than doubled that amount, raking in $11.8 billion.[83] The largest ICO ever occurred in 2018, when the company Block.one raised $4 billion for its EOS token, a blockchain-based platform that promised to enable decentralized programs of nearly any kind.[84]

But the rush to take advantage of investor appetite for these new and ever more exotic virtual currencies led to shoddy and, in some instances, fraudulent practices. Many ICO white papers shamelessly copied the text and wording of white papers from other ICOs: a *Wall Street Journal* study found that, of 1,450 white papers they analyzed, 111 contained plagiarized sections.[85] Other ICO projects claimed to have executive teams made up of individuals who either did not exist or had no knowledge of the ICO. Others had remarkably insulating legal language in their documents that purported to disclaim any value for their virtual currency. For example, the EOS token stipulated that it did "not have any rights, uses, purpose, attribute, functionalities, or features, express or implied."[86]

As one might have expected, many of these new virtual currencies failed, costing their investors real money. A website, deadcoins.com, sprang up to track the number of defunct currencies and by September 2018 had listed 911 such coins. This list appears to underestimate the failure rate of new virtual currencies; a study conducted by bitcoin.com found that 46 percent of the 902 crowdsale-based virtual currencies launched in 2017 had failed by February 2018.[87] Regardless of the precise numbers involved, it is clear that ICOs represented both a massive new market for companies interested in the blockchain and a significant risk for investors considering these projects.

One final virtual currency should also be mentioned, both because of its unique nature and because of the significant amount of attention it has received. This is Libra. When Facebook announced that it would be launching a digital currency in 2019 – a currency it hoped would form the backbone of a new global financial system – it immediately triggered a barrage of harsh criticism from observers. For some, the idea of the world's largest social media company coopting blockchain, a technology built for privacy and decentralization, for its own purposes was a betrayal of everything that the crypto-community stood for. For others, Facebook's clout could mean that Libra, unlike so many other virtual currencies, would finally present a real threat to the preeminence of national currencies – something to be feared by central banks and governments around the world. Within weeks of its announcement, Congress held hearings on the issue; one Facebook executive faced four hours of hostile questioning from the House Financial Services Committee, where committee members claimed that Libra was "a godsend to drug dealers and tax evaders"

that would "yield immense economic power that could destabilize government." A group of lawmakers proposed draft legislation to ban large technology
companies from issuing digital currencies (the measure was called the "Keep
Big Tech Out of Finance Act"). All of this, it should be noted, occurred before
any real details had been disclosed about the cryptocurrency. Facebook released
a white paper and announced that it would be partnering with other institutions
on the initiative (including Mastercard, PayPal and Uber), but hard details on
just how the cryptocurrency would work were sparse. Indeed, its own partners
said they didn't know how Libra would work or what their own roles would be in
running it. At the time of the writing of this book, Libra's future is uncertain and
fast changing. But its very creation sent shockwaves through the blockchain
world and showed just how quickly this world was evolving.

***

In 2018, IBM ran an ad promoting its newest service.

"This is a tomato you can track from farm to pot to jar to table, and serve
with confidence that it is safe," the commercial begins, as a series of stylized
(and stylish) individuals, representing a farmer, a chef, a grocery store shelver,
and a father serving his son spaghetti, hand a tomato to each other.

"This is a diamond you can follow from mine to finger, and trust it never fell
into the wrong hands," it continues, now showing a miner handing a raw
diamond to a cutter, who puts it in a box, from where it is taken by a rapturous
suitor who uses it to propose to his lover (who eagerly accepts).

"This is a shipment transferred two hundred times, transparently tracked from
port to port," the montage concludes, showing a variety of characters passing
a package amongst each other as an image of a globe turns in the background.

"This is the IBM blockchain, built for smarter business."

The fact that IBM, one of the world's largest technology companies,
launched an ad campaign entirely devoted to the blockchain is striking for
any number of reasons. First, and most obviously, it demonstrates the company's
belief that there is a market for blockchain technologies. If IBM did not believe
that people would pay for IBM's blockchain services, presumably they would
not be advertising them (unless it was some sort of elaborate form of virtue
signaling). But second, and more importantly, IBM's ad shows the extent to
which the blockchain had entered the public imagination. The headline of the
commercial was that IBM now had a blockchain product. And IBM believed
that this product could bring benefits to such diverse industries as food services,
mining and shipping. A group of marketers at IBM thus thought that "this is the
IBM blockchain" was a catchy slogan to attract the interest of consumers.

IBM's blockchain commercial was also symbolic of a wider shift within the blockchain ecosystem. Once bitcoin and the blockchain became household names, and reputable institutions began to recognize their innovative features, people started looking for new ways to use it, beyond the world of virtual currencies. Bitcoin, after all, was only one way to use the blockchain. The blockchain technology itself, however, had nearly limitless potential applications. In its essence, it was a way to store information in a decentralized manner, meaning that users did not need to go through a trusted administrator to access it. A virtual currency was one form of information that could be stored on a blockchain, but other sorts of information could be stored there as well.

One of the earliest efforts to use the blockchain for purposes other than virtual currencies was the blockchain platform Ethereum, mentioned at the beginning of this Chapter. Ethereum, as we have already seen, was the brainchild of a nineteen-year-old Russian-born Canadian named Vitalik Buterin. Buterin has been described alternately as a "prophet,"[88] a "teenage crypto-titan,"[89] and a "praying mantis" (for the way he perches over his keyboard when coding),[90] and he is widely acclaimed as one of the deep thinkers in the blockchain world. Buterin was a fan of bitcoin from early on (he founded a magazine devoted to bitcoin when he was just eighteen years old), but he soon came to the conclusion that bitcoin's real innovation was not in the currency itself but in the technology underlying it.[91] To Buterin, bitcoin's software seemed clunky and rigid. It had been designed with just one purpose in mind – the creation of a virtual form of money – and it did not lend itself to much else. But Buterin recognized that the blockchain, the building block with which bitcoin was built, could prove useful in almost any form of online interaction. It could be used to write enforceable contracts, or trade financial instruments or even create virtual corporations.

In order to do all this, though, Buterin would need to abandon bitcoin itself. So, just as Satoshi Nakamoto had done when he first launched bitcoin, Buterin wrote a white paper. The white paper, posted in November 2013, described a bitcoin-less blockchain that he called Ethereum. Ethereum, he wrote, would be a "next-generation smart contract and decentralized application platform."[92]

Satoshi Nakamoto's development of Bitcoin in 2009 has often been hailed as a radical development in money and currency, being the first example of a digital asset which simultaneously has no backing or intrinsic value and no centralized issuer or controller. However, another – arguably more important – part of the Bitcoin experiment is the underlying blockchain technology as a tool of distributed consensus, and attention is rapidly starting to shift to this other aspect of Bitcoin. . . . What Ethereum intends to provide is a blockchain with a built-in fully fledged Turing-complete programming language that can be used to create "contracts" that can be used to encode arbitrary state transi-tion functions, allowing users to create any of the systems described above [including smart contracts, digital assets, financial instruments, smart property and virtual corporations], as well as many others that we have not yet imagined, simply by writing up the logic in a few lines of code.[93]

Buterin's idea, in essence, was to create a blockchain for contracts. These con-tracts would exist on the Ethereum blockchain, a publicly available, distributed and cryptographically secure database. The contracts could set forth any variety of rules, just like real-world contracts. But, unlike traditional contracts, Ethereum contracts would be self-executing. All the rules would be contained in the code of the contract itself. A smart contract could, for example, state that Locke will send Hobbes $10 if Hobbes uploads *Leviathan* to the blockchain. The contract code would check that Hobbes uploaded *Leviathan* and, once it had confirmed this, send the money (likely in the form of Ethereum's native virtual currency, Ether) to an account controlled by Hobbes. All of these transactions would be recorded and maintained on the Ethereum blockchain. Buterin chose to call his new blockchain Ethereum because it "sounded nice and it had the word 'ether,' referring to the hypothetical invisible medium that permeates the universe and allows light to travel."[94]

The Ethereum blockchain launched to much fanfare in 2014, when it held a "presale" of the ether currency that would be used to create and maintain the ecosystem. In an interesting twist, investors who wanted to buy ether had to do so using bitcoin – a sign of the connection between the two competing blockchains, a connection that continues today. The Ethereum presale raised more than 29,000 bitcoins, which, at the time, would have been worth around $14.5 million, a tidy sum for an unproven new venture led by a teenager.[95]

The malleability of Ethereum made it a success in an arena that had largely resisted bitcoin's attractions – the world of large corporations and financial institutions. Whereas bitcoin could be used only as a currency – something that corporations and banks typically had a surplus of – Ethereum could be used to improve the internal functioning of businesses. It could reduce costs. It could speed up transactions. And it could thus make the infinite gears of commerce run more smoothly. Or at least, it promised to do so. Whether it could live up to this promise remained to be seen. But it was sufficiently innovative to gain the attention of major players in both business and finance.

While banks had largely shied away from bitcoin in its early days, they quickly jumped into the Ethereum ecosystem. Financial transactions, which typically involve large amounts of paperwork, numerous middlemen, and arms-length parties present a burdensome and expensive management problem. The idea of a smart contract that could automatically encode all of this information into a verifiable database, and that would automatically settle payments between parties in real time in a way that was both secure and unhackable, was thus intriguing to large banks. In 2015, a consortium of nine large banks, including J.P. Morgan Chase, Credit Suisse and Barclays, joined together in a venture to create shared standards for using blockchain in financial services.[96] J.P. Morgan Chase later designed its own blockchain program, known as Quorum, to speed up its derivatives and payments businesses.[97] Another industry consortium, the Enterprise Ethereum Alliance, attracted more than 500 firms.[98] While these efforts were slow to mature into real businesses with sustainable revenues, they demonstrated how far the financial sector had come in embracing blockchain technology.

Two tangible blockchain-related achievements in the financial sector offer a preview of things to come. In 2017, the French insurer AXA began offering a new product it called "Fizzy." Fizzy was a blockchain-based smart contract that insured airplane passengers against flight delays. The smart contract, which was written into the Ethereum blockchain, would automatically send compensation to passengers if their plane was delayed by more than two hours. As of August 2018, it had recorded 11,000 transactions.[99] Fizzy had a number of limitations: it originally applied only to direct flights between Paris Charles de Gaulle airport and the United States; the smart contract was in the form of code and thus difficult for the average consumer to interpret and understand; and the actual payment of money was subject to "banking delays."[100] But its founder, Laurent Benichou, was optimistic that it would quickly catch on. "Blockchain is useful because it allows me to say to the customer that you don't have to trust the insurer on the data we are using. . . . Your policy is on the blockchain. . . . Potentially, for a paranoid customer who assumes we cheat, we say it's not AXA anymore that's a party to the transaction that will decide whether you get indemnified."[101] But Fizzy appears to have fizzled out. An analyst that reviewed Fizzy's public information on the blockchain found that, between August 2018 and January 2018, the company was handling fewer than thirty insurance contracts a month.[102]

Second, in August 2018, the World Bank issued the world's first global blockchain bond. The issuance raised $80 million for the World Bank's development efforts and the entire process was handled on the blockchain. Part of the appeal of using the blockchain for debt issuances was that it could potentially greatly simplify the process of finding buyers, registering purchases and settling transactions. This process normally takes weeks. But with a blockchain-based bond, the issuance can be instantaneous, with buyers having their interests registered on an Ethereum-based blockchain network. The World Bank worked with an Australian bank, the Commonwealth Bank of Australia, to issue the bonds.[103] In a nod to the Australian roots of the project, the bond was called a Blockchain Operated New Debt Instrument, or bond-i, recalling Bondi Beach in Sydney.

The blockchain has also made inroads into other industries, particularly in areas that have expensive record-keeping requirements and multiple counterparties. The shipping industry, for example, was swift to embrace blockchain as a potential cost-cutting solution. It is easy to see why the blockchain might appeal to the shipping industry. The industry itself already has a significant amount of decentralization. Shipping a set of goods from an origin in one country to a destination in another involves a mind-numbing number of parties, from port authorities to ocean carriers to freight forwarders to customs officials. Each of these parties requires a different set of documents and approvals, many of which may be related to, but slightly different from, the documents and approvals required by another, and many of which must be signed in person. Just as importantly, each of these parties may not fully trust the other parties, due, perhaps, to a lack of previous interactions, divergent interests or some other source of uncertainty. By one estimate, a simple shipment of avocados from Kenya to the Netherlands requires 30 different companies and more than 200 documentary exchanges. But if all of the relevant information, such as the certificate of origin, the site of provenance of the goods, the invoice, the inspection of the goods, the payment of fees, the loading of goods on board transportation and the delivery of the goods at their ultimate destination, could be recorded in a single database that was trusted and unforgeable, then many of the costs of overlapping documentation and repetitive work could be eliminated.[104]

In 2018, Maersk, the world's largest shipping company, launched a joint venture with IBM to create a blockchain-based shipping platform that would put the entire shipping process on a decentralized network. TradeLens, the eventual result of this effort, called itself a "platform for transformation." The platform promised to enable "true information sharing and collaboration across supply chains, thereby increasing industry innovation, reducing trade friction and – ultimately – promoting more global trade."[105] On the TradeLens platform, all relevant documents would be stored in a distributed ledger, but in such a way that documents could be seen only by the people who needed to see them. An important component of the TradeLens blockchain is that it is "permissioned." What this means is that it is viewable not by any computer that decides to join the network but rather only by those individuals that have permission to do so. Similarly, only authorized individuals have the ability to make changes to a permissioned blockchain. This is important in a business environment where much of the relevant information is sensitive. Apple, for example, might not want to signal to the world the number of iPhones it is shipping to the United States or what the contents of these shipments are. This could give Apple's rivals an insight into its business practices and would presumably dissuade Apple from using a blockchain-based shipment provider in the first place. To further reassure its competitors that it would not be manipulating the platform for its own gain, Maersk decided to spin off the joint venture into its own company, thereby making it independent from the shipping giant. To date, however, these efforts have not been enough to convince competitors to join TradeLens. By March 2019, some small shipping companies had agreed to use the TradeLens platform, but none of Maersk's major competitors had signed on. The head of TradeLens remarked, "I won't mince words here – we do need to get the other carriers on the platform. Without that network, we don't have a product."[106]

The creation of permissioned blockchains was essential to convincing businesses to adopt blockchain technologies, but it also required a sea change in the technology itself. Whereas bitcoin and many other virtual currencies were premised on creating a system that was open to all, permissioned blockchains are premised on the opposite idea. They start with the assumption that the blockchain contains valuable information that should not be shared with the wider world. They take many of the technological innovations of the blockchain (such as its cryptography, its linked hashes and its system of grouped information) and put these innovations into a more centralized system, the better to respond to the demands of the corporate world.

***

But the most radical experiments in blockchain have occurred not in corporations but in governments. At the root of these efforts is the idea of blockchain elections. In recent years, there has been growing concern that elections are failing us. The causes of this are various (from partisan gerrymandering to the corrupting influence of money to the biasing effects of social media platforms, some of which may be manipulated by foreign sources attempting to skew the electoral process), but they can all be traced back to two general problems in election theory: accuracy and comprehensiveness. The two concepts are simple to understand, but devilishly difficult to put in practice. First, elections need to be accurate in the sense that votes should be counted correctly – we do not want a system in which citizens' votes are lost or tallied improperly. Second, elections need to be comprehensive in the sense that the final vote should reflect the preferences of society as a whole – we do not want a system where only one group, such as the wealthy or the powerful, get to vote. These seemingly basic concepts in election theory run into major problems, however, in current electoral processes.

From the perspective of accuracy, election officials have long struggled to ensure that the vote-counting process functions smoothly. One need only remember the controversy over the 2000 election contest between George W. Bush and Al Gore. In that close-fought election, Bush originally won 271 electoral votes, a number that included Florida's 25 electoral votes, while his Democratic counterpart, Al Gore, won 266. But the margin of victory in Florida was incredibly, almost imperceptibly, slim. On election night, out of a total of nearly 6 million votes cast, Bush was found to have a lead of 1,734 votes (less than 0.03 percent of the vote). Even a small error in counting could thus have swung Florida from Bush to Gore and, in the result, have made Gore president, not Bush. In the ensuing legal battles, the votes were recounted to check for accuracy, using both vote-counting machines and manual, human-led vote counting. Most of these recounts led to different results, making the flaws in the process readily apparent to most observers. One problem was that the ballots varied from county to county. Palm Beach County, for example, used something called a "butterfly ballot" that had punchholes down the center with the names of candidates branching out on either side, leading people to puzzle over which punchholes connected to which candidates. Democrats cried foul, arguing that the maze-like butterfly ballot disadvantaged them because, while the Democratic ticket was listed as the second option on the left side, voters had to "punch" the third punchhole in order to vote for them, with the second punchhole reserved for the Reform candidate, Pat Buchanan.[107] Other scintillating questions, such as how much of a "chad" (the round piece of paper that is punched out by voters in order to create the hole that indicates their vote) needed to be detached from a voting card in order for it to count, riveted the country for days. The entire process was only resolved when the Supreme Court held, in another closely contested partisan vote, that recounting the votes would violate the Equal Protection Clause, thus upholding Bush's victory.[108] A consortium of newspapers later reviewed the rejected ballots and concluded that, if the court had ordered a full statewide recount of all rejected ballots, Gore would have won the state under a variety of review standards.[109]

And while the Bush-Gore fiasco led to efforts to improve the accuracy of election processes in the United States, including the widespread adoption of electronic voting machines by states, these methods have also been criticized.[110] After it became clear that Russian hackers had targeted state election systems during the 2016 election, a number of experts came forward to express their belief that voting machines were vulnerable to malicious actors. As Gregory Miller, the head of the nonprofit OSET Institute said,

> There is a widespread belief that not being connected to the internet is a measure of security. But many of these vote-tallying machines are not

dedicated machines only used for counting ballots. Many of them are used for issuing fishing licenses and building permits. It would take a half-second for someone to infect a machine with a USB thumb drive.[111]

In a more practical experiment conducted at a convention of hackers named Defcon, held in July 2017, it took an associate professor from IT University of Copenhagen a mere hour and a half to break into an electronic voting machine from Advanced Voting Solutions. Another hacking group found that they could compromise the machine by plugging in a mouse and keyboard and clicking "control-alt-delete."[112] Indeed, hackers managed to breach every voting machine at the conference. It is little wonder, then, that prominent think tanks such as the Brennan Center for Justice have issued reports sounding the alarm about the vulnerability of voting systems.[113]

There are also concerns about the comprehensiveness of electoral processes. Even if electoral systems find a way to count votes correctly, it is equally important that those votes reflect society's preferences. This requires citizens to actually show up to the polls and vote on election day. If certain groups are systematically excluded or underrepresented, whether intentionally or unintentionally, then elections will fail to reflect the will of the majority. Low voter turnout in recent years has raised concerns that this is becoming more than just a theoretical problem. In the 2016 presidential election, just 61 percent of adult U.S. citizens showed up to vote.[114] This means that approximately two out of five citizens are not expressing their preferences in their country's most consequential elections. Turnout in midterm elections, which do not involve a presidential contest, is even worse. Just 49 percent voted in the midterm elections of 2018, for example.[115] These numbers might be less disturbing if we thought that the people who actually did show up to vote broadly represented the makeup of the country as a whole. But we know this not to be the case. White citizens are much more likely to vote than nonwhite ones.[116] Female citizens are more likely to vote than male ones.[117] And older citizens are more likely to vote than younger ones.[118] All of this suggests that the preferences of certain groups in society have more weight than the preferences of others.

Problems like accuracy and comprehensiveness are precisely the kinds of problems that the blockchain is designed to solve. Because the blockchain is in its essence a shared record of information stored in a way that is resistant to manipulation, it has features that make it attractive as an electoral tool. By making elections accessible to anyone who has access to a computer, and thus reducing the obstacles to voting, blockchain technology could potentially improve the comprehensiveness of elections. It also might make elections more secure, given that voters could theoretically go back and check that their vote was properly registered on the blockchain and counted in the election, all without broadcasting their identity to the rest of the world – something that voters cannot do under current electoral systems.

Blockchain's theoretical potential to improve elections has led to a number of real-world efforts to conduct elections through the technology. Some of these efforts have turned out to be less fulsome than reported. For example, in March 2018, it was widely reported that Sierra Leone had conducted its recent presidential elections over the blockchain. The story began when the blockchain start-up Agora issued a press release with the headline "Swiss-based Agora powers world's first ever blockchain elections in Sierra Leone."[119] Agora's chief operating officer told reporters that it was the "first time in history a blockchain has been used in any government election, ever." It was a remarkable story: Sierra Leone, one of the world's poorest countries, a nation that had suffered through years of brutal civil war, followed by an outbreak of the Ebola virus in 2014, had adopted cutting-edge technology to revamp its elections. It was the kind of story that media outlets fawned upon. But the story turned out not to be true. The government of Sierra Leone denied the news: its electoral commission released a statement explaining that its voting system "does not use blockchain in any way."[120] Sierra Leone citizens denied any knowledge of having used the blockchain or Agora's services. Agora itself soon backed away from its early claims: its CEO stated that "[t]here was some miscommunication on our behalf" and "[w]e made a few mistakes when speaking to journalists, and when we sought to clear it up, it was all too late." It turned out that Agora had simply been an observer at the election, not the official registrar. As an observer, it had simply recorded the votes, as they were announced by government officials, on its own proprietary blockchain. Agora's blockchain was not, however, used for any purposes by the Sierra Leone government. Agora's later description of the process shows just how limited its effort was. According to Agora:

> Votes were recorded as follows: Paper ballots were folded and placed into boxes by voters. Once they were full, ballot boxes were unsealed and emptied onto a surface by NEC [Sierra Leone's National Electoral Commission] polling station agents in front of observers. Boxes were emptied and refilled with the same ballots five times to conduct various election counts. NEC polling station agents showed each ballot to the international observers and announced each written vote out loud. Agora tallied results, which were manually recorded onto our blockchain using digital devices. Our recording of ballots differed from that of NEC polling station agents when votes were discarded as invalid; Agora still recorded them. Ballot boxes were later taken to NEC tallying centers, where regional counts were performed by the NEC. This is outside of Agora's scope of engagement in the election.[121]

Sierra Leone's "blockchain election" was thus not much more than a marketing ploy.

A somewhat more ambitious effort was made by West Virginia in 2018. In its primary elections of that year, the state tested out a new mobile phone application that allowed voters to register their votes on a public blockchain. The test was limited to two counties and was only open to voters located outside of the state, such as military members, but it appears to have gone off without a hitch. Eligible voters uploaded photos of their identification cards, along with a video of their face, to the app in order to prove that they were who they claimed to be. Once they had done this, they could cast their votes, which were anonymized and then recorded on a blockchain. Audits of the vote turned up no problems, and West Virginian officials soon announced that they would use the platform in their upcoming general elections. Again, the general election blockchain vote would be limited to overseas voters and counties would have the option of opting out of the system, but the effort was significantly more advanced than any previous one. The results were less than overwhelming. A mere 144 West Virginians voted using the technology. Later, when asked about whether West Virginia would expand use of the blockchain in elections, the chief of staff to the secretary of state of West Virginia responded that the secretary "has never and will never advocate that this is a solution for mainstream voting."[122]

These efforts have not been unanimously welcomed by election experts. The chief technologist of the think tank Center for Democracy and Technology, Joseph Hall, for example, denounced the West Virginia effort, arguing that "mobile voting is a horrific idea." To Hall, mobile voting added additional security concerns to an already flawed process. "It's internet voting on people's horribly secured devices, over our horrible networks, to servers that are very difficult to secure without a physical paper record of the vote." Marian Schneider, president of the nonprofit advocacy group Verified Voting, echoed those concerns. When she was asked by CNN whether she thought mobile voting was a good idea, she replied: "The short answer is no."[123]

Significant concerns continue to exist about the blockchain's potential to improve elections. While blockchain may solve some problems in modern election systems, it also creates new ones. Actual implementation of blockchain solutions in electoral processes have been fraught with limitations. Given that most citizens do not have the technical literacy to be able to navigate the complicated world of blockchain unaided, it seems likely that blockchain elections will require the active participation of middlemen, such as the companies that develop and maintain mobile voting apps. But while these apps make it easier for voters to understand the process, they also introduce a degree of centralization; everyone has to use the same app, for example. And centralization raises the risk of intrusion, as hackers who want to disrupt elections would naturally target these apps to look for vulnerabilities. Any step in the chain (from the development of the app's software, to the version of the app that is downloaded by users, to the information provided by the user to the app, to the app's registration of the information on a blockchain) could potentially be compromised. And all of that happens before the information is included in a blockchain itself. The security of the blockchain itself is, in a sense, a side matter, given that flaws in any earlier step could lead to incorrect information being included in the official blockchain register. And when the blockchain receives bad information, it will store that information just as surely as it will store good information. To put it mildly, there is no easy solution to these problems.

***

This Chapter has taken a look at some of the real-world applications of the blockchain. It began with a short history of bitcoin, the initial virtual currency that started off the blockchain craze. It then turned to how other virtual currencies, such as Ethereum, adopted blockchain technologies for their own uses, leading to new blockchain systems with different characteristics. It also examined some of the more innovative uses of the blockchain, such as businesses using it to record product supply chains and enact self-executing contracts. And finally, it explored potential uses of the blockchain in politics, such as maintaining government records or holding elections. As these stories show, the blockchain has evolved into a multifaceted technology, and enterprising technologists have tried it out on any number of problems. Equally clear, however, is that the blockchain's real-world deployment has generally underperformed expectations. To be sure, the blockchain has spread across the world of business, finance and government like wildfire, with pilot projects and industry groups launching nearly daily. In doing so, the blockchain has captured the imaginations, and the wallets, of individuals and businesses alike. But after the euphoria of discovery, many of these efforts have ended in disappointment and abandonment. What is more, a strange thing happened to the blockchain as it spread. What had initially been envisioned as a technology for decentralization turned more and more towards centralized structures. Whereas early adopters saw the blockchain as a way to make the world more democratic, later entrants saw it as a way to make money or, more simply, a way to improve upon (rather than replace) preexisting concentrations of power. Power in the industry slowly shifted from individuals to large corporations and governments. The stories in this Chapter have hinted at some of the reasons for this shift, from the benefits of economies of scale, to the inefficiencies of participative decision-making, to fears about loss of control, to worries about fraud and deception. The next Part will address these issues head-on.

PART II

WEAK LINKS

4

Crypto-Criminals

At the bottom of every great fortune without apparent source, there is always a crime –
a crime overlooked because carried out respectably.

Honoré de Balzac, *Père Goriot*

In the early morning hours of July 25, 2017, Greek law enforcement agents descended on a small beachside hotel in northern Greece. Their target was a man named Alexander Vinnik. Vinnik, a thirty-seven-year-old Russian national, ran a bitcoin exchange by the name of BTC-e. The U.S. Justice Department believed that BTC-e, and thus Vinnik, stood at the center of a global ring of hackers, money launderers and corrupt officials, all of whom used his services to cover up their illicit activity. FBI agents had been tracking Vinnik for more than a year, but they knew that Russia was not likely to extradite one of its own citizens. Now they had finally found him, and he was outside of the protection of his home country.

Greek authorities, acting on information provided by the U.S. Department of Justice, zeroed in on a hotel in Ouranoupoli, a small town in the sleepy Halkidiki region of northeast Greece. The town was popular with Russian tourists, and Greek authorities believed that Vinnik was there on vacation. They were right. When they raided the hotel, they found Vinnik there with his family. A police officer spotted Vinnik using his cell phone and managed to distract him for a moment, allowing another officer time to grab the phone before Vinnik could lock it. The officers searched his room and found a treasure trove of mobile phones, laptops and tablets. They quickly arrested Vinnik and took him to prison in Thessaloniki. Photos at the time show him being led to court, his hands handcuffed behind him, wearing a tight-fitting black Polo Ralph Lauren shirt bearing the image of boxing gloves and the words "Trained in the Bronx," a gold necklace dangling from his neck.

Vinnik was a high-priority target for the Justice Department. Justice Department officials had tied him to a number of bitcoin-related crimes, and they believed that shutting down his exchange, BTC-e, would strike a major blow against the criminals that used bitcoin in their ventures. According to a federal court indictment against Vinnik, BTC-e served as a veritable one-stop shop for criminals. Cybercriminals, hackers, ransomware creators, drug dealers, corrupt government officials – all of them frequented the company and its exchange. Its user list included accounts under the names of "ISIS," "Cocaine Cowboys," and "hacker4hire." And it functioned as an active marketplace as well. The Justice Department estimated that during its six years of existence, Vinnik's company had handled more than $9 billion of bitcoin transactions, and this does not even include the other cryptocurrencies, such as litecoin, that the exchange dealt in. Perhaps most explosively, U.S. authorities believed that Vinnik was either the mastermind behind or at least actively involved in, bitcoin's greatest robbery, the hacking of Mt. Gox. Hundreds of thousands of bitcoins stolen from the Mt. Gox account showed up in accounts controlled by Vinnik. In the words of the indictment, Vinnik's company was "an exchange for cybercriminals worldwide, and one of the principal entities used to launder and liquidate criminal proceeds from digital currencies."[1]

In addition to hiding other people's virtual currency, BTC-e also hid its own operations, using a maze of offshore companies in obscure locations. BTC-e's website stated that the company was located in Bulgaria but was subject to the laws of Cyprus. BTC-e's named owner, Canton Business Corporation, was based in the Seychelles but listed a Russian phone number. BTC-e's web domains were registered to companies in Singapore, the British Virgin Islands and New Zealand, among others.[2]

But perhaps what is most striking about the allegations leveled against Vinnik and his company is that many of the violations of law that Vinnik was accused of were in fact inescapable parts of the bitcoin ecosystem itself. For example, the prosecutors charged Vinnik with violating anti-money-laundering and know-your-customer rules by failing to identify his customers. As the indictment explained, "a user could create a BTC-e account with nothing more than a username and email address, which often bore no relationship to the identity of the actual user. Accounts were therefore easily opened anonymously."[3] But of course these features of Vinnik's exchange (its protection of personal identities and its refusal to inquire about the sources and destinations of currency transfers) were also features that defined bitcoin itself. The Justice Department's accusations against BTC-e were indictments not just of Vinnik and his shady business practices, but also of the entire cryptocurrency world.

Vinnik's arrest would prove to be just the beginning of a long and drawn-out diplomatic battle between the United States and Russia. The United States asked Greece to extradite Vinnik to the United States for prosecution. France intervened as well, arguing that it too desired to prosecute him on behalf of French nationals who had been defrauded through BTC-e. The Russian government objected to both of these claims, asserting that he was wanted by Russian authorities in connection with a $10,000 fraud claim. Vinnik, for his part, claimed both that he had nothing to do with BTC-e's administration and, at the same time, that he was committed to fighting U.S. dominance of the global financial system.

The judicial proceedings bounced from court to court, with conflicting rulings being handed down every few weeks. In October 2017, a Greek court ruled that Vinnik should be extradited to the United States. A few weeks later, another Greek court ruled that he should be extradited to Russia. The Greek Supreme Court appeared to settle the matter in December 2017 when it ruled in favor of the United States' claim, but after France's intervention, another set of Greek judges ruled that Vinnik should instead be extradited to France. In the aftermath of that decision, which also happened to coincide with a decision by the Greek government to expel Russian diplomats, the Russian government lashed out. "Several days after taking an unfriendly decision to expel Russian diplomats and to deny entry to several Russian citizens, [Greece has] adopted a decision to extradite Russian citizen Alexander Vinnik to France," the Russian Foreign Ministry said in a public statement. "It is obvious that Russia cannot leave these actions unanswered."[4] The barely concealed threat was effective. Two weeks later, Greek judges reversed direction again and ordered that Vinnik should be extradited to Russia. Then, in September 2018, the Greek Supreme Court appeared to settle the matter, ruling that he should be extradited to Russia. As of August 2019, he remained in jail in Greece. In the meantime, Russian news sources reported that Greek police had uncovered a plot by criminal elements to poison Vinnik in jail. The unnamed source assured the newspaper that there was no connection between Vinnik's attempted poisoning and the poisoning of Sergei Skripal, the former Russian spy, in England earlier that year.[5]

Meanwhile, investigations into Vinnik began to untangle the complicated web of criminal enterprise that surrounded his company. Two of BTC-e's customers, it turned out, were Carl Mark Force and Shaun Bridges, disgraced federal agents who had worked on the task force that brought down the Silk Road, the online marketplace for illicit goods. Force had been the lead undercover agent on the task force, while Bridges acted as the computer forensics expert. In the course of their work, they happened to interview one of the Silk Road's administrators, Curtis Green, whom they had identified and arrested for his work on the site. During the interview with Green, Bridges, who worked for the Secret Service, learned how to access user accounts at the Silk Road. Taking this information, and without informing his team, Bridges secretly logged into the Silk Road, locked users out of the website and drained their bitcoin accounts, sending the bitcoin to his own accounts at other exchanges. In all, he stole around $800,000 worth of bitcoin. The brazen theft, which Bridges had accomplished using Green's administrator account, led the Silk Road's owner, Ross Ulbricht, aka the Dread Pirate Roberts, to suspect that Green had made off with the money. In retaliation, he decided that it was time to "call on my muscle."

Fortunately for Green, Ulbricht's "muscle" was a user who went by the name of "Nob." Nob, who claimed to be a cartel operative, was in fact Carl Mark Force of the U.S. Drug Enforcement Agency. Force soon received a message from Ulbricht stating that he had a "problem" that needed sorting out and attaching a photo of Green's driver's license.

"Do you want him beat up? Shot, just paid a visit?" Nob wrote back.

"I'd like him beat up, then forced to send the bitcoins back," Ulbricht replied.

In order to maintain his cover as a cartel operative, Force played along. Together with other members of the task force, he asked for Green's consent and then staged an elaborate torture session in which his team dunked Green repeatedly into a bathtub. The entire session was filmed and then sent to Ulbricht. After receiving the video, Ulbricht changed his mind.

"Ok, so can you change the order to execute rather than torture?" he wrote. "He was on the inside for a while, and now that he's been arrested, I'm afraid he'll give up info."

Force again played along, this time arranging for staged photos of Green lying on the ground, covered in Campbell's chicken soup, apparently killed by Nob. After Nob sent the photos to Ulbricht as "proof" that he had murdered Green, Ulbricht sent Force $80,000 as payment. When Nob asked Ulbricht how he was holding up, Ulbricht replied that he was "pissed I had to kill him. But what's done is done."

In the months that followed, the Silk Road task force continued searching for the owner of the Silk Road. But Force, much like Bridges before him, could not resist the temptation to enrich himself in the process. Adopting a number of cover identities, Force began extorting money from Ulbricht, threatening to expose Ulbricht's identity if he didn't send him bitcoins. At the same time, and under a different cover, he sold confidential information from the task force's investigations to Ulbricht, thereby threatening the very viability of his own task force. Ironically, Nob claimed that he had acquired his confidential information from a corrupt agent working on the Silk Road task force. In any event, Force profited handsomely from all these nefarious activities, allowing him to pay off a mortgage on his house, invest tens of thousands of dollars in stocks and real estate and send $235,000 to an offshore bank account in Panama. It is estimated that Force made more than $8 million from his transactions. Many of these transactions were laundered through Vinnik's company, BTC-e.

Federal authorities eventually discovered Force's and Bridges' corruption and arrested them. But, in a final coda to the saga, after Bridges had been convicted of stealing bitcoin from Silk Road accounts, but before he reported to prison, he took one last parting shot. Using the private key of a bitcoin wallet that was controlled by the U.S. government, he transferred 1,600 bitcoins to other digital wallets he controlled at BTC-e, sending hundreds of thousands of dollars to himself, knowing that BTC-e would not ask questions about his identity or where he had gotten his funds from.[6]

One final element of the Vinnik story bears mentioning. In the aftermath of the 2016 U.S. presidential election, and amid worries about Russian efforts to influence it, special counsel Robert Mueller led an investigation into Russian interference. The investigation concluded, among other things, that an elite Russian hacking group housed in the Russian military intelligence agency known as the GRU engaged in wide-ranging efforts to sway the election in favor of the ultimate winner, Donald Trump. Among other things, Mueller accused the hacking group, which went by the nom de guerre Fancy Bear, of hacking into and then releasing embarrassing emails from Democratic officials. The investigation also discovered that the hacking group used bitcoin to finance its operations – it paid for websites, registered domains, bought computer servers and made a number of other payments, all through bitcoin transactions. The group also mined its own bitcoin in order to gain further funds for its covert activities. According to the indictment, bitcoin "allowed the conspirators to avoid direct relations with traditional financial institutions, allowing them to evade greater scrutiny of their identities and sources of funds." A later analysis by the cryptocurrency firm Elliptic found that many of Fancy Bear's bitcoin transactions passed through BTC-e.[7]

***

In the popular imagination, cryptocurrencies conjure up lurid images of the "Wild West" of the internet, where anything goes and where the worst elements of cyberspace gather together with impunity. And cryptocurrencies like bitcoin do, in fact, offer a variety of "malicious" features (such as anonymity, irreversibility and untraceability) that make them attractive to bad guys operating outside of the law. This has led some critics to broadly attack blockchain and virtual currencies as dangerous technologies that must be stamped out. Bill Gates has called bitcoin the "rare technology that has caused deaths in a fairly direct way."[8] Jamie Dimon has called it a "fraud."[9] Warren Buffett has called it "rat poison squared."[10]

Others, however, argue that crime on the blockchain is the exception, not the rule. They point out that the vast majority of blockchain applications are perfectly legal, and that a few widely publicized thefts have unfairly tarnished the reputation of a promising new technology. They also suggest that the so-called malicious features of blockchain are in fact often quite beneficial. More often than not, we actually value these features as deeply important to the functioning of society. Anonymity might be a great tool for criminals to hide their identities from government officials, but it is also an essential tool for protecting consumer privacy. Irreversibility might frustrate the recovery of stolen money, but it also prevents parties from reneging on contractual obligations. Thus, when people condemn blockchain as a magnet for criminals, they are really making a value judgment about the importance of privacy and certainty, not about the technology itself.

But regardless of whether they think that, on balance, the blockchain creates more harm than good, nearly all observers agree that if there are simple things that can be done to stop crime on the blockchain, without creating undue costs elsewhere, we should do them. Once we turn our attention to this problem – that is, away from a holistic analysis of blockchain's desirability and towards the more targeted question of how to minimize crime on the block-chain – the question becomes a much simpler one. "Simpler," of course, does not mean simple. As we will see, the decentralized nature of blockchain technology makes it particularly resistant to traditional forms of crime preven-tion. Without a central authority capable of monitoring and enforcing rules, we are left in search of more innovative tools to protect citizens from bad actors. In short, decentralization has important consequences for crime.

The accusations that the blockchain is a magnet for crime are not entirely baseless. One study found that around a quarter of bitcoin users are involved in some sort of illegal activity and that around a half of all bitcoin transactions have direct connections to criminal behavior.[11] These figures likely understate the severity of the problem, given that cryptocurrencies other than bitcoin promise even greater anonymity and untraceability, and thus are safer bets for criminals seeking to hide their cash. Another analysis found that, of the $812 billion exchanged through bitcoin transactions in 2018, $2.4 billion went to merchant service providers who handle payments for business,

$604 million when to darknet sites (for things like drugs and stolen credit cards), $857 million went to gambling sites, and the rest was pure speculation (that is, a bet that bitcoin would rise in value).[12] Another study estimated that, of the seventeen million bitcoins in circulation at the time, four million had been lost and two million had been stolen.[13] In 2017, security breaches at cryptocurrency exchanges led to the theft of $266 million in virtual currency. In 2018, hackers stole $865 million from exchanges.[14]

But statements about the crime wave sweeping the blockchain world obscure the fact that there are actually two things going on when we talk about blockchain crime. One of these is just garden-variety theft – people stealing virtual currencies from one another. The fact that it is virtual currency, rather than real currency, is, in a sense, just happenstance. Instead of robbing banks, criminals are robbing virtual currency accounts. The Mt. Gox hack is one example of this: hackers simply accessed Mt. Gox's bitcoins and siphoned them out to accounts that they controlled. But the list goes on: in January 2018, hackers stole $535 million in cryptocurrency from Japanese exchange Coincheck; in February, hackers stole $170 million from Italian exchange BitGrail; in June, hackers stole $40 million from Korean exchange Coinrail; in July, hackers stole $24 million from Israeli-Swiss exchange Bancor. In all, more than $1.7 billion have been publicly reported stolen from cryptocurrency exchanges and platforms since 2011.[15] Cryptocurrency exchanges tend to be the target of these thefts because they control the virtual currency wallets of large numbers of people, but individual thefts also occur.

The second phenomenon, and the one that causes even greater concern in policy circles, isn't so much crime *on* the blockchain, as crime *enabled by* the blockchain. One worry is that criminal organizations are taking their ill-gotten gains and storing them in bitcoin or some other form of virtual currency. Another is that people are selling illegal goods and services, such as drugs and guns and sex, and accepting in return bitcoin or virtual currency. Another is that hacking groups, after launching ransomware attacks on companies, are demanding bitcoin as ransom for decrypting infected computers. When hackers – widely believed to be working for the North Korean government – unleashed the WannaCry cyberattack in May 2017, locking up thousands of computers around the world, including computers owned by Nissan, Renault and the United Kingdom's National Health Service, they asked infected users to send them $300 in bitcoin in return for unlocking their computers. Affected users ended up sending the hackers $140,000 in bitcoin as ransom payments.[16] One reason why this use of virtual currencies by criminals to buy, sell and store their assets is so problematic is that it eliminates one of the most effective mechanisms for tracking down criminals – the use of the banking system. There is a reason why prosecutors often adopt a strategy of "following the money." It is a lot simpler to track down financial flows from one bank to another than it is to monitor criminals in their daily activities. If criminals never have to use banks, though, they will never "touch" the financial system in a way that others can track.

So, when people say that the blockchain has a crime problem, they are generally saying one of two things: blockchain is a *target* of criminals, in that it is being stolen by them, and blockchain is a *currency* of criminals, in that it is being used by them. It's worthwhile to keep in mind that these two aspects of blockchain criminality are different and may require different policy solutions. What works to stop one element of crime may not work to stop another. Interventions to prevent hackers from accessing bitcoin addresses might not be particularly effective in stopping organizations from laundering money through them. And interventions to prevent criminal organizations from being paid in bitcoin might not be particularly effective in stopping hackers from stealing it.

***

Why is it that the blockchain has such high rates of crime? Is it a necessary feature of the technology? Or are there ways to reduce or even eliminate crime on the blockchain? These questions are essential to the future development of the technology, and industry participants and law enforcement agencies alike are hard at work trying to solve them. The answers they find may end up determining whether blockchain emerges as a world-changing technology or, instead, returns to the dustbin of history. But while crime on the blockchain certainly comes in its own unique forms and variants, the problems themselves are not new. Criminologists, sociologists and psychologists have been studying the causes of crime, and how to prevent it, for centuries. Many of their lessons are directly relevant to the blockchain and shed light on how we might go about busting crime in decentralized technologies. They also suggest some of the inherent limitations of these approaches.

Imagine that you are John Locke, and you desperately desire to have a copy of Hobbes' *Leviathan*, but you simply cannot afford it. The price (in bitcoin) that Hobbes has placed on the book is beyond your means. But imagine, further, that you know that your next-door neighbor has a bitcoin address filled with coins. He keeps the private key to this address written on a slip of paper on his bedside table. He is leaving town this weekend, and you know he never locks his door. You could simply slip inside his house while he is gone, take his private key and send the bitcoin to an address you own. Then you can finally have that copy of the *Leviathan* you have been pining away for.

Would you steal the bitcoin?

The question gets at a very basic problem in criminal law. Why do people commit crimes? And of course, there are many reasons – greed, envy, lust, anger. All the cardinal sins are prime suspects here. But one particularly influential theory comes from Plato's *Republic*, in perhaps the most famous thought experiment in the history of the philosophy of crime. It is the Ring of Gyges. In the story, the shepherd Gyges comes upon a golden ring while out tending his flock. By accident one day, he twists the sleeve on the ring and discovers that it turns him invisible. By twisting it twice, he becomes visible again. After several test runs with the ring, Gyges finally decides to use it. He travels to the royal court in Lydia and then, in short order, seduces the queen, murders the king and takes control of the kingdom.

The legend ends there. But it is Plato's take on the legend that has made it legendary. Glaucon, who is conversing with Socrates on the nature of justice, brings up the ring of Gyges to prove a point.

> Suppose now that there were two such magic rings, and the just put on one of them and the unjust the other; no man can be imagined to be of such an iron nature that he would stand fast in justice. No man would keep his hands off what was not his own when he could safely take what he liked out of the market, or go into houses and lie with any one at his pleasure, or kill or release from prison whom he would, and in all respects be like a God among men. Then the actions of the just would be as the actions of the unjust; they would both come at last to the same point. And this we may truly affirm to be a great proof that a man is just, not willingly or because he thinks that justice is any good to him individually, but of necessity, for wherever anyone thinks that he can safely be unjust, there he is unjust. For all men believe in their hearts that injustice is far more profitable to the individual than justice, and he who argues as I have been supposing, will say that they are right. If you could imagine any one obtaining this power of becoming invisible, and never doing any wrong or touching what was another's, he would be thought by the lookers-on to be a most wretched idiot, although they would praise him to one another's faces, and keep up appearances with one another from a fear that they too might suffer injustice.[17]

Glaucon here is presenting a theory of crime. According to Glaucon, everyone would commit crimes if they thought they could get away with them. In other words, given perfect anonymity, everyone is a criminal. For Glaucon, even the strongest sense of morality cannot withstand the power of a tool like Gyges' ring. Only a fool would refrain from taking what he wanted if he knew he could get it for free.

The ring of Gyges has thus come to stand for the proposition that what deters crime is not so much morality or psychology but rather detection and punishment. In order to fight crime, we need to ensure that crime doesn't pay. Glaucon's beliefs about the criminal lurking within all of us line up neatly with broader utilitarian theories of criminal law.[18] These theories assert that the criminal, like other individuals, is simply a rational actor. He will commit a crime if, and only if, it is in his interest do so. Crime, then, is the result of rational calculation. Or, as the economist Gary Becker has put it, "a person commits an offense if the expected utility to him exceeds the utility he could get by using his time and other resources at other activities. Some persons become 'criminals,' therefore, not because their basic motivation differs from that of other persons, but because their benefits and costs differ."[19] The results of this calculation depend on three key factors: the benefits to be gained from the crime; the likelihood of detection; and the punishment, if detected.

Utilitarians, thus, have a clear formula for fighting crime. Assuming we can't change the benefits of crime (something is either stolen or it isn't, after all), then we need to work on either detection or punishment. One way to reduce crime would be to increase the chance of detecting it. We could, for example, deploy more police on the streets or have them work longer hours in order to catch crime as it occurs. We could increase the power of investigators to track down criminals after the fact. Or we could install video cameras on street corners to record shady activities. The problem with a detection-oriented approach to crime, though, is that it can be expensive. It would be costly to society to have to pay policemen to work around the clock, or hire new investigators, or to install video cameras around the country. So, many utilitarian theories of criminal law argue, the better solution, the more efficient one, is to focus not on detection but on punishment. Instead of trying to catch more criminals, we just need to punish the ones we do catch very harshly. If criminals really are rational, then they should be less willing to commit crimes if the punishment is sufficiently draconian. After all, even if it is highly unlikely that someone will catch me jaywalking on an empty street, I might still refrain from doing so if the punishment were life in prison. It just is not worth the risk. "The efficiency of substituting severity for certainty," Dan Kahan, a law professor at Yale, has written, "is generally regarded as a foundational insight of the standard economic conception [of crime]."[20] The advantage of punishment-oriented approaches to crime is that they tend to be cheaper. Instead of spending lots of money increasing law enforcement activity, we can simply ratchet up the punishments of the few criminals we do catch, and the effect should be the same. It seems like a no-lose situation.

But increasing the harshness of punishments has some problems as well. For one, there may come a point at which increasing punishment just doesn't seem fair. Many individuals harbor an instinct that punishments should be proportionate to the severity of the crime. The punishment should fit the crime. It seems unfair to punish jaywalking with life in prison. It seems unfair to punish shoplifters with million-dollar fines. Even if we knew that most jaywalkers or shoplifters were not caught, and that these punishments were necessary to deter the unwanted behavior, we might still hesitate before we actually imposed them on individual violators. So, punishment-oriented approaches to crime deterrence run into fairness-oriented critiques. But second, and perhaps just as importantly, it is unclear that potential criminals really do weigh the potential punishment for the crime when deciding whether to commit it. They may well not even know what the range of punishments are (the Federal Sentencing Guidelines are notoriously complex). But even if they did know, there is strong evidence that they care much more about the likelihood of detection than the severity of punishment. After all, if I think I can get away with it, I may not care much about whether the punishment for committing a crime is five years, rather than ten, or even twenty.

A number of recent psychological studies have provided support to Glaucon and the utilitarians. One particular area of research that has received attention is cheating in academic environments. In one study, conducted at the University of North Carolina at Chapel Hill in 2010, researchers split participants into two groups, placing one group in a well-lit room and the other in a dimly lit room. The participants were then given a worksheet and asked to solve simple math problems. For each problem that they solved, they would receive a reward of $0.50. Importantly, however, participants were asked to report their own results, and it did not appear that there was any way for the researchers to double-check that they had reported their results honestly. Their worksheets appeared to be anonymous and participants gave themselves their own reward (out of an envelope stuffed with dollar bills). Thus, participants had a financial incentive to overreport how many problems they solved. But unbeknownst to the participants, their worksheets were in fact identifiable, allowing the researchers to determine who had cheated and who had not. The results were clear and compelling. While both groups overreported the number of math problems they had solved, the rate of cheating was significantly higher among participants placed in the dimly lit room. The researchers interpreted the results to suggest that when people feel that their identities are hidden, they are more willing to engage in unethical behavior. The darkness in the room, in other words, made the participants less principled.[21]

Thus, to Glaucon and the utilitarians, crime is a rational act based on a calculation of the costs and benefits of committing it. In order to reduce crime, we need to increase either the rate of detection or the severity of punishment. And a surefire way to increase crime is to introduce more anonymity into the environment.

A utilitarian approach to blockchain crime might, then, take aim at its anonymity. We know that there are high levels of crime within the blockchain ecosystem. Cryptocurrency exchanges are hacked on a regular basis. Criminals use bitcoin and other virtual currencies to launder their money. Ransomware attacks use bitcoin as their preferred method of payment. There is one obvious reason for these phenomena. Bitcoin (and, to an even greater extent, other cryptocurrencies) promise anonymity to their users. This makes blockchain-based cryptocurrencies attractive to people who would prefer to keep their transactions secret. Cryptocurrencies like bitcoin have long promoted anonymity as the underpinning of their technology. In Satoshi Nakamoto's original white paper on bitcoin and the blockchain, he wrote that the key to privacy on the network was keeping public addresses anonymous. And while it is possible for outsiders to observe transactions and see where bitcoin is coming from and going to, there is a high level of anonymity within the system because public addresses have no connection with real-world identities. Other virtual currencies have added on additional layers of privacy and thus can claim even greater assurances of anonymity. But just as importantly, blockchain transactions take place over the internet. It is entirely possible for someone to send bitcoin to a stranger over the internet without ever coming face to face with him. So, even if cryptocurrencies such as bitcoin are not perfectly anonymous (they may leak *some* information about the owner of the bitcoin, such as patterns of behavior or sources of funds), they have many of the trappings of anonymity that we know can affect individuals' behavior. All of these suggest that the barriers to criminality that exist in real-world scenarios are weakened within the virtual world of the blockchain.

But it turns out that bitcoin is not quite as anonymous as it is sometimes made out to be, and there are mechanisms for reducing its anonymity. To be sure, it appears to be anonymous to outside observers, at least at first glance. An outsider looking at the blockchain will see only a list of public addresses that are made up of a random string of numbers and letters, and these addresses will be associated with a number of bitcoins that reside at the address. Here is one public address: 18BUZZSmW1yZ6g88CYn6wmuUdGnTpjY6aT. The address has no link to the real-world identity of its owner and, thus, should provide some level of privacy. The problem, though, is that the addresses themselves are public. Even if we do not know the real-world identity of the owner of an address, we can still learn something about the owner by looking at the transactions that go through the address. For example, if a hacker says that he will only unlock your computer if you send bitcoin to a particular address, we might suspect that the hacker owns that address. If a public address receives $10,000,000 in bitcoin immediately after $10,000,000 in bitcoin has been stolen from a wallet, then we might suspect that the thief owns that address. This does not allow us to identify the owner, but it does give us some information. In reality, the process is a bit more complicated than this, as people can create multiple public addresses and send money between them or to newly created addresses. They can use "tumblers" and "mixers" to make it harder to tell which bitcoin went where. All of these strategies make it harder to associate public addresses with identities, but researchers have found ways to resolve or at least mitigate many of these problems. This is why scholars refer to bitcoin as a pseudonymous, rather than anonymous, virtual currency. People interact in the bitcoin network through the use of pseudonyms, or false names, but they cannot refrain from using names at all.

But who cares if governments can know where stolen bitcoin reside if they cannot identify the real-world owner of the bitcoin? They can't send a court order to a central administrator ordering the money to be returned. The blockchain has no central administrator. The money, it would appear, is irrecoverable. Well, it turns out that there are a number of ways in which pseudonymous public addresses might be linked with real-world identities.

For one, an owner might simply reveal that he owns a particular address. This is more common than one might expect. In December 2013, for example, Matt Miller, a TV anchor for Bloomberg, gave his two cohosts a Christmas gift of $20 worth of bitcoin, but in doing so, he briefly turned the slip of paper containing the address and private key to the video camera. The money was promptly stolen, by a reddit user going by the name of milkywaymasta. This is also one way that researchers learned of Alexander Vinnik's identity. A number of coins stolen from Mt. Gox had gone to an account associated with the name WME. Someone using the name WME had also posted on blogs that he was running a virtual currency exchange business in Moscow. Later, in posts on bitcointalk.org, one "WME" claimed that he had been scammed by a bitcoin exchange. WME also posted screenshots of his conversations with the alleged scammer, conversations that showed he went by the name of "Aleksandr," demanded payments to KBME Bank (a Tanzanian bank that was later labeled by the United States as involved in terrorist financing, transnational organized crime and sanctions evasion) and eventually had money transferred to a bank owned by "Vinnik Alexander." It didn't take investigators long to connect the dots.[22]

Another route to de-anonymizing bitcoin is connected to the process of converting bitcoin into more traditional currency. Bitcoin, after all, is a closed ecosystem: people can send bitcoin between themselves, but there is no way to convert bitcoin into dollars or euros or yen through the bitcoin software itself. If somebody wants to convert their bitcoin into traditional currency, they have to go through an exchange. The number of people using cryptocurrency exchanges has grown exponentially in recent years, with one popular platform, Coinbase, boasting twenty-five million users.[23] And these exchanges require information about the identities of their users. So any time that an individual uses an exchange to facilitate a transaction, he loses some of the anonymity that bitcoin provides. Indeed, this has been one of the primary methods that regulators have used to crack down on lawbreakers. In 2016, for example, in order to uncover tax evasion in the cryptocurrency world, the IRS ordered Coinbase to turn over the records of all customers who bought virtual currency in the period from 2013 to 2015. Central repositories thus serve a critical role in law enforcement in the industry.

So bitcoin is not quite as anonymous as some commentators make it out to be. And in some ways, it is even less anonymous than traditional currency. After all, the blockchain records all transactions in the currency on an immutable database, a database accessible to all. If someone knows the owner of a particular address, they can also trace back all transactions that that address ever entered into, all the way back to the creation of the currency. It would be as if you could trace a dollar bill everywhere it had ever been just by having it in your hands. Thus, bitcoin and other cryptocurrencies are not anonymous, and in some ways provide less in the way of privacy protection than traditional currency.

At the same time, cybercrimes tend to attract very low rates of punishment. In 2013, law enforcement agents found and recovered the money taken in physical bank robberies 21 percent of the time.[24] In comparison, very few cybercrimes lead to punishment. In 2010, victims reported 304,000 complaints of internet crimes. These led to just six convictions.[25] The difficulty of identifying, tracking and prosecuting internet crimes is high. These difficulties are only increased by the fact that internet crimes do not require a physical presence in a country. It is just as easy (perhaps easier) to launch a cyberattack from abroad than it is to do so domestically. And foreign law enforcement agencies may be less willing to assist in the prosecution of their own citizens for crimes committed against individuals abroad.

Targeting large actors within the industry, such as cryptocurrency exchanges, might be one way of increasing detection rates. After all, even if the blockchain itself is decentralized and peer-to-peer in nature, there are a few major companies that control a significant portion of the day-to-day transactions in bitcoin. But the problem, as amply demonstrated by the BTC-e case, is that often these large actors are located in offshore jurisdictions and, at least in some cases, are operated through shadowy and vague structures intended to hide their real owners.

And what is more, even when they are not located offshore, they often resist efforts by regulators to impose burdensome requirements on them. One example is ShapeShift AG, a Swiss cryptocurrency exchange that is run out of Denver, Colorado. ShapeShift's stated goal is to be the "fastest, most private, and most convenient way to swap digital currencies."[26] One way in which it does this is to allow users to exchange one cryptocurrency, such as bitcoin, for another, such as Monero, with the company not registering the identity of its users. It just so happens that Monero is a blockchain-based cryptocurrency that is even more anonymous than bitcoin, and thus provides a useful outlet for criminals seeking to hide their assets. ShapeShift is run by a towering figure in the blockchain world, thirty-four-year-old Erik Voorhees. He was an early adopter of bitcoin and founded one of the most famous and successful of bitcoin companies, a site called Satoshi Dice that allowed people to gamble using bitcoin. But Voorhees has been vocal in his criticism of regulatory efforts to lessen or eliminate the privacy-oriented protections in the blockchain. "I don't think people should have their identity recorded to catch an occasional criminal," he told one interviewer. Voorhees founded ShapeShift in 2014 under the pseudonym "Beorn Gonthier," a reference to a character from J.R.R. Tolkien's *The Hobbit* who could shapeshift into a bear. A *Wall Street Journal* investigation of the company discovered that almost $9 million of dirty money had been laundered through the site. This included money from North Korean hackers and Ponzi scheme operators. The *Wall Street Journal*'s analysis also concluded that, of the $89 million laundered through ShapeShift and other exchanges, less than $2 million had been seized by law enforcement. So just 2 percent of money laundering through cryptocurrencies gets detected – a woefully small amount.[27] So, even when large actors are located within a jurisdiction, it may be difficult for regulators to constrain them. Such efforts to target large actors within the industry are limited in scope and effectiveness.

All of this suggests that efforts to deter crime on the blockchain through purely legal methods will meet with substantial obstacles. The illusory anonymity provided by bitcoin and the more fulsome forms of anonymity provided by other cryptocurrencies make virtual currencies an attractive form of value for criminals and may also encourage bad behavior by individuals who might not have committed crimes in real-world situations. Low rates of crime detection may embolden criminals even further. And the decentralized nature of the blockchain make it difficult for regulators to impose better discipline on the industry: there is no single actor that they can impose regulatory requirements upon.

***

But if Glaucon and the utilitarians suggest that people will commit crimes if they think they will not be caught, another important field of criminal law theory argues that what truly stops people from committing crimes is the belief that it is wrong to do so.[28] These normative theories of crime assert that people have all sorts of opportunities to commit crime in their daily lives, but rarely do they do so. What stops them is not so much that they fear that the police will catch them but rather that doing so violates their ideas of what is right and good, of what people *should* do. Another way of putting this is that while utilitarian theories of crime tend to focus on reason – the ability of individuals to make rational choices based on the costs and benefits of given behaviors – normative theories of crime focus on norms – those informal understandings about appropriate behavior that contribute to order and civility in a community. Normative theorists argue that social and moral standards regulate the behavior of individuals much more effectively than law ever can. Utilitarian theorists would consider this nonsense. Norms of behavior not backed by sanctions do not restrain individual decision-making, they argue. As long as crime pays, criminals will exist. We need to focus on incentives, the utilitarians argue, not beliefs. But to believers in the efficacy of norms, material incentives are only a part of what determines people's actions. Values, beliefs and communities are just as important. Thus, if we want to stop crime, we need to find ways to ensure that individuals believe that the law is legitimate and its dictates worthy of obedience.

Normative theories of crime have identified a number of ways in which the social environment affects individual beliefs and behavior. One conclusion is that individuals are deeply influenced by the beliefs, and the actions, of their peers. "If a person is surrounded by persons who are (or appear to be) morally opposed to crime, she is likely to share their aversion," writes Dan Kahan. "If they find (or appear to find) criminal behavior innocuous or even desirable, she is likely to feel the same way."[29] This insight leads to a number of potential avenues for addressing crime.

One is simply informing the community of what other people actually do and what they believe. This type of intervention, known as social proof, can work well when most of the community is law-abiding and finds crime morally repugnant. It has been used, for example, in reducing binge drinking on college campuses. It turns out that college students tend to believe that their peers are more comfortable with binge drinking than they really are, and this misconception leads them in turn to be more willing to binge-drink themselves. In order to correct this incorrect belief about social norms, one group of researchers simply gave students information about the systematic misperception of other students' comfort with campus drinking. Doing so led to a significant decrease in drinking.[30]

But normative theories of crime also highlight some of the dangers of attempting to regulate social norms. The law, after all, affects social meaning. If it does so in pernicious ways, it might end up accomplishing the exact opposite of what it intends. In the words of Kahan, "*what* it punishes (drug possession, sodomy) can tell us what kind of life the community views as virtuous; *how* it punishes (imprisonment, corporal punishment, fines) can tell us what forms of affliction it views as appropriate to mark wrongdoers' disgrace; how *severely* it punishes (the death penalty for the killers of whites, life imprisonment for the killers of blacks) can tell us whose interests it values and how much."[31] If these messages are inconsistent with the broader views of the community, or if punishments are regarded as unduly harsh, they may well undermine the legitimacy of law in the eyes of citizens.

One famous example of this comes from the world of drug sentencing. In 1986, in response to growing public concern over an epidemic of drug use in the country, Congress passed the Anti-Drug Abuse Act, imposing severe mandatory prison sentences for a long list of drug offenses. But the Act also included a notable discrepancy: if an offender was found in possession of crack cocaine, they would receive a mandatory ten-year sentence if they had just 50 grams of the drug on them; but if an offender was found in possession of powder cocaine, they would receive a ten-year sentence only if they had 5,000 grams of the substance. In other words, there was a 100-to-1 disparity between crack cocaine and powder cocaine under the sentencing laws. This disparity alone might not have been a problem if there had not also been strong racial implications in the disparity. One study of federal prosecutions found that 91 percent of crack defendants were African American, while only 3 percent were white. Conversely, 32 percent of powder cocaine defendants were white, while only 27 percent were African American. A consequence of this disparity was that black defendants often faced the harsh sentencing requirements applicable to crack, while white defendants only faced the (comparatively) lenient sentencing requirements applicable to powder cocaine. And while many explanations have been offered for the difference (the differing physical effects of the drugs, their addictiveness, their association with crime, etc.), the overall effect of the disparity was hard to ignore. Its harms fell overwhelmingly on African Americans. This had knock-on effects on community views of the law. As Laura Murphy of the American Civil Liberties Union said of the law:

> It is both unfair, impractical, and unwarranted. How can you go to an inner-city family and tell them their son is given 20 years, while someone in the suburbs who's using powdered cocaine in greater quantities can get off with 90 days' probation? When people understand the truth about the way these laws are imposed, the fact they've had no deterrent, and the race-based nature of these prosecutions, then I think a sleeping giant is going to roar.[32]

In other words, the disproportionately severe punishments given to the community led to an outcry against the fairness and legitimacy of the law itself. Eventually, Congress was forced to pass a new law, the Fair Sentencing Act, reducing the disparity in sentencing regimes between crack and powder cocaine.[33]

Thus, normative theories of crime assert that crime depends on beliefs, both about what is virtuous and good, and about what others believe is virtuous and good. If we want to deter crime, then we need to pay attention to the social environment in which it takes place. We need to change the informal social and moral beliefs of the relevant community. And we need to appeal to ideas of fairness and equality. What might a normative approach to blockchain crime look like? If legal sanctions are ineffectual at deterring crime on the blockchain, then perhaps norms-based interventions can step in to fill the void. Blockchain users often refer to the network as a "community," one where individual users have a say in the way the system is governed. They tout the democratic nature of the blockchain and its open-source approach. Thus, at least rhetorically, there seems to be some support for the proposition that social norms within the blockchain have powerful behavioral effects. This suggests that social sanctions could potentially provide an effective substitute for legal sanctions in policing problematic behavior.

There certainly do seem to be instances of community-oriented cooperation for the common good on the blockchain. Prominent examples include the community's efforts to resolve the unintentional hard fork created in the bitcoin network in 2013 by the release of a new version of the software, as well as the efforts in 2016 within the Ethereum community to create a hard fork to resolve the hack of the DAO venture. In each of these scenarios, large actors cooperated to prevent harm to other users, even when there were no direct benefits to themselves (they of course benefited indirectly by preventing disastrous consequences that might have imperiled the very existence of the virtual currencies). Chat rooms also are filled with examples of Good Samaritans helping other users out after they have had their bitcoins stolen or their accounts hacked.

But there are reasons to be skeptical about the scope and effectiveness of social sanctions in rooting out criminality on the blockchain. For one, as a purely empirical matter, they do not seem, to date, to have done a particularly good job at it. Money laundering, thefts and hacks are rampant in bitcoin and other cryptocurrencies. In 2018 alone, around $1.7 billion in cryptocurrencies were stolen from exchanges or scammed from investors.[34] Kaspersky Lab, a prominent cybersecurity group, estimates that 1,811,937 users were affected by ransomware in 2017 and 2018, with many of these users being forced to pay bitcoin or some other virtual currency to regain access to their computers.[35] And other nefarious behaviors are also springing up such as "malicious crypto-mining," in which hackers take control of a user's computer and harness the computing power to mine for cryptocurrency for their own account.[36] As Kaspersky Lab wrote in one recent report, "cryptocurrencies have opened up new and unprecedented ways to monetize malicious activity."[37] So, at least for now, social norms have not been effective in deterring criminal behavior on the blockchain.

Of course, social norms take time to develop. The very idea of a "norm" is that it comes from the normal or usual form of behavior in a community. Until people have been interacting with each other and observing the behavior of others for a certain amount of time, these conceptions about what is normal and appropriate in the community just cannot develop. David Axelrod, the game theorist, has argued that norms require repeated interaction; otherwise, learning just cannot occur.[38] Thus, it could be that, as the blockchain industry develops, more cooperative forms of behavior will become a social norm and criminal behavior will decline as a result.

But there are additional obstacles to cooperative social norms in the blockchain. One other reason to be skeptical about the effectiveness of social sanctions on the blockchain is that, even if these sanctions manage to deter a substantial portion of crime, even a small number of bad apples can wreak substantial harm. Even if we can convince the vast majority of users to refrain from using the blockchain to promote crime or launder money, this could still leave a number of hardened criminals who see it as an opportunity to make off with their loot. And just a few hacks can lead to massive losses for users.

This gets at an important point. Social sanctions are most effective when communities are small and closely knit. This is a problem for the blockchain. The blockchain community, after all, is vast and impersonal: its membership comprises thousands of anonymous computers around the world, with real-world interactions rare or nonexistent. In his pivotal study of the development of social norms in the world, Axelrod found that it was significantly more likely for stable forms of beneficial norms to develop within communities that were small and close-knit, where there were expectations that members would interact with each other in the future. Sometimes, norms can develop in surprising places, so long as the participants believe that they will interact again. He cites, for example, the development of norms between opposing soldiers in World War I. Troops often developed a kind of "live-and-let-live system" with the other side. In battles, soldiers would often intentionally avoid harming soldiers in opposing trenches. As one British officer wrote:

> It was the French practice to "let sleeping dogs lie" when in a quiet sector . . . and of making this clear by retorting vigorously only when challenged. In one sector we took over from them they explained to me that they had practically a code which the enemy well understood: they fired two shots for every one that came over, but never fired first."[39]

Importantly, the community within World War I armies was sufficiently small and cohesive for social norms to stick. If someone violated the norms, they would be immediately reminded of their mistake by receiving shots from the enemy side. Within the blockchain community, it is unclear that such cohesiveness currently exists or is even capable of existing. Users typically do not interact together in the real world. There are many more people within the community. And it is unclear how "punishment" could be dealt out by other members of the community.

Finally, and perhaps most importantly, the actual norms of the blockchain community appear to include a certain amount of what can only be described as a laissez-faire attitude towards selfish behavior. "It's not a bug if it is included in the code," is not an uncommon sentiment. After the Mt. Gox hack, for example, a number of bloggers came out arguing that the Mt. Gox investors "should have known better." One thread was titled: "Can somebody tell me how anybody with money on MtGox was not a greedy awful and stupid speculator?"[40] When one user responded that some people might have been relatively new to bitcoin and simply not have known where else to store their currency, he was quickly criticized for his lack of knowledge.

"I'd say your as [sic] at fault as the importance of the money to you," wrote one user. "If that money meant a lot to you and you were depending on it then you should have been more involved in the community so that you knew what was happening to that very important investment you made."

"It's always best to blame the victim," wrote another user, apparently ironically.

"Yes, especially when those victims are idiots," responded another.

"Sounds to me like you lost a lot of money with Gox," the user continued. "Well if so, I can say that I am genuinely happy that you are hurting for this.

Speculators are worth less than nothing, contribute nothing to society, and ultimately deserve this."

Emin Gün Sirer, a professor of computer science at Cornell and the codirector of the Initiative for Cryptocurrencies and Contracts, has looked at this problem in some depth. Having studied peer-to-peer systems and distributed networks for years, he quickly took an interest in the cryptocurrency phenomenon and was soon writing frequently on the industry. And although often optimistic about the potential of blockchain, he also had questions about the perceived security of bitcoin from harmful cyberattacks. In 2013, he cowrote a paper with Ittay Eyal, a colleague of his in the computer science department at Cornell, titled *Majority Is Not Enough: Bitcoin Mining Is Vulnerable*.[41] The paper demonstrated that it was possible for a group of miners commanding less than 25 percent of all computer power on the network to compromise the bitcoin system, earning more than their fair share of bitcoins. The paper received much attention in the bitcoin community because it disproved the widely held belief that bitcoin could be compromised only if bad actors managed to control 51 percent of the mining power on the network. Sirer's paper showed not just that bitcoin was less impregnable than some thought it was but also that its proper functioning required significantly more than a majority of the network to behave honestly. If even a small minority of its actors set out to take advantage of others, they could very well succeed.

Bitcoin's reliance on honesty led Sirer to a further question. Were people inclined to behave honestly when they interacted through the blockchain? The system was anonymous, after all. What incentives did they have to behave appropriately if their misbehavior could not be punished? Curious about how the increasingly mechanized world affected human behavior, Sirer did what any respectable academic faced with a seemingly intractable question does: he polled Twitter. In a post, he asked his followers the following question:

> You find a system bug that, if you used it, would make you X dollars. The bug bounty is a flat $10 k. Assume you won't get caught. Above what value for X do you use the bug to make money, instead of reporting it and settling for the bounty?[42]

In other words, he asked his followers to put a monetary value on just how honest they were. If a company had launched a new product and offered users $10,000 to identify any vulnerabilities in the product – the "bug bounty" – would they willingly identify the vulnerabilities if that meant giving up a chance of exploiting those vulnerabilities for their own gain? How much money would it take for them to sacrifice their honesty?

The responses were overwhelming. More than two-thirds of people would exploit the bug if the personal gains from doing so were sufficiently high. Only one-third of people reported that they would never exploit the bug. So twice as many people would exploit a known vulnerability in a program if it would make them money than would voluntarily report the vulnerability. Users responded with a number of rationales, but a common one was that there was nothing wrong with taking advantage of a computer program that had a flaw in its code. "Bug = undocumented features," wrote one user, continuing: "Burden on vendor. Why not." "Bug exploiting is not theft," wrote another. "IMO, its [sic] incompetence from the part of the developers and the investors," wrote yet another. "Bugs should be exploited. Darwinism applies in the crypto space too."

Sirer's study was admittedly unscientific, but it did give a sense of the norms within the industry. Many, perhaps even most, blockchain and cryptocurrency enthusiasts were willing to exploit other users for personal gain, even when the exploitation was caused by a "bug," so long as they could be sure they would not be caught. This caveat emptor mindset, reminiscent of Glaucon's argument about the ring of Gyges, was prevalent in the industry. If someone was unwilling or unable to fully understand a technology, then they had to bear the costs of their ignorance. They should not expect to be protected by the norms of ethical behavior in the real world.

This is problematic for blockchain from a governance standpoint. Even the best-written programs, ones issued by the world's largest companies, have unknown vulnerabilities when they are launched. "In spite of decades of steady technological progress that has made computers better in almost every way, virtually all software still suffers from bugs," Matt Blaze, a computer scientist at Georgetown, has said. "Every computer, every smartphone, every piece of software is delivered to the user with a plethora of hidden security flaws preinstalled. We just haven't found them yet."[43] The problem is that computer programming is notoriously fickle. Unlike human beings, who at least nominally have the ability to spot a glaring error and refuse to execute it, computers must respond to actions in the way that they are ordered to do by their code. This means that even small errors in a code, or even oversights, can cause large problems. In 2018, an iPhone hack known as the "black dot bug" began circulating that allowed hackers to freeze victims' iPhones simply by sending them a text message with a black dot in it (the black dot was accompanied by malicious code). In 2017, a security expert for Google discovered the worst Windows vulnerability "in recent memory," a bug that would allow hackers to remotely access target's computers without any action by the target itself. Both problems were eventually discovered and resolved. But the presence of such vulnerabilities, even in software developed by some of the world's most sophisticated and powerful companies, demonstrates the extent of the problem. It is why software companies regularly issue patches and updates. They are waging a constant battle against known and unknown bugs.

Vulnerabilities in the blockchain could potentially be quite harmful. For example, the error in version 0.8 of the bitcoin source code led to a fork in the bitcoin network in March 2013, a small mistake that nearly destroyed the virtual currency entirely. It was only resolved by the concerted action of a few large miners, who had to sacrifice their hard-earned currency in the name of preserving the system itself. But, of course, the incentives to identify errors in code, and thus exploit them, grow when the assets behind the code grow. And Bitcoin's total value has grown tremendously, from a market capitalization of approximately $40 million at the beginning of 2012 to a market capitalization of $238 billion at the end of 2017.

Here, for example, is a page of Bitcoin's code from July 2010:

```
Case OP_RETURN
{
    c = pend;
}
break;
```

Notice anything problematic? Probably not. But in late July 2010, a German programmer going by the name ArtForz did. He realized that the line allowed someone to spend money from another person's wallet. This was back when Satoshi Nakamoto was still active in the community. Nakamoto, so worried about the problem, decided that it was too dangerous to acknowledge. So instead of announcing the flaw, he simply hid it from the rest of the network. He instructed the small group of people who had become aware of the problem to keep it secret. "For now, don't call it the '1 RETURN' bug to anyone who doesn't already know about it," Nakamoto wrote to Gavin Andresen, another bitcoin developer. In order to fix it, he wrote a patch to the bitcoin software and buried the fix in the revised code of an otherwise anodyne update to the software. Because the revised software "has a dozen changes in it, it won't necessarily be obvious what the worst vulnerability was. That may give people a head start to upgrading if any attackers are looking for the vulnerability in the changes." Nakamoto's patch worked: the 1 RETURN bug was fixed and, at least for a while, the threat of people spending other people's bitcoin receded.[44] But Nakamoto remained deeply concerned about the security of the network. It is worth remembering his final message, posted to Bitcoin's forum on December 12, 2010: "There are still more ways to attack than I can count."[45]

***

To a number of criminologists, the neat dichotomy between utilitarian and normative theories of crime obscures the practical reality that most people, at most times, have mixed motives for their actions. People are guided not just by their ideas of the good, but also by their ideas of what is good for them. They might be willing to sacrifice some amount of well-being for their broader moral commitments, but not too much. They might be willing to break some of society's norms to get ahead, but they aren't willing to break them too flagrantly. As Max Weber wrote, "[i]t is understood that, in reality, obedience is determined by highly robust motives of fear and hope – fear of the vengeance of magical powers or of the power-holder, hope for reward in this world or in the beyond."[46] This sensible approach – and one adopted by many criminal law theorists – is something of a hybrid of the two models described above. Norms matter, but so do incentives. If we want to stop crime, we need to change norms of behavior within a community, *and* we need to change the incentives for individuals. We cannot simply do one or the other. Even the strongest norms will not stop committed outlaws, while even the strongest punishments will not deter criminals in communities where crime is an accepted, even laudable, way of life.

One particularly influential hybrid theory of criminal law is the theory of broken windows. James Wilson, a criminologist at Harvard, and George Kelling, a criminologist at Rutgers, first articulated the broken windows theory of crime in a 1982 article in *The Atlantic*. In the article, they argued that "untended" or disorderly behavior leads to a breakdown in community controls. Once communal barriers of mutual regard and civility are lowered by actions that signal that no one cares, crime tends to spread quickly. They gave the example of windows in a building.

> Social psychologists and police officers tend to agree that if a window in a building is broken and is left unrepaired, all the rest of the windows will soon be broken. This is as true in nice neighborhoods as in rundown ones. Window-breaking does not necessarily occur on a large scale because some areas are inhabited by determined window-breakers whereas others are populated by window-lovers; rather, one unrepaired broken window is a signal that no one cares, and so breaking more windows costs nothing. (It has always been fun.)[47]

In other words, according to Wilson and Kelling, what prevents crime is not so much monitoring and detection as outward signals of community norms of good behavior. We should fix broken windows and paint over graffiti, not just because it changes the cost-benefit analysis of an individual deciding whether to rob a bank, but also because it sends a message about what kind of community it is. "This is a community that cares about its members." "This is a community of upstanding citizens." "This is a community that maintains peace and order for its members." When these signals of community behavior break down, so too do the norms preventing criminal or lawless behavior.

In support of their position, Wilson and Kelling gave an example drawn from the work of Philip Zimbardo. Zimbardo, a psychologist at Stanford, was famous for his "prison experiment." In the experiment, Stanford students were asked to play the role of either guards or prisoners within a mock prison. Within a matter of days, the situation spiraled out of control, with the "guards" abusing the "prisoners" with real punishments, including physical assault, psychological abuse and other degrading behavior, such as forcing the prisoners to urinate and defecate in buckets they placed in their cells. Eventually, Zimbardo had to call the experiment off in order to prevent further harm. Interestingly, Wilson and Kelling do not refer to this study in their paper, perhaps because its results might have led readers to discount the results of the study they did cite. Instead, they focus on another prominent study of his, this one involving abandoned vehicles. For the study, Zimbardo parked a car with no license plates and the hood up on a street in the Bronx and a street in Palo Alto. In the Bronx, it took a mere ten minutes before someone stole the radiator and battery from the car (the perpetrators, Zimbardo notes, were a mother, father and son). Within a day, thieves had removed everything of value from the car, and then people simply started smashing windows and ripping the upholstery. Things went differently in Palo Alto. The car parked in Palo Alto stood untouched for over a week. Eventually, Zimbardo went and smashed the car with a sledgehammer. Only then did other passersby join in in desecrating the car.[48] Wilson and Kelling take from this experiment the lesson that outward appearances, such as untended property or untended behavior, heavily influence individual decision-making. "Because of the nature of community life in the Bronx – its anonymity, the frequency with which cars are abandoned and things are stolen or broken, the past experience of 'no one caring' – vandalism begins much more quickly than it does in staid Palo Alto, where people have come to believe that private possessions are cared for, and that mischievous behavior is costly. But vandalism can occur anywhere once communal barriers – the sense of mutual regard and the obligations of civility – are lowered by actions that seem to signal that 'no one cares.'"

In their broken windows theory of crime deterrence, Wilson and Kelling draw on the Zimbardo experiment to propose a number of potential solutions to crime, many of them community focused. Rather than relying on the police to impose order, communities might try to enforce order themselves, either through "community watchmen" who patrol informally or by vigilante groups that take the law into their own hands. But these community efforts, Kelling and

Wilson conclude, are unlikely to keep the peace without more. The police are needed as well. Simple changes, such as having police officers travel on public transportation on buses and subways, in order to see and be seen, and heightened enforcement of rules against smoking, drinking and disorderly conduct, might have substantial effects on crime more generally.

If the problem is outward signs of social decay and disorder, then the answer, under the broken windows theory, is more police monitoring. Cops on the street. The more that we can stop low-level crime and even behavior that does not amount to crime but simply contributes to an overall sense of disorder, the more we will deter crime before it happens. The broken windows theory has been so influential in criminal law circles that it has leaked into real-world policing strategies. New York City hired Kelling as a consultant in the 1980s and subsequently started to implement many of his ideas, such as strictly enforcing rules against graffiti, subway fare evasion and public urination. Chicago adopted a slightly different approach, referred to as "community policing," in which the city government was proactive in removing graffiti, responding to complaints about rundown buildings and generally engaging with residents. Los Angeles has also adopted elements of the broken windows approach. Studies assessing the effects of the broken windows approaches have reached conflicting conclusions, some finding that it is an effective strategy for high crime areas, while others finding that it is largely unhelpful. The broken windows theory has also met with criticism for its association with a number of problematic consequences, such as the stop-and-frisk policies that have been criticized roundly for leading to racially discriminatory results. But these criticisms notwithstanding, broken windows theory continues to play an important part in criminal law theory and in real-world policing behavior.[49]

Broken windows theory has been bolstered by studies on the influence of environmental cues on individual behavior. In one set of studies conducted in the Netherlands in 2008, researchers set out to examine whether other signs of disorder and neglect would make people more willing to engage in bad behavior. In order to answer this question, the researchers lodged an envelope halfway into a mailbox, so as to make it look like the mailer had failed to secure it in the mailbox, and placed a five-euro note visibly in the envelope. Researchers then subtly changed the environment to see how it would affect the behavior of passersby. In one scenario, the mailbox was covered in graffiti. In another, the ground around the mailbox was cluttered with litter. In the final scenario, both the mailbox and the surrounding ground were clear and uncluttered. The researchers found that the surrounding conditions had a large effect on people's willingness to steal the envelope (and the five-euro note) from the mailbox. When the mailbox and its environs were clear and uncluttered, passersby stole the envelope 13 percent of the time. But when the surroundings had signs of disorder, passersby were much more likely to steal the envelope. When the ground near the mailbox was covered in litter, 25 percent of people who passed ended up stealing the money. When the mailbox itself was covered in graffiti, 27 percent did. In other words, the mere presence of graffiti and litter doubled the number of people who were willing to steal.[50]

If broken windows theory suggests that effective crime-fighting requires fixing windows, repainting buildings and punishing minor infractions of law, all in order to send a signal of community order, how might it apply to the blockchain? At the core of any broken windows approach is a belief in the importance of visible signals of social norms and law enforcement priorities. Thus, as a starting point, we might attempt to identify the behaviors and actions that are most visible to the blockchain community. For example, we know that cyberintrusions into cyptocurrency exchanges like Mt. Gox and BitInstant receive substantial attention in the press and message boards. We also know that major darknet sites, such as the Silk Road and AlphaBay, have gained notoriety in blockchain circles as well. Thus, we might start by focusing law enforcement efforts on cleaning up these sites, by bolstering security procedures, prosecuting low-level offenders and making clear that law enforcement agents are actively monitoring these sites. One approach might be to follow what the FBI did after it shut down the Silk Road in 2013. Instead of taking the site entirely offline, the FBI instead posted a replacement site that visitors would be directed to. This site would greet visitors with a prominent message proclaiming "THIS HIDDEN SITE HAS BEEN SEIZED," along with a message about the investigation and images of the seals of the FBI, the Drug Enforcement Administration and the Department of Homeland Security. The FBI adopted this approach as an ex post strategy, posting the notice only after they had already shut the site down. But broken windows theory suggests that an ex ante approach might work even better, alerting potential criminals that sites are actively being watched by law enforcement agencies.

But, of course, there are some real difficulties with adopting a broken windows approach to blockchain crime. For one, it is expensive. The idea behind broken windows is that we need active monitoring of communities and frequent prosecutions of lawbreakers, even minor ones. Adopting such an approach in cyberspace would require a much more proactive and intrusive approach from regulators, visiting sites, posting messages and launching cases. This takes time, money and resources.

It also goes against the trend in cybercrime enforcement of focusing on only the largest cybercrimes, and in particular ones with national security implications. The Vinnik case illustrates such an approach: it touches on a number of high-priority problems – from global money-laundering networks to corrupt federal agents to Russian espionage. And there are good reasons for authorities to focus on these types of megacybercrimes. Prosecuting hackers is hard to do, both because attribution is hard (how do we prove that the hacker is the one that actually did it in a world of anonymous browsers and virtual private networks?) and because the crimes often cross borders (how do we catch a criminal in a foreign country without the cooperation of local authorities, who may well want to protect their own nationals, particularly if the victims are all abroad?). A broken windows approach to blockchain would require a major shift in law enforcement priorities.

But, finally, it's not even clear whether the mechanisms that make broken windows theory work in the real world also work in cyberspace. Broken windows policing involves cleaning up physical spaces, putting cops on the street, and increasing interactions within a community. Part of the intuitive appeal of the theory is its personal nature: we are affected by the things we see in the world and the people we speak to. But when people are communicating through computers, this physical element is eliminated. What is the "space" that needs to be improved? This is a problem with cybercrime more generally as well. As Neal Katyal, the former solicitor general, has written, "[s]ocial norms cannot operate as effectively to prevent crime on the net because its users are not necessarily constrained by the values of realspace."[51] One of the major concerns about the sociology of the internet is that it gives extremists an outlet for finding communities of like-minded believers, ones where radical and hateful ideologies can be spread without fear of condemnation. It is unlikely that law enforcement will be able to target all of these sites. Thus, regulators likely have neither the means nor the will to engage in the kind of intrusive monitoring that broken windows theory suggests is necessary to prevent crime effectively.

✳✳✳

Utilitarian theories of crime suggest that criminal activity will be highest where the probability of detection and the sanctions for violation are low. Normative theories suggest that it will be highest where individuals cease to view the legal order as legitimate or worthy of respect. Broken windows theories suggest that it will be highest where general signs of disorder abound. These insights lead to different recommendations about how to fight crime. Under utilitarian theories, we need to focus on improving our ability to monitor and detect crime and to set punishments at efficient levels to deter crime from occurring in the first place. Under normative theories, we need to instill in individuals a respect for the rule of law, either by educating them about the content and desirability of the law or by, potentially, changing the law itself. Under broken windows theories, we need to focus our efforts on fighting low-level crime and even things that do not amount to crime but contribute to signs of disorderly communities, such as graffiti and littering. The three approaches might, of course, overlap in some instances. For example, a broken windows theory to policing might propose that we increase the number of policemen walking the streets – a proposal that might also increase the likelihood that a given crime would be detected and punished and that might also increase the respect of citizens for legal authorities. But they might also conflict. In some instances, utilitarian theories of crime suggest that we should forget about improving the rate of detection and instead focus on ratcheting up jail time and punishments – something that broken windows theories do not generally recommend and that might undermine respect for the legitimacy of the legal system as well. Similarly, broken windows and normative theorists have at times recommended simple, non-crime-related police action, such as cleaning up graffiti or abandoned buildings – something that utilitarian theorists generally do not focus on.

These alternative theories of crime suggest some of the avenues governments might take to target crime on the blockchain, but they also demonstrate the limitations of all of these approaches. One of the unifying problems that all of the theories struggle with is decentralization. From a utilitarian standpoint, it is hard to change the incentives of dispersed actors because there are so many actors to monitor. From a normative standpoint, it is hard to change social values when the community is large and diffuse. And from a broken windows standpoint, it is hard to send messages of community order when there is no single physical space to act on. The mechanisms of crime prevention run into trouble when they deal with decentralized systems.

But of course, in a way, this is the very intention of the blockchain. It is a technology purpose-built to resist government intrusion. It is based on ideas about the proper limits of government and the inherent rights of individuals. Thus, the criminality problem is more than just an unhappy coincidence. It is rooted in the blockchain system. The history of individualism and antiauthoritarianism within the industry suggests that efforts to constrain crime within the blockchain will necessarily meet with substantial obstacles.

5

The Energy Hunt

The cost of a thing is the amount of what I will call life which is required to be
exchanged for it, immediately or in the long run.

Henry David Thoreau, *Walden*

In the far northern reaches of Sweden, where snow blankets the countryside
for more than half the year, where winter temperatures regularly reach minus
fifteen degrees Fahrenheit or lower, and where the Northern Lights blaze
across the dark sky during winter months, a massive new industrial complex
hums away night and day, its work never stopping. It is known as the "Node
Pole," and it is powering the blockchain.

Boden, Sweden, is an odd place for blockchain miners to have set up shop.
The small town was founded at the junction of two railways, the Northern
Line and the Ore Line, built in the 1800s to facilitate the transport of rich iron
ore from the mines in the north to the cities in the south. The extremeness of
the geography is hard to exaggerate. If you started in Fairbanks, Alaska, and
drew a line eastward along the latitude towards Sweden, you would end up at
the town of Kage. You would then need to drive an hour and a half north to get
to Boden. If you drove another hour, you would hit the Arctic Circle. Boden's
main claim to fame is that it is strategically located near the northeastern edge
of the country and, thus, near Russia. As a result, Boden has long been home to
large detachments of the Swedish army. In fact, to this day the Swedish army
maintains its largest garrison in all of Sweden in the town. The town fortress,
now decommissioned, still brims with bunkers, shelters and dragon's teeth
fortifications. But, beyond that, the town is somewhat unremarkable. As Nils
Lindh, an official at the Boden Business Agency, put it to me, quite simply,
"Tourists come here because it is quiet, and they can see the Northern
Lights."[1] Indeed, just down the road is the world-famous Treehotel, a series
of minimalist, but nonetheless luxurious, treehouses in the middle of thick
forest.

In the last few years, however, Boden has started to make a name for itself in the blockchain world. Because of its northern location and its access to cheap energy, Boden turns out to be an attractive destination for companies seeking to mine cryptocurrencies. Companies have flocked to the city in droves. In 2014, KnCMiner, an ASIC manufacturer, opened a mining facility in an old helicopter hangar that had been used by the Swedish army. In February 2017, Canaan Creative, a Chinese miner, announced that it too was setting up a facility in Boden. And then in May 2017, two large cryptocurrency miners, Hive Blockchain and Genesis Mining, announced that they were opening a major mining farm in the town as well. Suddenly, Boden, an isolated town near the Arctic Circle, had become the center of some of the world's most powerful blockchain mining operations.

"It all started when we got the Facebook investment," Nils Lindh, the head of business development at Boden Business Agency, explained. In 2013, Facebook had set out to find a location for its first data center outside of the United States, and it ultimately decided on Lulea, a university town near Boden. Facebook decided on Lulea because of its cheap electricity from renewable sources and its energy efficiency; the cold winter air acts as a natural coolant for the hot-running servers that process Facebook's tremendous amount of international data.

"After we got the Facebook investment, we started asking if we could attract more data centers," Lindh continued. "And when we started looking at it, we realized we had nearly perfect conditions from an infrastructure point of view for attracting energy-intensive industries."

One of their first investors was KnCMiner, the ASIC manufacturer. In 2014, when KnCMiner went looking for places to open a new cryptocurrency mining farm in Sweden, it finally settled on an old aircraft hangar used by the Swedish armed forces for storing helicopters. It then proceeded to fill it to the brim with mining rigs – a total of 45,000 in all.[2] This facility was a 10 MW facility. But it was such a success that they then decided to build a second facility, this one a 20 MW facility. This was followed by a third and then a fourth facility, all of them located in and around Boden. But the company's rapid success came to an abrupt halt in 2016. In July of that year, bitcoin's block reward was halved from 25 bitcoins to 12.5 bitcoins, meaning that newly mined blocks paid out only half as much as before. Recognizing that their business model would not be profitable under the new regime, KnCMiner declared bankruptcy.[3] As Lindh told me:

> If they could have managed to find the cash to survive for another week, they would still be running today. Bitcoin was trading for around $240 when they

declared bankruptcy, but two weeks later, it was up at $600. But they put us on the map. After they came, we started to get calls from miners. We started attending blockchain events and data center events. We went to one in San Francisco in 2013. It was filled with angel investors and entrepreneurs and Silicon Valley execs. And there we were, these government employees from an Arctic town in Northern Sweden. But that was our Eureka moment. We understood what the blockchain was. It is not about bitcoin, or cryptocurrencies, or anything like that. It is about what you can use the blockchain for. And we realized we were perfectly set up to attract it.

In 2018, Hive Blockchain, a major cryptocurrency mining company based in Canada, announced that it would be investing $100 million in a new mining farm in Boden. Hive's background was unusual. The company had originally been formed, way back in 1987, as a gold mining operation, Leeta Gold Corp. But in 2017, the company pivoted to the blockchain industry and changed its name to Hive Blockchain Technologies Inc. Within three days, its stock rose 633 percent.[4] Its mining farm in Boden was its largest gambit yet, increasing its mining capacity almost twofold. The massive facility is filled with mining rigs, tens of thousands of them, specifically designed to mine for cryptocurrencies, primarily bitcoin and ethereum. These cutting-edge mining computers run twenty-four hours a day, seven days a week, solving the difficult problems that are required to earn the rewards that come from finding new blocks to add to the blockchain.

"Here in an undisclosed remote region of Sweden, less than thirty kilometers from the Arctic Circle, one of the world's large digital currency mines has just been constructed," the company boasts in a video tour of the facility, set to a musical score that would not be out of place in a high-tech thriller movie. "Welcome to Hive."

"Across nearly every industry that exists, centralization, corruption and security are major problems and support for decentralized solutions grows every day," the video continues. "The benefits of blockchain technology extend far outside of just currency, and many predict it will play a critical role in transforming our world one decentralized industry at a time. As the industry matures, mining facilities like this will play a critical role in powering our much-needed decentralized world."[5]

For Hive, the decision to move to Sweden was largely an economic one: the price of electricity in Sweden was 6.5 euro cents per kilowatt hour in 2018, while the average price in Europe was 11 cents per kilowatt hour.[6] When the primary driver of a mining farm's costs is electricity, these cents can make a big difference.

"We're on a global hunt to secure as much power as we can," Hive director Olivier Roussy told one interviewer.[7]

But other factors played a role as well, including the political environment, energy sources and climate. Hive's CEO explained the decision to locate in Boden in the following terms: "I am delighted to launch Hive's largest and most advanced mining facility to date in Sweden, another stable, cold climate jurisdiction with access to abundant green energy, to further capitalize on rising cryptocurrency prices."[8] The Swedish facility happens to be powered by hydroelectricity provided by a local hydropower plant, giving Hive an abundant source of cheap, renewable energy.

Indeed, energy consumption is so important to blockchain companies that they brag about it. In January 2018, Hive issued a press release stating that that they had just finished the first phase of the build-out of the facility in Boden. The release announced that the new facility "increases [Hive's] energy consumption dedicated to cryptocurrency mining by over 175% to 10.6MW." More was to come: "Hive is fully financed to add an additional 13.6MW of GPU mining capacity in Sweden by April 2018 and a further 20.0MW of ASIC mining capacity, facilities capable of mining Bitcoin and Bitcoin Cash, by September 2018."

In late 2018, though, signs of trouble emerged for the cryptocurrency mining industry. A steep drop in bitcoin prices put pressure on the companies, who earn the majority of their profits from selling bitcoin. Mining farms, after all, have large fixed costs: they have to build facilities, buy mining rigs and maintain them – all while upgrading, when necessary, to take into account any increases in capacity in the network (remember that the difficulty of mining equations increases automatically in the bitcoin network if miners start solving the equations more quickly than expected). The hope is that these costs are offset by the revenue they earn from block rewards granted when they verify transactions, find new blocks and add them to the blockchain. But when the value of those rewards (currently set at 12.5 bitcoins) drops, profit drops as well. At the peak of the market at the end of 2017, a single bitcoin was worth $20,000, meaning that miners were earning $250,000 every time they found a block ($20,000 times 12.5 bitcoins). But by October 2018, the price of a single bitcoin had dropped to $6,500, meaning that miners were earning only $81,250 every time they found a block. The price had dropped by more than 67 percent, severely cutting into the profits of miners. This led Genesis Mining, one of the companies that had relocated to Boden, to rethink its business model. It began forcing clients to enter into five-year subscriptions if they wanted to continue using Genesis Mining's services. The company explained that the change was necessary because "some user contracts are now mining less than the daily maintenance fee requires to be covered." In other words, it was no longer profitable to continue mining at the price that clients were paying.

Another miner, Hashflare, announced in June 2018 that it was closing for the same reason – "the payouts [from mining] were lower than maintenance for 28 consecutive days."[9]

But at least some observers believe that the Node Pole, and the crypto-currency mining boom powering it, will continue. "Our end goal is to get start-ups developing blockchain use cases here," Lindh, the head of business development at the Boden Business Agency, said. "This is our goal. There is a lot of talent here, even in the forest. Entrepreneurs and programmers, many of them want the country life. We want to prove that they can do it all here."

✳✳✳

"Bitcoin mining poses threat to Paris climate-change accord."[10]

"Bitcoin is destroying the planet."[11]

"Bitcoin mining on track to consume all of the world's energy by 2020."[12]

Judging from the headlines of recent years, one might be led to conclude that the blockchain presents the greatest threat to human existence since the dawn of nuclear warfare. And while these headlines may be alarmist, they certainly paint a stark picture of the inefficiencies of blockchain technology and the harms these inefficiencies are visiting on the planet. They suggest that bitcoin and the blockchain are gobbling up massive amounts of energy and polluting the environment on a major scale. If something is not done about it soon, they suggest, the repercussions for our global ecosystem will be catastrophic.

A cursory look at the numbers shows why. Studies of the energy used by blockchain-based virtual currencies have consistently shown large and grow-ing consumption in the industry. A study published in 2018 concluded that the bitcoin network was consuming 2.55 GW of electricity and estimated that it would soon grow to 7.67 GW. To put these numbers in perspective, they are equivalent to the consumption of the entire countries of Ireland (population: 4.8 million) and Austria (population: 8.8 million), respectively.[13] Digiconimist, a site that tracks energy use in the bitcoin system, estimates that as of October 2018 the bitcoin network was using 73 tWh per year, more than the vast majority of countries in the world.[14] And these numbers are just for bitcoin itself. Other cryptocurrencies consume significant amounts of energy as well. Ethereum, for example, is estimated to consume a smaller but still massive 19 tWh per year.[15]

The numbers are even more shocking when viewed from a per-transaction perspective. After all, it would be one thing for a virtual currency to be consuming large amounts of energy if it were powering the entire global economy. But even at its feverish peak in 2018, bitcoin handled only a small fraction of the number of transactions that occurred through banks, credit card processors and cash. One study concluded that each bitcoin transaction consumes between 300 kWh and 900 kWh of electricity. The lower end of this estimate would be enough to power the average Dutch household for a month. The higher end would power an American household for the same length of time.[16]

This extensive energy use gives the blockchain a massive carbon footprint. One report found that the bitcoin network emits approximately 17.7 million tons of carbon dioxide per year.[17] Another concluded that bitcoin's carbon footprint was even larger, at 69 million tons of carbon in 2017.[18] Another report found that a single bitcoin mining farm in Mongolia was emitting between 24,000 and 40,000 kilograms of carbon dioxide an hour. The farm consisted of eight buildings, all of which were filled with mining rigs, a total of 25,000 in total. The factory received its energy from a nearby coal-fired power plant, from which it had received a 30 percent discount by the local government. Its daily electricity bill was $39,000. But these costs were dwarfed by the farm's profits: its daily revenue was $250,000.[19] For a small factory located in a desert in Inner Mongolia, these were astounding sums.

And while some commentators have criticized these studies for adopting unrealistic assumptions, even the most conservative estimates of blockchain's energy use are still massive. It is thus a worthwhile question to ask why precisely the blockchain requires so much energy to operate, and whether anything can be done about it. Bitcoin, after all, still remains a relatively little-used currency. Other currencies are even less functional. If they are already consuming electricity at such high rates, what would happen if they grew to the sizes that the more optimistic prognosticators assume? Is the blockchain an environmental disaster in the making?

This Chapter will begin to explore these questions, but it will also position them within a broader debate about the costs and benefits of decentralization. The last Chapter explored how spreading out power can affect individual incentives and social norms. It showed how doing so can lead to damaging feedback effects between self-interested behavior and community morality. This Chapter, on the other hand, will explore how spreading out power can affect efficiency, potentially leading to duplicative processes that slow down decision-making and increase its costs. This doesn't mean that democratizing technologies are always inefficient. But it does mean that they require input and action from many different

actors, often located in different places. Finding efficient ways to coordi-
nate their activities can often present a challenge.

***

To understand blockchain's energy problem, we have to revisit the structure of
the blockchain itself. Satoshi Nakamoto, the creator of bitcoin, coded the
blockchain so that the only way in which new bitcoins could be issued was by
adding new blocks – which contain lists of pending transactions in the currency – to the blockchain. In a very real way, this is what the blockchain is. It is
simply a long list of blocks that show where bitcoins reside. Thus, it is deeply,
perhaps existentially, important that individuals are incentivized to add blocks
in a responsible and accurate manner. This explains why Nakamoto introduced
the concept of a block reward – if you add a block, you are compensated for your
effort with a few bitcoins (originally, the reward was 50 bitcoins, but it has since
declined to 12.5 bitcoins, as set by Nakamoto's code). At the same time, it was
also important to ensure scarcity in the blockchain system. Nakamoto did not
want new bitcoins to be minted too quickly or easily, or else the currency could
become devalued. In order to ensure scarcity, Nakamoto intentionally made it
difficult for computers to add new blocks to the blockchain. To add a block,
miners must package together the previous block plus any new transactions into
a proposed new block, and then hash all those together such that the hash of the
previous block, the new transactions and a random number known as a nonce is
equal to or lower than a given value. The given value might, for example, be

ooooooooooooooooooo1oooooooooooooooooooooooooooooooooooooooooooooooo.

What makes this calculation so difficult is that, given the hashing equation
that Nakamoto chose (the cryptographically secure hashing algorithm known
as SHA-256), it is impossible for miners to know ahead of time which nonce
will give a hash value beneath this target. The only way for them to solve it is
through brute force. Computers must simply guess . . . and guess . . . and guess.
Eventually, they will luck into the right combination of inputs. This concept is
what is known as proof of work: in order to mine new blocks and be issued
newly minted bitcoin, nodes have to prove that they did a certain amount of
computational work.

Of course, over time, as more miners have thrown more computing power
at the hashing algorithm, the bitcoin network has gotten very good at solving
these hashing algorithms quickly. They are making guesses so rapidly that, if
the difficulty of the equation had stayed the same as it was when Nakamoto
first instituted it, computers would be mining new bitcoins by the second.

Nakamoto recognized that this might be a problem and, to address it, introduced an evolutionary quality into the hashing game. If, in any given period, computers mined new bitcoins at a rate faster than desired (a rate he set at one block every ten minutes), the difficulty of the hashing algorithm would automatically adjust so that, in the next period, new blocks would again be found at the desired rate.[20] So, for example, if a new mining farm came online in the last period and the network started mining new blocks at the faster rate of one every five minutes, rather than one every ten minutes, then bitcoin's algorithm would order the difficulty level to double in the next period so that bitcoin mining would reset to its desired pace. What this means, of course, is that the bitcoin mining game is a virtual version of the Red Queen's race: no matter how fast bitcoin miners run, they will always stay in the same place.

But while it may be true that, as a collective matter and over the long term, miners cannot beat the system, this does not mean that miners have no incentive to beef up their computing power. In fact, the opposite is true. They have strong economic reasons for creating bigger and faster mining rigs. For one, it takes some time for the bitcoin network to notice changes in hashing power, so miners that quickly add new mining rigs to the network find themselves mining new blocks at a higher rate for a short time. Thus, there is a short-term but tangible reward for increasing your hash power. But, perhaps more importantly, if a miner adds new hash power, while others don't, it will gain a competitive advantage over its rival miners and be able to mine a greater proportion of new blocks. This means that the miner with the biggest, fastest computers will earn more bitcoins than other miners, even if the miner ecosystem, taken as a whole, is still earning new bitcoins at the same rate. In other words, miners have incentives to devote ever more computing power to bitcoin in order to stay ahead of their competitors, even if it is a zero-sum game from a mutual, industry-wide perspective.

These economic incentives led to the so-called arms race in mining power in recent years, as companies developed faster and faster mining chips and deployed more and more of them in an effort to keep ahead of their competitors. One important factor in encouraging this race was bitcoin's rising value during much of the 2010s. In 2012, a single bitcoin was worth $100. At the end of 2017, it was worth $20,000. The price of bitcoin has real practical consequences for the behavior of miners: their primary reward for performing hashing equations is the new bitcoins they earn every time they add a block to the blockchain. As a result, higher bitcoin prices justify higher expenditures in terms of energy and computing power. Miners have developed newer and faster chips in response. In January 2012, the total hash power of the bitcoin network was 8.8 terahashes per second – meaning that all the computers on the bitcoin network combined could calculate 8.8 trillion hash equations per second (a terahash is equal to a trillion hash equations). That is a lot of hash calculations. But by 2018, the company BitMain was selling a single mining device, called the Antminer S9-Hydro, that weighed just thirteen pounds, and that had more than double that hash power, all for the price of just $700.[21] In October 2018, the entire network had a combined hash rate of around 52 million terahashes a second. In other words, bitcoin miners were running hash equations at a rate six million times faster in 2018 than they were in 2012.[22] And of course, as miners have gotten faster and faster at running hashing equations, the network has adapted to make the problems harder and harder to solve. This, in turn, means that it is more expensive for miners to mine new bitcoin.

This situation might strike observers as nonsensical. Why would someone ever design a system that required such massive amounts of computing power to run? Or, what is more, why would someone ever design a system that directly incentivizes companies to devote more and more energy to performing worthless calculations? After all, solving these hash equations is not providing useful new knowledge to the world. They are not solving world hunger or developing driverless cars. They are simply proving what data, when put through the SHA-256 algorithm, hashes to an arbitrarily chosen number. And the only way to solve this problem is simply to guess! As a practical matter, this means that the primary determinant of who earns money in the bitcoin world is who expends the most energy guessing. To put it bluntly, this seems bad.

It turns out, however, that there is a very important reason for structuring the blockchain system in this way. That reason is security. Requiring miners to perform these difficult math problems, and forcing them to expend real money and energy doing so, makes it very hard for malicious actors to go into the blockchain and alter it after the fact. Hashing is at the heart of blockchain's cybersecurity. Without it, the blockchain would be dangerously susceptible to hacking, theft and fraud.

In order to understand this point, it is worthwhile to return to the basic function that miners perform in the bitcoin network. Miners add transactions and blocks to the blockchain, but they also maintain the blockchain by validating these transactions and blocks as they are added. They do this by checking to ensure that newly added transactions are real transactions – that is, that the person who is trying to send the bitcoins really is the person he claims to be (by confirming his digital signature) and owns the bitcoins he claims to own (by confirming the contents of the sending address). All of these transactions are connected through a chain of blocks, with each block referencing the previous block in the chain (technically, each block includes a hash of the previous block, a concept known as a hash pointer). What this means is that anyone can trace a bitcoin from where it resides today back to the point in time when it was first created, simply by working backwards through the long chain of blocks in the blockchain. It also means that a change anywhere in the blockchain leads to changes everywhere in the blockchain, or at least in every block after the change. After all, each block contains a hash of the previous block. So, if a malicious actor wants to go back and secretly add a transaction somewhere in the middle of the blockchain, he cannot simply change the contents of that one block from many months ago. He has to change the contents of every block thereafter.

The proof-of-work system at the heart of blockchain's mining infrastructure makes it prohibitively expensive for him to do so. Adding a block, after all, requires lots of computing power, energy and time. And the only way that the malicious actor's blockchain will come to be accepted by other nodes is if he can somehow make his blockchain longer than the real, nonfraudulent blockchain. As long as lots of nonmalicious miners are out there devoting computing power to mining new blocks, it should be nearly impossible for the malicious actor to re-mine all the blocks that he has to change and still overtake the other blockchain. And even then, other miners will likely see that the malicious actor's blockchain looks nothing like the other version they had been working on, and could easily reject it. Mining, thus, makes the blockchain remarkably tamper-resistant.

Putting all this together, the seemingly inefficient mining game spurred on by the bitcoin network, as well as other blockchain networks, serves to protect the blockchain from hacking. In order to tamper with the blockchain, hackers have to amass such an enormous amount of computing power to overwhelm the system that doing so becomes unprofitable. They are better off simply playing by the rules of the game and mining their own bitcoin with all that computing power. Nakamoto's system thus creates strong incentives for the community to act honestly to validate and maintain the system.

The problem is that all of this computing power requires electricity to run. A single mining machine like the Antminer S9-Hydro has a power consumption of around 1,700 watts. This is a large, but not inconceivable, amount of energy – many hairdryers, for example, use upwards of 1,500 watts of electricity. The problem comes from the fact that, unlike hairdryers, which are typically used for only a few minutes a day, mining rigs are packed together into small spaces and run all day. Per square foot, an average cryptocurrency mining farm might use 2,100 kWh per year, compared with 12 kWh per year for an average residential home.[23] And mining farms are much bigger than your average home. KnCMiner's mining farm in Sweden is housed in an aircraft hangar and contains 45,000 mining rigs.[24]

The effects of this massive energy consumption are already being felt. Cryptocurrency miners in some cities have grown so large that they are putting strains on local utility infrastructure. Consider, for example, Chelan County in Wenatchee, Washington. Chelan County happens to be the location of the Rocky Reach Dam, a hydroelectric power facility along the Columbia River that, along with other dams in the area, provides energy to seven million people in the northwest of the United States. Because of its close proximity to these hydroelectric projects, Chelan County has always been known for its cheap energy. Electricity there typically costs between two and four cents per kilowatt-hour, significantly less than the average of twelve cents per kilowatt-hour in the rest of the United States.[25] It did not take long for cryptocurrency miners to realize that Chelan County would be a great place to set up shop. By 2018, thirty cryptocurrency miners had moved there. In fact, the Chelan County Public Utility District was so swamped with applications and inquiries from cryptocurrency firms hoping to open facilities there that they had to place a moratorium on new applications. Other local businesses complained that the influx was raising energy prices for everyone else and even leading to energy shortages. This worried local political officials. "We are getting requests for service that are just astounding," Steve Wright, the general manager of Chelan County Public Utility District, told the *Wall Street Journal* in an interview. "We do not intend to carry the risk of bitcoin prices on our system." The president of the board of commissioners for the utility district stated that placing a moratorium on new miners was essential to "safeguard the county's precious jewel, our hydropower."[26] Eventually, the county decided to implement a new pricing structure that raised electricity prices specifically for cryptocurrency and blockchain companies.[27] A similar move by a neighboring county, which had received requests from cryptocurrency miners that would have more than tripled the entire county's electricity use, was quickly challenged in court by miners who argued that the rate change unfairly and arbitrarily discriminated against the industry.[28]

But these kinds of problems pale in comparison with what might happen if blockchain scaled up on a global scale. In September 2018, there were, on average, around 230,000 bitcoin transactions a day.[29] In comparison, a single credit card company, Visa, handles 150 million transactions a day.[30] If bitcoin or other currencies were to take off, their energy use would increase as well. The Bank for International Settlements concluded that it would be nearly impossible for cryptocurrencies to scale to handle the types of volume that traditional payment processors handle:

To process the number of digital retail transactions currently handled by selected national retail payment systems, even under optimistic assumptions, the size of the ledger would swell well beyond the storage capacity of a typical smartphone in a matter of days, beyond that of a typical personal computer in a matter of weeks and beyond that of servers in a matter of months. But the issue goes well beyond storage capacity, and extends to processing capacity: only supercomputers could keep up with verification of the incoming transactions. The associated communication volumes could bring the internet to a halt, as millions of users exchanged files on the order of magnitude of a terabyte.[31]

In other words, if virtual currencies were to become truly global, they would paralyze world commerce.

The blockchain thus has an energy problem. It is consuming massive amounts of electricity, computing power and engineering effort, all for the sake of solving simple but time-intensive mathematical problems that are arbitrarily set by computer code. What is more, energy use has risen rapidly in recent years, driven largely by the economic incentives of miners to devote more and more power to minting new blocks for the blockchain. If the trends continue, maintaining the blockchain could eat up greater and greater swathes of the world's energy.

At least so far, however, the consequences of this pending environmental dilemma have not changed mining behavior. Miners continue to build new mining facilities around the world in a constant search for cheap energy. The world's largest miner, BitMain, for example, announced in August 2018 that it would invest $500 million in a new cryptocurrency mining factory in Rockdale, Texas, taking over an old aluminum smelting facility.[32] In January 2018, a Russian company bought up two old power stations in the Ural Mountains in Perm, Russia, and converted them into crypto-mining facilities.[33] In May 2018, two Australian companies agreed to develop a decommissioned coal power plant into a mining complex for $142 million.[34] Iceland, one of the more popular destinations for miners, has been overwhelmed with new crypto-facilities; in 2018, the energy consumption of miners exceeded that of all the country's homes combined.[35]

At least part of the reason why miners have not reduced their energy consumption is that they are making a lot of money from it, particularly the largest miners. Remember that the reward for mining a new block is currently set at 12.5 bitcoins. When bitcoin was at its peak price of $20,000 in December 2017, this meant that roughly every ten minutes (the interval for adding a new block to the blockchain) one lucky miner was handed out a gift of $250,000. This works out to daily issuances of $36,000,000. Annual issuances of bitcoin would amount to more than $13 billion. To be sure, this did not all land in the lap of a single miner. Rewards are issued to whichever miner was fortunate enough to mine the last block. Success in the race to mine new blocks is determined partially by luck ("Were you lucky enough to guess the nonce that hashed to the desired value set by the bitcoin software?"), but also, and to a much greater extent, by computing power ("How many guesses were you able to make in the last time period?"). This means that the largest miners were capturing the lion's share of the profits. And while information about miners and their shares of the market is not transparent, some commentators have argued that BitMain alone may well control more than 50 percent of the bitcoin network's hash power, meaning that they could earn a majority of all newly issued bitcoin.[36]

The secretive world of crypto-mining became a bit less opaque in 2018 when BitMain announced that it was filing for an initial public offering on the Hong Kong Stock Exchange. In order to sell shares to the public, the Beijing-based mining company was forced to disclose information about how it worked and how its finances looked. The documents provide a remarkable look at the business of cryptocurrency mining. To start with, BitMain made profits of $1.1 billion in the first quarter of 2018. Interestingly, however, most of these profits came, not from mining itself, but from selling mining equipment to other miners. These sales accounted for 90 percent of its profits in 2017 and 94 percent of its profits in the first six months of 2018. BitMain held a global market share of 74.5 percent in ASIC chips (the specialized mining chips, known as application-specific integrated circuit chips, that are used for bitcoin mining). Their mining power was a significant share of the market too; according to their prospectus, the two mining pools they managed "contributed to approximately 37.1% of the aggregate hashrate of the Bitcoin network calculated by their aggregate block rewards as a percentage of the total block rewards generated from the Bitcoin network for the preceding 12 months." In other words, BitMain's mining farms likely won 37 percent of all the bitcoin issued during the year. Given the company's massive market share in mining power, you might have expected that mining would have contributed a significant portion of the revenue for the year. But you would be wrong. Proprietary mining accounted for just $94 million in revenue for the first six months of 2018.[37] Mining hardware sales, on the other hand, accounted for $2.7 billion in revenue. To put this another way, the biggest miner on earth, an entity that controlled 37 percent of the bitcoin mining system, made twenty-eight times as much money from selling mining equipment to other prospective miners as it did from mining bitcoin itself. It gives a sense of where the profits in the industry come from: servicing the industry, not partaking in the business of the industry itself.[38] Selling shovels to gold miners is a profitable business.

The international reach of miners has also expanded, as large operations search the world for new locations to place their crypto-facilities. BitMain itself has facilities in Sichuan, Inner Mongolia and Texas. Other miners have set up shop in the countries of Georgia, Canada, Iceland, Sweden and Russia. They generally seek out places with cheap energy (their primary cost of doing business), cold weather (making it easier to keep their servers from overheating), speedy internet (to ensure their access to the network) and friendly regulatory environments. They have also benefited from special deals with local energy companies, such as BitMain's arrangement with the Mongolian city Ordos for subsidized energy.[39]

To be clear, not all of the energy used to maintain the blockchain is wasted. Solar power farms, wind farms and hydroelectric power stations often generate more electricity than is demanded by local users, and thus are looking to find potential buyers so the energy does not go to waste. Cryptocurrency miners can fill that gap. Hydro-Québec, the Canadian state-owned power company, actively sought out cryptocurrency miners to purchase up to 5,000 MW of excess energy it was producing in 2018. As the CEO of Hydro-Québec said at the time, "I tell them, in the winter, you just have to open the garage door and windows to stay cool."[40] And of course, some of the energy consumed by the blockchain comes from renewable sources. Hydropower is one of these sources, but so are wind, solar and even geothermal energy drawn from the heat of the earth, such as hot springs, hot rocks and even magma from volcanoes. The cryptocurrency miners that set up shop in Iceland were drawn by the country's cheap geothermal power generated from volcanoes.

But regardless of these mitigating factors, it is hard to deny that the blockchain ecosystem requires significant amounts of energy, much of which would not be consumed if it were not for the blockchain. And much of this energy is decidedly not from environmentally friendly alternatives. One study found that 58 percent of major mining pools were located in China, where coal is used heavily in electricity production.[41] BitMain itself has its largest mining farms there.

***

One might wonder whether all this apparent inefficiency in the blockchain system would have a market solution. In other words, if all these miners are engaging in destructive behaviors that harm the world and do not, collectively, benefit them (since bitcoin is issued at a set rate regardless of the energy consumption of miners), certainly there should be incentives to find a better system. Functioning markets might be expected to drive out these inefficiencies, rewarding companies that provide better products at cheaper prices.

The problem is that blockchain has created a system that is prone to a well-known phenomenon in markets known as the tragedy of the commons. The tragedy of the commons generally refers to the problematic incentives that arise when a common resource is shared among many participants. It draws upon the following insight: when a common resource can be accessed and utilized by many different actors, it will tend to be overused by those actors because the actors do not bear the full cost of their use of it. For example, if everyone has the right to graze their cows in a common pasture, people will tend to graze their cows more often than they would if the pasture were owned by a single individual. The single individual knows that if he overgrazes his cows on his own pasture, the pasture might be damaged and be rendered unusable in future years, a cost that he would bear fully, and he would thus rationally reduce his usage of it. But in a commons-type scenario individuals do not bear the full cost of overgrazing their cows on the pasture; by overgrazing, they get all the benefit of having better-fed cows and only some of the cost of damage to the pasture, since the damage will be shared by all the other users as well. Since each individual farmer will have similar incentives and, importantly, will know that all the other farmers do as well, they will all have strong incentives to rush in and overuse the pasture as soon as possible. The result is the tragedy of the commons: because the resource is shared, it will be lost.[42]

The blockchain ecosystem is similarly premised on the ability of miners and other users to take advantage of a shared resource (energy and electricity) without bearing the full cost of its use (the environmental harm from the consequent carbon emissions). To be clear, this problem is not unique to cryptocurrencies. It is in fact a problem shared by all companies, markets and countries. It is a problem that is bedeviling government decision-makers around the world. But the blockchain's structure is particularly pernicious because of its built-in incentives: rewards in the system are allotted based primarily, even exclusively, on people's willingness and ability to consume this shared resource. It would be as if we set up a common pasture and told farmers that they would be paid based on how much of the pasture their cows ate up. They already had informal incentives to overuse. Now those incentives are built into the rules of the system.

The strategic incentives of blockchain miners also happen to mirror those of the classic prisoner's dilemma, a related concept from game theory. The prisoner's dilemma is a famous hypothetical developed by game theorists to analyze when people will cooperate for mutual gain and, perhaps more importantly, when they will not. It was first described in formal terms by

Albert Tucker, a game theorist at Princeton. The terms of the game, as described by Tucker, are as follows:

Two men, charged with a joint violation of law, are held separately by the police. Each is told that:
(1) If one confesses, and the other does not, the former will be given a reward of one unit and the latter will be fined two units.
(2) If both confess, each will be fined one unit.
At the same time each has good reason to believe that
(3) If neither confesses, both will go clear.[43]

The incentives of the two prisoners can thus be described as follows:

		Prisoner B	
		Confess	Not Confess
Prisoner A	Confess	-1, -1	1, -2
	Not Confess	-2, 1	0, 0

The best outcome for the prisoners, from a mutual perspective, is for both prisoners to stay silent and not confess. If they both refuse to talk, they will each get off without any punishment, for a combined aggregate value of zero. On the other hand, the worst outcome for the prisoners, from a mutual perspective, is for both prisoners to confess. If they both confess, they will each be fined one unit, for a combined aggregate value of negative two. Since zero is better than negative two, one might think that the prisoners would just stay silent, thus ensuring the best-case scenario from a collective standpoint.

There is a problem, however. The problem arises because of the strong individual incentives for each prisoner to confess. Imagine that you are prisoner A. You do not know if prisoner B has chosen to confess or remain silent. All you can control is what you end up doing. If prisoner B has stayed silent, then you can either stay silent as well, in which case you will neither be fined nor rewarded, or you can confess, in which case you will be given a reward of one unit. Clearly, confessing is a better choice. But what if prisoner B, instead of staying silent, actually confessed? Well, in that case, you can either stay silent, in which case you will be fined a whopping two units, or you can confess as well, in which case you will be fined just one unit. So again, confessing is a better choice. But that means that, regardless of what the other prisoner does, you are better off confessing. And the other prisoner has exactly the same incentives.

This is the dilemma. Assuming that both prisoners act rationally, they will end up at the worst possible outcome from a collective standpoint. The prisoner's dilemma is often viewed as a counterpoint to Adam Smith's conception of the invisible hand: when actors face a prisoner's dilemma, their private incentives will lead them to socially suboptimal results, not optimal ones. If they could only cooperate, they would both end up ahead. But their pursuit of individual rewards creates a mutually destructive outcome in which everyone is worse off.

I should perhaps note at this point that all of this discussion has taken the perspective of the prisoners. One might reasonably ask why we should care about the problematic incentives of prisoners; after all, we want them to confess to crimes they have committed. What is a dilemma from the perspective of the prisoners might actually be a perfectly desirable outcome from the perspective of prosecutors. This is why one of my criminal law colleagues who used to serve as a policeman refers to the prisoners' dilemma as the "policeman's opportunity."

But the genius of the prisoner's dilemma framework is that it fits any number of real social situations – ones where we would like individuals to be able to cooperate for mutual gain. If all bicyclists would stop using performance-enhancing drugs, all bicyclists would benefit, but each individual bicyclist has an incentive to dope in order to gain a competitive advantage. Yet that competitive advantage disappears if everyone else is also doping. If all companies would stop paying bribes to politicians for lucrative government contracts, all companies would benefit, but each individual company has an incentive to bribe in order to gain a competitive advantage. Yet that competitive advantage disappears if everyone else is also bribing. If all countries would abandon nuclear weapons, all countries would benefit, but each individual country has an incentive to build nuclear weapons in order to gain a military advantage. Yet that military advantage disappears if everyone else is also building nuclear weapons. In each of these scenarios, the rational pursuit of individual interests leads to socially harmful results.

The prisoner's dilemma, of course, is a formalized model that cannot take into account the many ways in which cooperation can develop in the real world. For one, actors in the real world often expect to interact with each other in the future, so the game is rarely a one-off game. This means that they can see whether the other actor cooperated last time, and adjust their behavior accordingly. Repeat play also introduces the possibility of learning (gathering information about what types of behavior are acceptable) and the possibility of punishing (responding to antisocial behavior by imposing costs on the offending party). In addition, actors in the real world can often communicate in real time and tell the other side what they plan to do. Thus, they can commit to taking actions that maximize both sides' gains. They could, for example, sign a contract that imposes legal liability in the event that one side cheats. All of these possibilities in the real world are hard (but not impossible) to capture in the prisoner's dilemma model, and thus the possibilities for cooperation are perhaps higher than a strict reading of the problem might suggest.

At the same time, there are reasons to believe that, despite these limitations, the prisoner's dilemma provides a powerful analytical tool. Not all problems are amenable to contractual agreement. Governments may enter into treaties with one another, but there is no supranational body with the power and authority of traditional judges to enforce these treaties. Companies can contract with one another, but if the behavior at issue is already illegal, and just hard to monitor (like bribery), then contracts may not be particularly helpful in preventing the behavior. And, just as importantly, when there are many actors that could potentially undermine cooperative norms, then developing the means to enforce cooperation can be hard to do. When these dynamics are present, the prisoner's dilemma incentives kick back in.

The miners that form the backbone of the blockchain face the same basic incentives presented in the prisoner's dilemma. Collectively, they would be better off if they refrained from spending massive amounts of resources on developing newer, more specialized chips to compute hash equations at faster and faster rates. These resources are not put to productive use, and the bitcoin network automatically adjusts its difficulty based on the collective speed of the network's hashing power, so miners would earn more rewards relative to expenses if they spent less money powering up their mining rigs. But individually each miner has an incentive to "cheat" and deploy faster mining rigs. This is a classic prisoner's dilemma. And it is something that Satoshi Nakamoto feared, almost from day one. In December 2009, he wrote that: "We should have a gentleman's agreement to postpone the GPU arms race as long as we can for the good of the network. It's much easier to get new users up to speed if they don't have to worry about GPU drivers and compatibility. It's nice how anyone with just a CPU can compete fairly equally right now."[44] Nakamoto recognized that an "arms race" was a real possibility in the blockchain world and that the only way to prevent it was a "gentleman's agreement." And it quickly became clear that this gentleman's agreement was not a very sticky one, and it unraveled almost as soon as it was proposed.

***

Not everyone believes that the miner's dilemma is unfixable. Some miners, for example, are doing what they can to make the arms race less environmentally harmful. In some instances, as in Boden, they have sought out locations where established renewable energy projects can provide a significant portion of the power needed to run their operations. Other companies have gone a step further, launching renewable energy projects themselves. One mining company, Soluna, announced that it would start work on a 37,000-acre wind farm in southern Morocco in 2019. The wind farm would power the company's bitcoin mining rigs, but it would also have surplus power that it could provide to local citizens or companies. In this way, the founders hoped that the blockchain industry could start to offset its energy consumption with newly developed renewable energy sources that might help reduce society's carbon footprint as well.[45]

Another, more radical approach to solving the blockchain's seemingly insatiable appetite for energy focuses on changing the structure of blockchain itself. Much of the blockchain's wasteful energy use stems from Satoshi Nakamoto's initial decisions regarding how to protect the blockchain from cyberattacks and how to incentivize users to maintain the system. His strategy was to pay out bitcoin rewards to miners who performed maintenance "work." This system is now known as a proof-of-work blockchain. But some powerful figures in the world of the blockchain have suggested that proof of work is not the best structure for the blockchain and that, instead, we need to find new systems.

This is what Vitalik Buterin, the founder of Ethereum, set out to do. "I would personally feel very unhappy if my main contribution to the world was adding Cyprus's worth of electricity consumption to global warming," he told one interviewer.[46] In his search for alternative structures for the blockchain, he has become a vocal proponent of something that is known as "proof of stake." Proof-of-stake blockchains reward users not on how many resources they expend on mining puzzles but rather on how much currency they hold. Currency holders would be able to add new blocks to the blockchain at a rate correlated with their overall ownership or "stake" in the currency.

There are two primary advantages of a proof-of-stake system. First, it reduces, or even eliminates, incentives for miners to increase computing power and thus energy use. In proof-of-stake systems, it does not matter if you have a factory filled with servers in Mongolia churning out SHA-256 computations. All that matters, for the purpose of adding new blocks and being rewarded with new currency, is that you own the virtual currency in question. A second and related advantage of a proof-of-stake system is that it incentivizes miners to actually own the virtual currency they are mining. In proof-of-work systems like bitcoin, there is no requirement that miners hold virtual currency; they can mine a new block, receive their bitcoin reward and then immediately sell the bitcoin to someone else. A proof-of-stake system is thought to encourage stability in a currency because the people who are performing the hard work of maintaining the system also have some skin in the game. They want the virtual currency to succeed because they own it.

While some proof-of-stake systems exist today, most of them are relatively small and unproven. Buterin has spoken publicly about plans to revise the Ethereum blockchain to convert it from a proof-of-work system to a proof-of-stake system, a project dubbed "Casper," but these plans have yet to be finalized and deployed. The plans started as early as 2014, and the community has fiercely debated the pros and cons of the transition.[47] But, at least as of the writing of this book, proof-of-stake remains an aspiration, not a reality.

***

For political theorists, the fact that the blockchain's decentralized structure leads to inefficiency would not come as a surprise. This is a well-known feature of systems with diffuse power structures. Decentralized decision-making is by its very nature a slow and cumbersome process. It requires many people to get together to decide on an action, and often requires duplicative and repetitive processes. Centralized systems, on the other hand, can take action quickly and decisively. They do not need to wait for other people to weigh in or to engage in extended discussion about the merits of a given action. The central authority simply decides. This is why Socrates called democracy a "noble but sluggish steed."[48]

This debate about the merits of centralized versus decentralized decision-making has played an important role in fashioning, of all things, the American government. In particular, it has informed debates about the respective powers of president and Congress. Presidents are often thought to be speedy and decisive. Congress, on the other hand, is believed to be slow and deliberate. The framers of the United States Constitution thus sought to identify the kinds of problems that required speedy and decisive decision-making, and the ones that required slow and deliberate decision-making, and separate the powers of government accordingly. War, however, proved to be a contentious topic. In *The Federalist*, Alexander Hamilton defended the decision to give the president extensive war powers by extolling the virtues of centralized decision-makers. "Of all the cares or concerns of government," Hamilton wrote, "the direction of war most peculiarly demands those qualities which distinguish the exercise of power by a single hand."[49] Only presidents had the unity of mind and action necessary for the successful prosecution of war. Charles Pinckney of South Carolina argued that large legislatures were "too slow" to be able to effectively administer a war.[50] James Madison wrote that "the larger a country, the less easy for its real opinion to be ascertained, and the less difficult to be counterfeited."[51]

On the other hand, others have worried that presidents, acting alone, might be too efficient at dragging the country into war. As John Jay wrote in *The Federalist*,

> Absolute monarchs will often make war when their nations are to get nothing by it, but for purposes and objects merely personal, such as a thirst for military glory, revenge for personal affronts, ambition, or private compacts to aggrandize or support their particular families or partisans. These and a variety of other motives, which affect only the mind of the sovereign, often lead him to engage in wars not sanctified by justice or the voice and interests of his people.[52]

Supreme Court Justice Joseph Story echoed these sentiments in his classic commentaries on the U.S. Constitution: a declaration of war was "in its own nature and effects so critical and calamitous, that it requires the utmost deliberation, and the successive review of all the councils of the nations."[53] James Wilson of Pennsylvania argued that legislatures would be more circumspect than presidents, stating that giving the legislature the power to declare war would ensure that the government "will not hurry us into war; it is calculated to guard against it. It will not be in the power of a single man, or a single body of men, to involve us in such distress."[54] In other words, the very slowness of legislatures was the precise reason why they should be tasked with deciding on a matter as important and dangerous as a war. As George Mason put it, "[h]e was for clogging rather than facilitating war."[55] The decentralized legislature was a way to do that.[56]

Ultimately, the U.S. Constitution opted for a mixed approach, granting some war powers to the unitary executive and others to the dispersed legislature. Under Article II of the Constitution, the president serves as the commander-in-chief of the army and the navy, while, under Article I, Congress has the power to declare war. Alexander Bickel, a constitutional law scholar, has written that this structure represents a careful apportionment based on the respective merits and dangers of centralized and decentralized decision-makers. Quoting Justice Oliver Ellsworth, he wrote that "[i]t should be more easy to get out of war than into it," and that "[the presidency]'s errors are active ones ... sins of commission," while Congress's "errors are those of irresolution, sins of omission."[57] When action, speed and efficiency are necessary, centralized decision-makers are the best option. But when deliberation and discussion are wanted, decentralized decision-makers may be better at gathering the necessary information and working through the various pros and cons.

These arguments about executive versus legislative war powers are enlightening for debates about the blockchain's environmental issues.

Decentralized decision-making can be slow and cumbersome, but it also can lead to more stable, desirable results. Legislatures may be inefficient at deciding where and when to go to war, but the cost is thought to some to be worth it in order to clog the machinery of warfare. In the blockchain, decentralized mining structures may be an inefficient way of maintaining a record of information – they require many different users to be in constant dialogue, downloading, verifying and maintaining the blockchain – but they are justified by the desire to improve the security of the network and prevent bad actors from rashly taking actions that affect the rest of the network.

One major difference, of course, is that the inefficiency of decentralized decision-making in the legislature is, in a sense, a direct result of its benefits, namely, that allowing Congress time to debate and discuss will lead it to make better decisions. In other words, inefficiency is the point. But in the blockchain, the inefficiency of decentralized miners and their harmful carbon emissions is unrelated to the purpose of the system. We could imagine, and indeed a number of blockchain engineers have imagined, a decentralized system that would not require such massive energy use. Some of these costs might of course be mitigated by, for example, changing the structure of the blockchain, or by miners switching to renewable energy. But some are inevitable. Decentralized systems are unavoidably and purposefully slow and cumbersome.

***

This Chapter has examined the impact of blockchain on the environment. It has surveyed the dramatic levels of energy that the blockchain consumes. It has identified the sources of this energy use. And it has discussed tentative efforts to reduce or mitigate blockchain's environmental footprint. If the last Chapter was about morality (how do we stop crime?), this Chapter was about efficiency (how do we make technology less costly?). Both are equally important questions. But they also raise a broader question of how societies ensure that new technologies are used for good, not ill. How do they make sure that innovation does not fall into gaps in the interstices of the law? How do they fashion laws that addresses the particular set of costs and benefits that technology offers? It is to those questions that we turn in the next Chapter.

6

The Penumbra Problem

Wherefore it has been said that as poverty and hunger are needed to make men industrious, so laws are needed to make them good. When we do well without laws, laws are not needed; but when good customs are absent, laws are at once required.

Niccolò Machiavelli, *Discourses on Livy*

Maksim Zaslavskiy is a self-proclaimed philanthropist, digital entrepreneur and real estate guru. Born in Ukraine in 1979, he moved to the United States when he was twelve years old and settled in Brooklyn. He has a degree in finance from Baruch College and an LLM in law from Cardozo. He is the author of several books (including *Real Estate Investment: Learn About the Passive Income That Everyone Is Talking About*; *Real Estate Marketing: Proven Marketing Tools for Real Estate Brokers & Agents*; and *Foreclosures: The INS and OUTS of Buying*). He has also been charged with securities fraud conspiracy and faces up to five years in jail for a cryptocurrency scheme he launched in 2017.

According to the Securities and Exchange Commission, in 2017 Zaslavskiy founded a company called REcoin in Nevada.[1] He marketed the company as a real estate venture developing real estate-related smart contracts, where brokers, tenants, purchasers, developers and architects could all come together and use digital tokens to interact with one another. Over the course of the year, he offered investment opportunities to investors in the cryptocurrency tokens being created by the company. He described the REcoin token as a blockchain-based virtual currency that would be backed by domestic and international real estate investments. It would give investors an "easily accessible financial platform through which people from all over the world convert their savings into real estate-backed currency for the potential of high returns to protect their earnings from inflation." He also claimed that REcoin had "some of the highest potential returns," which he estimated would be between

9 and 67 percent a year. He created a website for REcoin and published a white paper describing how it worked. The white paper stated that the currency could grow "at least in two ways through the steady increasing value of the real estate investments that REcoin is used to purchase, and a higher REcoin value when the demand for REcoin rises." The white paper also claimed that "REcoin is led by an experienced team of brokers, lawyers and developers and invests its proceeds into global real estate based on the soundest strategies," and that "an international team of attorneys and programmers have been working tirelessly on creating solutions for REcoin holders." In a nod to his humanitarian side, Zaslavskiy also promised that 2 percent of the "funds emitted during the mining process" would be sent to charitable organizations such as the Red Cross or the Save the Children Foundation, and that "up to 70% of the profit from REcoin is dedicated to a range of different charities and is written into the program code." Zaslavskiy announced that REcoin would launch an initial coin offering that would run from August 2017 to October 2017, and that early investors would receive a 15 percent discount on REcoin tokens. The company generated significant interest among investors, with around 1,000 individuals purchasing REcoin tokens. Zaslavskiy would later state that REcoin had obtained approximately $300,000 from investors.

In September 2017, Zaslavskiy issued a press release – through Reddit – claiming that the ICO was a success. He now claimed that REcoin had raised "over $1.5 million" during the first three days of the presale and that "trust in our project became so vast that another $2.3 million in expected earnings were generated as a result of the REcoin pre-sale success." But Zaslavskiy had bad news for the investors:

> Unfortunately, at that point the US government did what it does best – interfered. In no uncertain terms, it let us know that we're not allowed to take steps to maintain the level of liquidity of our real estate holdings to keep your investments safe and secure, and our community truly decentralized and rid of any outside influence.

So, Zaslavskiy informed his investors, the REcoin tokens would have to be shut down.

But, Zaslavskiy continued, all was not lost. He had created a new company, called the Diamond Reserve Club. In connection with the club, Zaslavskiy was creating another blockchain-based cryptocurrency called a Diamond Reserve Coin. Zaslavskiy published another white paper, this one claiming that investors would earn "a minimum growth of 10% to 15% per year." Diamond Reserve Coins were "hedged by physical diamonds stored in secure locations in the United States and fully insured for their value." The Diamond

Reserve Club would give members the ability to exchange their tokens for physical diamonds. Zaslavskiy told REcoin investors that "all of your REcoin holdings will be seamlessly converted into Diamond Reserve Coin at the rates favorable to you." They would also receive a "10% bonus" out of gratitude for their early confidence in his company.[2]

All of these plans came crashing down on November 1, 2017, when Zaslavskiy was arrested and charged with securities fraud. According to documents filed by the Securities and Exchange Commission and the Department of Justice, Zaslavskiy's "virtual currencies" were nothing but a scam. The first company, REcoin, never owned any real estate. It did not have an international team of attorneys, brokers and developers; it had never hired a broker or a lawyer or a developer, and Zaslavskiy later admitted that his team was largely made up of individuals in Ukraine. And it did not sell the 2.8 million tokens it claimed to have sold. Zaslavskiy had never even developed or created a digital token or coin in connection with REcoin. As for the Diamond Reserve Coin, again, no digital token or coin was ever created. His company never bought any diamonds. There was no insurance. The entire scheme was a sham.

The SEC conducted a remarkable interview of Zaslavskiy in September 2017, from which a better picture of the scheme and its protagonist emerges.[3] In the interview, Zaslavskiy comes off as alternately humorous, dismissive and defensive. Asked how to spell the name of a street in Kiev where he had met one of his investors, he replied, "Google will help." Asked for his home address, he replied, "That's a tough one to answer. About a thousand miles up in the air." When the SEC pushed him to be more responsive to its subpoena, Zaslavskiy took issue with the subpoena's use of the word "token" in describing the sales. "It's not a point of a game. It's the point, when I went to law school here, and I did went to law school here, each word matters. That's what you've been taught in any law school."

At one point, the SEC asked him about passages included in REcoin's press releases:

Q: The next paragraph, sir, says: "Unfortunately, at that point the U.S. government did what it does best, interfere. In no uncertain terms it let us know that we're not allowed to take steps to maintain the level of liquidity of our real estate holdings to keep your investment safe and secure. And our community truly decentralized and rid of any outside influence." Did I read that correctly?

A: Yes, you did.

Q: What is that?

A: Fuck-up.

Q: I'm sorry?

A: I didn't write all of that. But, the person who wrote this, this and this, he screwed it up. And –

Q: Did anyone in the U.S. government let you know in –

A: No.

Q: So, that's not true?

A: No.

Q: Continuing on with Exhibit 7, is this one of the – I'll just continue reading from the second page, which is MZ26: "However, the good news, my fellow REcoin holders and investors, is that . . . we're not going to let your tremendous faith in our collective project, its strategical and tactical objectives go to waste. We all want to make a world" – et cetera. Do you see that?

A: Yes.

Q: Okay. Is this – what is that about? What is it this about?

A: He is artistic person, so he tried to make nice of something.

Q: Let me ask a clearer question.

A: Okay.

Eventually, Zaslavskiy described how he first hit upon the idea for REcoin.

Let's begin where I got it. I got the idea from old times, from, like, a thousand years ago, 2,000 years ago . . . . The old days how it worked, if you have a second, you have the guy, elder, in the village. I come to the elder, for example, you give a thousands dollars or a dollar, any coins, you could write me a letter, "Yeah, I keep a thousand of his," I guarantee that he's going to be, basically, 100 percent financial set. And then you go to next village. So, this way you don't get robbed. That's how it was a thousand years ago. I love history. That's where I got the whole idea.

He also expressed some skepticism of how the blockchain industry worked. "I look after everything that's going on with ICOs. And you read a couple of them, I'm serious, if you have five cents of understanding – five cents, I'm not saying they have to be genius – it's a rip-off." "Can you explain why bitcoin is fine? No. It's unexplainable. I call it UFO."

If the facts alleged by the SEC and the DOJ are true, this would appear to be an open-and-shut case. The securities laws prohibit individuals from making untrue statements of material fact or engaging in any course of business that operates as a fraud upon another person in connection with the sale of securities.[4] Zaslavskiy told investors that he had purchased real estate and diamonds, hired lawyers and brokers, and sold millions of tokens, when, in reality, none of these things had occurred. It would be hard to imagine a more straightforward case of fraud.

But here is where things get tricky. The SEC charged Zaslavskiy with violating the securities laws. Thus, in order to determine whether he had violated these laws, it was necessary to show that his fraud was not just any kind of fraud, but fraud in connection with the sale of *securities*. Which brings us to the key question: Are cryptocurrencies securities?

This is not an easy question. When most people think about securities, they think about stocks and bonds. They represent some kind of financial claim upon a company, such as a right to dividends or a guaranteed stream of fixed payments for some period of time. But all sorts of more or less exotic hybrid instruments also fall under the classification, such as derivatives, preferred stock, debentures and warranties. So what about cryptocurrencies? Where do they lie? Are they securities?

As an initial matter, at the time that Zaslavskiy was charged, no court had ever ruled on the question of whether cryptocurrencies qualified as "securities," and thus no clear answer existed in the law. It was what legal scholars call a matter of first impression: because no directly binding legal precedent existed, the judge was forced to decide the question on the basis of abstract legal principles. To use an analogy often resorted to by judges, calling a ball or a strike here was not easy to do. No one had ever said what the strike zone was for cryptocurrencies. Thus, in order to call a ball or a strike, the court would need to create a strike zone in the first place.

Zaslavskiy, for his part, argued that, whatever that strike zone might be, his virtual currencies decidedly did not fall within it. For one, the digital currencies he offered were precisely that, currencies. And, as Zaslavskiy pointed out, both the Securities Act and the Exchange Act expressly exclude currencies from the definition of a security. Thus, Zaslavskiy argued, if his digital currencies were currencies, they could not possibly be securities. As a result, he could not have violated the securities laws when he sold them. But, even if his digital currencies were not truly "currencies," Zaslavskiy argued, he should still win. Whatever they might be, they definitely were not "securities" as that term had been defined by the Supreme Court. Under something called the Howey test (named after the Supreme Court decision that first established the principle), an arrangement is deemed a security if it "involves an investment of money in a common enterprise with profits to come solely from efforts of others."[5] But, as Zaslavskiy pointed out, his virtual currencies did not look like a typical investment in a company. Instead, "REcoin and DRC Coin were nothing more than software code that provides a purchaser access to the blockchain and the blockchain can only be useful if the purchasers keep it updated with transactions." How could software code ever be considered a common enterprise like a corporation or a partnership could be?

Finally, Zaslavskiy argued, even if one could conclude that his virtual currencies fell under the Howey test, that was only because the test itself was flawed. Its definition was so "overbroad, ambiguous, and dated" that it had come to sweep in all sorts of things that it should not. How could Zaslavskiy have known that, when he created his digital currency, he was violating, of all things, the securities laws? If he couldn't have known this, then it would be unfair to punish him after the fact for it. It was so unfair, Zaslavskiy claimed, that it even violated the U.S. Constitution and its guarantees of due process. In support of this position, he quoted from the public statements of SEC officials themselves. Former SEC Chair Mary Jo White, he pointed out, had stated in a speech in 2016 that "[o]ne key regulatory issue is whether blockchain applications require registration under existing SEC regulatory regimes." If even leading SEC officials did not know if virtual currencies were covered by the securities laws, how could Zaslavskiy have known?

The court did not find Zaslavskiy's arguments persuasive. It summarily rejected his claims that the case against him was fundamentally flawed or unfair. In doing so, it went to some length to explain why virtual currencies were similar to regular investments. "Stripped of the 21st-century jargon," the court wrote, "the challenged indictment charges a straightforward scam, replete with the common characteristics of many financial frauds."

And, the court noted, the law is amply clear about what a security is. "The test expounded in *Howey* has – for more than 70 years – provided clear guidance to courts and litigants as to the definition of 'investment contract' under the securities laws."

With his arguments rejected, Zaslavskiy was out of options. He pled guilty.[6]

***

As the Zaslavskiy case demonstrates, the blockchain presents difficult problems for law. Some of these problems are straightforward, requiring nothing more than a yes or a no answer from a judge or a regulator. Are virtual currencies securities? Do antifraud rules apply to initial coin offerings? But others are harder and require more complex analysis. When is it fair to punish creators of blockchains for illegal actions that occur on them? How far can the government go in regulating the actions of crowds?

We tend to think of law as a body of on-off switches that, once tripped, trigger certain consequences. If you sell a security, then you have to register with the Securities and Exchange Commission. If you earn income, then you must file a tax return. But, when it comes to the blockchain, these mechanisms become jumbled. For one, the unique structure of blockchains makes it unclear when and how actions will trip a switch and thus trigger obligations. For another, by spreading out decision-making to large groups of actors, blockchains complicate the question of who owes the obligation in the first place. It is important to keep in mind that the Zaslavskiy case involved a single individual running the relevant scheme. There was no true decentralized platform that underpinned the REcoin or Diamond Reserve Coin. But if there had been, prosecutors would have found themselves in a different and more difficult position.

This Chapter will address head-on the conflict between blockchain and the law. It will examine how blockchains challenge existing models of regulation. It will explore how regulators have responded to this challenge. And it will begin to sketch out some of the more radical attempts to implement block-chains in a manner that circumvents legal regulation. At the heart of all these problems is the idea of decentralization. The law, in short, is ill-adapted to deal with the kind of radical democratization that blockchain enables.

***

At some point early on in every law student's first year in school, sometimes as early as his very first class in law school, he is exposed to a problem known as the "no vehicles in the park" hypothetical. It is a classic problem in legal interpretation, one that provides law students with an early introduction into the methods of legal analysis that they will deploy throughout the rest of their legal careers. It is also a notoriously deceptive problem.

The professor tells the class to imagine that they have walked to a local park. It is a beautiful spring day, with clear blue skies and a cool breeze. The park is bustling with people, with children at play, parents walking strollers and the elderly out for strolls. Outside the park, however, they see a sign. The sign states, in bold letters, "No vehicles in the park." The professor instructs the class that the sign accurately states the law: that you may not take a vehicle into the public park. With that background, the professor asks the class, what does the sign mean?[7]

At first glance, the answer is obvious. The rule is simple: you cannot take a vehicle into the park. It also seems clear: it is a bright-line ban on all vehicles. The rule, thus, would not appear to open itself up to much debate. The rule does not provide wiggle room to argue that, say, in this case, it would be reasonable or advisable to bring a vehicle into the park, or, in that case, it would be unreasonable to do so. The answer is always the same: all vehicles are prohibited, no matter what. The professor's question, then, seems easy.

But it turns out that this seemingly simple question is devilishly difficult to answer.

Most students agree that "no vehicles in the park" means that you cannot drive a car into the park. They also tend to agree that you cannot drive a motorcycle. But then things start to get difficult. What about bicycles? What about skateboards? Wheelchairs? Electric scooters? Electric cars? What about that stroller the parents have their baby in? Or toy cars for the children? In recent years, professors have added a new wrinkle: What about driverless cars? And if a driverless car did go into the park, who would be liable?

As the hypothetical demonstrates, even as simple a rule as "no vehicles in the park" is rife with ambiguity. And, as might be expected, students take different approaches to resolving the ambiguity. Some simply state that they know a vehicle when they see one, and that a bicycle isn't one, while a motorcycle is. This approach, which some students dismiss as not being very "lawyerly," in fact has an illustrious legal pedigree. Supreme Court Justice Potter Stewart once famously remarked, in a case about pornography, that "I know it when I see it, and the motion picture involved in this case is not that."[8] But other students are more analytical: they look up the dictionary definition of vehicle and see whether a bicycle, a roller skate, a toy automobile or an airplane would fit neatly under the definition. The Oxford English Dictionary defines "vehicle" as a "means of conveyance provided with wheels or runners and used for the carriage of persons or goods." If vehicles only include things that transport people or goods, then bicycles, roller skates and airplanes would be prohibited, and toy automobiles likely would not (but perhaps those strollers would be verboten). Still other students delve into the intent of the rule: the rule is there to protect the safety of pedestrians in the park, so if bicycles and electric scooters are dangerous, then they fall within the statute. Strollers seem pretty safe, so they should be permitted. Finally, many students use a form of analogical reasoning: they look at the features of automobiles, which they are pretty sure are banned under the rule, and then compare them to other things. Automobiles have engines, so perhaps things with engines, such as motorcycles and airplanes, are banned, but things without engines, such as bikes and strollers, are not. But of course, electric cars do not have engines, so perhaps they are permitted. We might ask whether electric cars are like regular automobiles, which we know to be vehicles, but, of course, the answer is yes and no. Bikes are like automobiles in some ways, and unlike them in others. The question is whether they are relevantly like automobiles, and that, ultimately, is not answered in the law itself.

The "no vehicles in the park" hypothetical is drawn from H.L.A. Hart, a giant in the history of legal theory. Hart used the hypothetical to illustrate a problem that he called the "problem of the penumbra." According to Hart, every law has a set of core activities to which it clearly applies. Everyone agrees on these cases. But, Hart continued, outside of these core activities, a vast penumbra of other related activities extends. In this penumbra, it is unclear how or whether the law applies. The problem of the penumbra, Hart argued, is an essential and unavoidable feature of law. As Hart explained:

> If we are to communicate with each other at all, and if, as in the most elementary form of law, we are to express our intentions that a certain type of behavior be regulated by rules, then the general words we use – like "vehicle" in the case I consider – must have some standard instance in which no doubts are felt about its application. There must be a core of settled meaning, but there will be, as well, a penumbra of debatable cases in which words are neither obviously applicable nor obviously ruled out. These cases will each have some features in common with the standard case; they will lack others or be accompanied by features not present in the standard case . . . . [I]f we are to say that these ranges of facts do or do not fall under existing rules, then the classifier must make a decision which is not dictated to him, for the facts and phenomena to which we fit our words and apply our rules are as it were *dumb*. The toy automobile cannot speak up and say, "I am a vehicle for the purpose of this legal rule," nor can the roller skates chorus, "We are not a vehicle." Fact situations do not await us neatly labeled, creased, and folded, nor is there legal classification written on them to be simply read off by the judge. Instead, in applying legal rules, someone must take the responsibility of deciding that words do or do not cover some case in hand with all the practical consequences involved in this decision.[9]

As Hart explains, the law deals in categories. This type of behavior is a tort, while that type of behavior is a crime. This type of behavior is a felony, while that type of behavior is a misdemeanor. Whether a particular behavior or action falls within the ambit of a rule has important consequences (it may mean the difference between spending the rest of your life behind bars and remaining free). As a result, much of law, and legal analysis, depends on our ability to accurately and reliably place behaviors into various, conceptually distinct buckets.

The problem of the penumbra is particularly pronounced when new technologies come around. These new technologies often do not perfectly fit the buckets that lawyers, judges and legislators have established, and this can create uncertainty for all involved. In recent years, for example, the U.S. Supreme Court has faced numerous questions about how the Constitution – a document written in 1789 – applies to global positioning systems, laptops, cell phones, smartphones and any number of other modern-day accoutrements. To say that they have struggled to present a coherent body of law on the question is to put it mildly.[10]

But if legal interpretation is always hard, the problems become only more acute when the technology at issue becomes more radical and innovative. It is one thing to analogize cellular phone records to "papers" from the eighteenth century. It is another to analogize the blockchain to money, property, commodities or anything else. It is, in a sense, all of these and none of them. Attempts to analogize to past facts with a technology as unique and *sui generis* as the blockchain become strained, perhaps to the point of breaking. As Justice Neil Gorsuch has said, "Talk of kings and common-law writs may seem out of place in a case about cell-site records and the protections afforded by the Fourth Amendment in the modern age." If that is true of cellular phones, one can only imagine how law might apply to the blockchain. It is a technology that is so new and innovative, that is so different from older technologies, that it makes a muddle of our outdated and cumbersome legal structures.

And yet the legal system must adapt. It must sort out the difficulties and ambiguities in the law and identify which rules apply to the blockchain and which do not. But as may be clear from the discussion above, the blockchain presents a number of particularly pernicious legal problems because it is in a sense *sui generis*. There are not many other technologies that are of the type of the blockchain. It is in a very real sense in a category of its own. This makes it very difficult for judges and regulators to apply old rules to it.

***

Henry Kissinger is said to have once asked, "Who do I call if I want to speak to Europe?"[11] He was lamenting the inability of European countries to speak with a single voice, and thus the difficulty of dealing with them. But the decentralized structures enabled by the blockchain raise many of the same problems–about decisionmaking, responsibility and liability–that the fragmentation of Europe did. Who do you sue if you want to sue bitcoin?

The first problem presented is a categorization problem. In order to determine what rules apply to the blockchain, we need to know how the blockchain should be categorized under current law. Is it a security? Is it a currency? Is it a commodity? Is it a property? Is it all of these things? Or is it none of them?

Second, the decentralization of the blockchain presents a monitoring problem. Once we know what rules apply to the blockchain and its participants, we need to know how to monitor participants in order to ensure that they are complying with those rules. But decentralized structures are notoriously difficult to monitor. Because they are by definition run by many different actors, effective monitoring requires extensive efforts to identify and observe the behaviors of many different relevant actors. This can be hard to do when those actors are anonymous, difficult to find or located abroad.

Third, the decentralization of the blockchain creates a number of difficulties from an enforcement perspective. After we know what rules apply, and we find effective ways to detect violations of those rules, we ultimately need to be able to penalize actors for the violations. But when a system is devised in a way that responsibility for its functioning is dispersed among many different actors, apportioning responsibility and punishing acts of noncompliance can be hard. If a blockchain develops in such a way that it becomes a magnet for money laundering, who do we hold responsible? The original code developer? The miners who maintain the network? The exchanges that facilitate conversions into real currency? The answer might be (a), (b), (c), none of the above or all of the above. And if regulators have jurisdiction to punish only a small subset of the actors, should they? What if this will have no effect on the overall level of crime itself? Welcome to the world of blockchain and the law.[12]

These problems should by now be familiar. Theories of crime deterrence revolve around many of the same concepts – identifying problematic behavior, monitoring it and sanctioning people when they engage in it. But they can also be generalized to law and regulation more broadly. Until regulators have established the rules of the road and clarified how they apply to blockchain, uncertainty will remain, both for governments and for blockchain participants. As Franz Kafka said, "Our laws are unfortunately not widely known, they are the closely guarded secret of the small group of nobles who govern us. We like to believe that these old laws are scrupulously adhered to, but it remains a vexing thing to be governed by laws one does not know."[13]

***

Imagine that a mysterious online developer creates a blockchain-based virtual currency called LockeChain. LockeChain is designed to be a better, more decentralized version of bitcoin. Each person that downloads the software will have an equal say in how the virtual currency is run, which transactions are verified and how the software is amended and updated over time. All users have an equal chance at mining new blocks to add to the LockeChain blockchain, and whenever they do, they are rewarded with a few new LockeChain coins. Its motto is "life, liberty, and the pursuit of LockeChain." The system is fully anonymous, with individuals identified only by a randomly generated address. After uploading the LockeChain software onto the web, the developer disappears and has no further role in the running of the network.

From a legal perspective, the first question that arises is what laws apply to LockeChain. This is the categorization question from earlier: in order to know what legal regimes apply to LockeChain, we need to know what LockeChain is. Is it a currency? Is it an organization? Is it a security? Or is it something else? Or is it all of these things?

Let us begin by looking at whether LockeChain is a security. As noted above, in at least one case a court has held that virtual currencies are securities (or at least that a jury could reasonably conclude that they are), but Congress has not passed any specific laws on the issue, and the Securities and Exchange Commission, which is tasked with regulating securities, has not issued any rules on it either (although they have hinted at what their ultimate legal position will be). So, at least for now, virtual currencies exist within the "penumbra" of securities law, neither firmly within nor firmly without.

One thing that is clear, however, is that, in order to determine whether a cryptocurrency like LockeChain is a security, courts and regulators will apply the Howey test. As mentioned before, the test draws its origin from the case of *SEC v. W.J. Howey Co.*, a Supreme Court decision that dates back to 1946. The case involved a scheme by a Florida company, the Howey Company, to take advantage of its large holdings of orange groves. The company owned thousands of acres of citrus groves in Lake County, Florida (an area just west of Orlando), but was in need of cash in order to finance additional developments. In order to get this cash, it created the following scheme. The company offered interested investors (primarily wealthy patrons of resort hotels that the Howey Company owned in the area)[14] a sales contract, in which the investors would purchase portions of the grove from the company, paired with a service contract, in which the investors would simultaneously lease the land back to the company and give the company full authority over the cultivation of the grove. Investors were promised a portion of any profits the company made from the sale of oranges, which the company projected to be around 10 percent a year for a decade. When the SEC heard of this arrangement, it filed a lawsuit to enjoin the company from continuing the scheme, arguing that the contracts constituted "securities" under Section 2(1) of the Securities Act of 1933 and thus were required to be registered with the SEC (something that the Howey Company had not done). The Supreme Court agreed. Looking at the totality of the arrangement, the Court explained that it was clearly an "investment contract," in which individuals "were led to invest money in a common enterprise with the expectation that they would earn a profit solely through the efforts of the promoter or of some one other than themselves." The purchasers, although nominally "owners" of the land, were in all practical senses just investors in the Howey Company business. They had no right to enter onto their land or take the oranges, and even if they had wanted to, the separate tracts that they purchased were not even separately fenced or identifiable to an outside observer. The purchasers were thus not looking to enjoy the land. They were looking to earn a profit from an investment. The arrangement looked much more like the sale of stock in a company than the sale of land. In reaching its conclusion, the Court held that the test for determining whether a transaction constitutes a security under the Securities Act is "whether the scheme involves an investment of money in a common enterprise with profits to come solely from the efforts of others." Using this test, it was clear that the arrangement in *Howey* was a security: purchasers invested money in a common enterprise (that is, the cultiva-tion of the grove) and were led to expect profits solely from the efforts of others (that is, the Howey Company employees that were to cultivate the grove). The test has since been applied in thousands of cases and has largely remained untouched as the lodestar of securities law.[15]

So is LockeChain a security? Let us apply the Howey test to find out. The Howey test has three elements: (1) an investment of money; (2) in a common enterprise; (3) with the expectation of profits to be derived solely from the efforts of others. Only if all three of these elements are satisfied will LockeChain be deemed a security and, thus, subject to the extensive dis-closure and antifraud provisions of the securities laws. So, a lot rides on the answer.

To start with, the first prong seems clear: any time that someone purchases LockeChain, they are investing money, so we can dispense with the first prong relatively easily. (Of course, even this relatively anodyne prong could raise difficulties if the "currency" that is used to purchase the LockeChain is a different virtual currency, but we will leave that aside for the moment.) In any case, that is where the clarity ends, and the ambiguity begins.

Next, with respect to the second prong of the Howey test, are LockeChain purchasers investing in a common enterprise? In a certain sense, they are. The blockchain, after all, is a distributed network that is maintained and run by its users. As bitcoin.org describes it, "bitcoin uses peer-to-peer technology to operate with no central authority or banks [where] managing transactions and the issuing of bitcoins is carried out *collectively by the network*."[16] Thus, there could not be a more *common* enterprise: everyone participates in the enterprise itself. But in another sense, LockeChain, like bitcoin, is not a common enterprise. It is not a company or a corporation or an LLC. There is no single entity at all, and investors' assets are not pooled into any specific vehicle or location. Instead, they simply receive an entry on a blockchain (that exists on different computers located around the world), and the blockchain simply records that certain transactions have occurred. This certainly does not look like any kind of common enterprise that has ever existed before. So, in one sense, LockeChain decidedly is a common enterprise; and yet in another, it decidedly is not. Which of these two senses is the correct one? Courts have provided some guidance, stressing factors such as whether there is "horizontal commonality" – related to whether the investors' fates are linked to each other – or "vertical commonality" – related to whether the investors' fate is linked to the work of the manager or other third parties – but they also are not particularly helpful here.

And what about the third prong, the expectation of profits to be derived solely from the efforts of others? Again, the answer is a strong *maybe*.[17] As an initial matter, there is some question about whether investors in LockeChain, like investors in bitcoin or Ethereum, are seeking a profit at all. Certainly, a good portion of the investors will be speculators, hoping to buy low and sell high. But another portion will not. It is worth remembering that the initial idea behind bitcoin was to create a currency that was not controlled by the government and big banks. The idea of making a profit out of it was secondary. Perhaps LockeChain investors are simply hoping to be able to buy digital goods sold by LockeChain merchants. That is one complication. The other relates to the "solely from the efforts of others" language of the prong. Are the profits from LockeChain investments made "solely from the efforts of others"? Again, the answer is unclear. Profits from virtual currencies like bitcoin come from a number of potential sources: the regular nodes that validate transactions, the miners that mine new bitcoin, the cryptocurrency exchanges that facilitate access, and so on. Bitcoin's success, and thus profits, are highly dependent on the efforts of many different people. At the same time, they are not dependent on the efforts of any single institution or body or manager – something that courts have often looked to determine the third prong. And, in many cases, the purchaser of the bitcoin will participate as a node or miner in the market, and thus the success of the venture will depend partially on the purchaser's activities. Therefore, profits might not be dependent solely on the efforts of others. They are also dependent on the purchaser.

As I hope this discussion makes clear, applying securities law to the block-chain is an exercise in mind stretching. And we haven't even gotten past the definition of a security! The blockchain makes legal analysis difficult because the radically decentralized structures created by the blockchain just are not familiar to the law or to regulators.

The SEC has attempted to address some of these ambiguities in press releases and public statements. In a widely covered speech in June 2018, for example, SEC commissioner Bill Hinman stated that "when I look at bitcoin today, I do not see a central third party whose efforts are a key determining factor in the enterprise," suggesting that bitcoin would not satisfy the third prong of the Howey test related to profits coming from the efforts of a manager or third party. As he explained:

> This also points the way to when a digital asset transaction may no longer represent a security offering. If the network on which the token or coin is to function is sufficiently decentralized – where purchasers would no longer reasonably expect a person or group to carry out essential managerial or entrepreneurial efforts – the assets may not represent an investment contract. Moreover, when the efforts of the third party are no longer a key factor for determining the enterprise's success, material information asymmetries recede. As a network becomes truly decentralized, the ability to identify an issuer or promoter to make the requisite disclosures becomes difficult, and less meaningful.

For Hinman, the key factor is centralization. If a cryptocurrency is so decentralized that no identifiable person or group carries out essential functions for the network, then it cannot be deemed a security. If, instead, a central group (such as the developers or the promoters of the virtual currency) remains responsible for the cryptocurrency after its launch, it will likely be deemed a security. Hinman justified this distinction by referring to the overriding purpose of the securities laws. "The impetus of the Securities Act," Hinman asserted, "is to remove the information asymmetry between promoters and investors." When investors buy stock in a company, they know much less about the company than the company's managers do. This puts them at a disadvantage, since they don't know whether the price they are paying for the stock is appropriate given the company's future prospects and plans. The securities laws help reduce this information asymmetry (where the managers have lots of information, and the investors have none) by requiring companies to provide mandatory disclosures to investors on topics such as the company's background, its financial results and its managers. But, Hinman argued in his speech, this disclosure-oriented remedy is not needed when cryptocurrencies are decentralized. The disparity of information between investors and managers just does not exist in a truly decentralized cryptocurrency. There is no single actor with superior knowledge. Everyone is in the same boat. And when everyone is in the same boat, it is pointless to force one group to disclose information to another. Indeed, it is even unclear whether you could identify a group on which to impose these disclosure obligations in the first place. For all these reasons, Hinman seemed to suggest, decentralized cryptocurrencies do not need the securities laws, and the securities laws do not need them. At the same time, Hinman shied away from making an explicit statement that bitcoin could never be a security:

> I would like to emphasize that the analysis of whether something is a security is not static and does not strictly inhere to the instrument. Even digital assets with utility that function solely as a means of exchange in a decentralized network could be packaged and sold as an investment strategy that can be a security. If a promoter were to place Bitcoin in a fund or trust and sell interests, it would create a new security.[18]

In other words, despite all the discussion about decentralization versus centralization and its application to bitcoin, bitcoin could be a security depending on the circumstances. The SEC largely followed Hinman's analysis in a digital assets framework it issued in 2019, so Hinman's approach appears to represent the views of the agency devoted to regulating securities.[19]

So there you have it. LockeChain might be a security, but it also might not. And, even more confusingly, it might be a security for some purposes but not for others. The SEC has indicated that, at least in garden-variety purchases and sales of bitcoin, bitcoin is not a security. Other, more centralized cryptocurrencies, on the other hand, may well be. SEC Chairman Jay Clayton has even gone so far as to say that "I believe every ICO I've seen is a security."[20] But, at least as of the writing of this book, neither Congress nor the SEC has issued any binding legal rules on securities regulation in the cryptocurrency sphere. So, at least for now, and as Zaslavskiy noted, cryptocurrencies and their promoters will have their fate determined by "decisions from 1946 about fractional interests in an orange grove."

You might be asking yourself at this point why it matters whether LockeChain is a security. And the answer is that it matters quite a lot. If it is a security, then it is subject to the Securities Act of 1933 and the Securities Exchange Act of 1934, as well as the massive body of law surrounding these two acts. Most importantly, purchases and sales of securities must be registered with the SEC in a lengthy, time-consuming and expensive process. An initial public offering costs, on average, $3.7 million, and this is not even considering the disclosure and compliance costs that the company must bear on an ongoing basis for as long as it remains public.[21] So the ambiguity around whether cryptocurrencies are securities has substantial consequences for the industry as a whole.

But just because LockeChain is considered a "security" does not mean that it is not other things as well, such as a commodity, a currency or property. Commodity regulators, currency regulators and the Internal Revenue Service have all weighed in on these questions and, perhaps unsurprisingly, have typically concluded that the cryptocurrencies they have surveyed fall under their respective jurisdictions. For example, the Bank Secrecy Act imposes a variety of obligations on so-called "financial institutions," a term the statute defines to include a number of different more or less banklike companies such as investment banks, credit card companies, currency exchanges and telegraph companies (yes, the law considers telegraph companies to be "financial institutions").[22] Most of these subcategories of financial institution, however, require the institution to be dealing with "currency" before they will fall under the regulation's requirements. Are virtual currencies "currency"? One might suspect that they are, at least judging from the name. But the Bank Secrecy Act defines currency as "the coin and paper money of the United States or of any other country that is designated as legal tender and that circulates and is customarily used and accepted as a medium of exchange in the country of issuance."[23] And of course, virtual currencies are neither coins nor paper money (nor, for that matter, "of the United States" or any other country), so they appear to fall outside the definition. As a result, companies that operate in the virtual currency industry have an argument that they are not subject to the Bank Secrecy Act's requirements. The Treasury Department's Financial Crimes Enforcement Network, or FinCEN, however, takes a different view of the matter. FinCEN has issued guidance indicating that it considers cryptocurrency exchanges to fall under the category of "money transmitters," one of the subcategories of "financial institution." Helpfully for FinCEN, money transmitters are defined much more broadly than other types of financial institutions. They include anyone who offers money transmission services involving the "acceptance of currency, funds, *or other value that substitutes for currency.*"[24] So anyone who transmits "value that substitutes for currency" may fall under the definition of a money transmitter, and thus the Bank Secrecy Act would apply to them. This would mean that they would be subject to FinCEN's registration, reporting and record-keeping regulations.[25] One of these requirements is that money transmitters implement effective anti-money-laundering programs that are reasonably designed to prevent money laundering and the financing of terrorist activities.[26] As one might imagine, implementing a system to prevent money laundering in an anonymous cryptocurrency like bitcoin is difficult to do without requiring identifying information that effectively eliminates the "anonymous" feature of the currency.[27] Just as importantly, there is substantial ambiguity about what activities involving a blockchain would cause someone to become a money transmitter. Do you have to open a cryptocurrency exchange? Is it enough that you are mining cryptocurrency? What if you are simply operating as a node on a blockchain? The questions could go on.

The IRS, on the other hand, has said that, while virtual currency may be used to pay for goods and services (like a currency) or held for investment (like a stock), the IRS views it as property, and thus does not afford it the tax treatment it gives either currencies or stock. This has one major (and detrimental) consequence: every time owners of virtual currency use that currency to pay for something, they must pay tax on any increase in value of the currency from the time they received it. This means that they must keep track of the value of each bitcoin they buy at the time of purchase, track those bitcoins over time, figure out the value of the bitcoin at the time they pay for something with it, calculate the gain in value from the time they purchase the currency to the time they used it, and then report it to the IRS at the end of the year. This is a tremendously burdensome process. It is no wonder, then, that very few people are voluntarily reporting cryptocurrency transactions in their tax filings; between 2013 and 2015, for example, between 800 and 900 people a year reported bitcoin transactions to the IRS, while Coinbase, the largest U.S. bitcoin exchange, had 5.9 million customers and 6 billion transactions.[28] Just as importantly, the IRS's stance creates real, substantive obstacles for bitcoin and other similarly situated cryptocurrencies to develop into usable currencies. People would undoubtedly think twice about using dollars if they had to account for the dollar's exchange rate every time they made a purchase. But that is how the IRS treats cryptocurrencies.

Perhaps the most comical juxtaposition of old law and new facts is the application of commodities law to the cryptocurrency realm. The regulator here is a body called the Commodity Futures Trading Commission, which has the responsibility of overseeing the commodities industry as a whole. The CFTC has asserted that cryptocurrencies, like bitcoin are commodities, and thus subject to its jurisdiction. But the manner in which it did so reached new heights of interpretive flexibility. The Commodity Exchange Act defines a commodity as:

> wheat, cotton, rice, corn, oats, barley, rye, flaxseed, grain sorghums, mill feeds, butter, eggs, Solanum tuberosum (Irish potatoes), wool, wool tops, fats

and oils (including lard, tallow, cottonseed oil, peanut oil, soybean oil, and all other fats and oils), cottonseed meal, cottonseed, peanuts, soybeans, soybean meal, livestock, livestock products, and frozen concentrated orange juice, and all other goods and articles, except onions . . . and motion picture box office receipts . . ., and all services, rights, and interests . . . in which contracts for future delivery are presently or in the future dealt in.[29]

Are blockchain-based cryptocurrencies like wheat, cotton, grain sorghums and tallow, which are commodities? Or are they more like onions and motion picture box office receipts, which are not? According to the CFTC, the answer is clear: virtual currencies are commodities, just like cottonseed meal, livestock products and frozen concentrated orange juice. And at least one court has agreed with that position, holding that the CFTC has jurisdiction to prosecute the creators of a virtual currency for violating the Commodity Exchange Act.[30]

So LockeChain might be a security, a commodity or a property, or potentially all of these at the same time. Anatole France once said, "The law, in its majestic equality, forbids the rich as well as the poor to sleep under bridges."[31] He meant it as a condemnation of the corrupt core of the French government of the time, which, in his view, was nothing but a mechanism for promoting the interests of wealthy elites. But France's statement might equally serve as a warning about how seemingly neutral laws can have unequal effects. If they are not applied in thoughtful and tailored ways, they can impose harmful consequences on certain groups and companies. The vast array of regulations that could potentially apply to blockchain-based companies acts as a constraint on companies considering operating in the sphere. As the CEO of Goldman Sachs, David Solomon, has said:

> Like others, we're watching and exploring and doing work in terms of trying to understand the cryptocurrency market as it develops. We have some clients that have certain functionality that we've engaged with them on clearing physical futures, but other than that, we never had plans to open a cryptocurrency trading desk. We might at some point in time, but there's no question when you're dealing with cryptocurrency, it's a new area, there are a lot of issues, it is unclear from a regulatory perspective, and it's not clear whether or not, in the long run, as a currency, those technologies are going to work and be viable.[32]

It is hard to imagine a virtual currency gaining traction if users have to report gains to the IRS every time they use it. It is hard to imagine small companies launching ICOs if they must go through a multimillion-dollar registration process with the SEC. How regulators decide to categorize cryptocurrencies carries important consequences for the future of blockchain as a technology.

Thus, the blockchain presents a foundational problem for law. Because its decentralized structure allows people to organize their affairs in fundamentally different ways than they were able to before, the blockchain defies easy categorization into the typical "boxes" that legal frameworks use. One consequence of this is that many of even the simplest transactions using virtual currencies could potentially implicate any number of legal regimes. Regulators have struggled to find ways to shoehorn virtual currencies into their existing legal frameworks, with varying degrees of success. But overall, the blockchain remains in a legal penumbra.

***

So it is unclear which legal rules apply to the blockchain. This is problematic because we need to know the rules of the road before we can start implementing them. But the law requires more than just a clear set of rules to be effective. It also requires observers who are capable of seeing when those rules are broken. And monitoring is a problem in the blockchain world.

Let us take the example of Monero, a cryptocurrency that launched in 2014. Monero is widely touted as the "untraceable" alternative to bitcoin. Unlike the bitcoin network, where identities are obscured but addresses and transactions are publicly available, the Monero network hides all relevant information. If you own Monero, no one can see where it came from or where it went to. It is simply a black box.[33] This has important consequences for the wider cryptocurrency world as well. For example, users of traceable currencies such as bitcoin can exchange their bitcoin for Monero, and then reconvert it to the original currency. As a result, the owner can sever any connections with their previous activity on the traceable blockchain. If a bitcoin address is connected to a bad action, such as a theft or a ransom payment, the owner can use Monero to launder their dirty bitcoin and turn it into clean bitcoin. A *Wall Street Journal* investigation found that hackers from North Korea who had launched the WannaCry ransomware attack used Monero to launder the ransom payments they had originally received in bitcoin. So did the fraudsters who founded Starscape Capital, a company that raised $2.2 million in bitcoin from investors in 2018 and then promptly disappeared.[34]

But even when virtual currencies are not stealth coins like Monero, they still raise monitoring problems due to their decentralized structure. Imagine, for example, that the federal government had reason to believe that a criminal organization was using a bank to hide the proceeds of their robberies. All they would need to do in order to locate the proceeds and identify the people behind them would be to ask the bank for them. They might need to get a subpoena to figure out which account it was, but this would be a relatively simple process, and one that federal prosecutors are well versed in handling.[35] Once they had this information, the bank would be obliged by law to act accordingly.

But there is no single entity that the government can go to with similar requests in the cryptocurrency world. There simply is no one with this kind of information, or this kind of control over the money supply. That, after all, is the point of the blockchain. Bitcoin and the blockchain were created in order to take control over money and private transactions out of the hands of large entities and give that control back to the people. In order to get information about cryptocurrency users, then, the federal government must resort to indirect methods, such as tracking where assets move on the blockchain and then hoping that someone makes a mistake that gives up their true identity. Certainly, cryptocurrency exchanges – the companies that offer to buy or sell cryptocurrencies to customers – play an important role in this ecosystem and give regulators some ability to monitor the flow of funds in cryptocurrencies. In 2017, for example, the IRS forced Coinbase, one of the largest virtual currency exchanges, to turn over the records of thousands of account holders whom the IRS suspected of evading taxes.[36] But Coinbase is a U.S. company, headquartered in San Francisco, with American owners. Many cryptocurrency exchanges are harder to reach, either because they are located abroad or because they have less scrupulous business practices. It is worthwhile remembering that prosecutors only managed to find out who owned BTC-e, the cryptocurrency exchange connected to the Mt. Gox hack and other infamous incidents, through a series of lucky turns.

One might argue that the monitoring problems here are no different than those posed by, say, Swiss banks, which have long been known for their fearsome protection of client privacy. For years, it was widely believed that criminals and tax evaders were depositing their money in Swiss bank accounts, with no questions asked, and thereby ensuring that their home governments could never come snooping around to see how much they had stashed there. But one big difference between Swiss banks and the cryptocurrency world was that, at the end of the day, Swiss banks depended heavily on access to the U.S. banking system. So, when an American whistleblower who worked at UBS, the largest Swiss bank, came forward to the American government to reveal that UBS was facilitating tax evasion, prosecutors had leverage to force the bank to change its ways.[37] UBS ultimately paid a fine of $780 million to the U.S. government, handed over information on thousands of its U.S. customers and agreed to provide ongoing reports to the U.S. government on its U.S. banking clients.[38] The blockchain simply does not respond to these same levers. The decentralized structure of the blockchain spreads power out to many different people, none of whom have access to (or control over) the rest of the network. There is no single company like UBS to ask for information. There is no person to subpoena to start taking down everyone's names. There is no single point of entry.

***

We have seen how blockchain-based industries make it hard to figure out what the rules of the road are. We have also seen how they make it hard for regulators to identify when the rules of the road have been broken. But the final piece of the puzzle, the one that ultimately all legal systems rely on, is the ability to punish people when they break the rules.

The sociologist Max Weber, in his seminal lecture *Politics as a Vocation*, famously argued that the state, in its essence, depends on a threat of violence. As he explained:

> If no social institutions existed which knew the use of violence, then the concept of "state" would be eliminated, and a condition would emerge that could be designated as "anarchy," in the specific sense of this word. Of course, force is certainly not the normal or the only means of the state – nobody says that – but force is a means specific to the state. Today the relation between the state and violence is an especially intimate one . . . . Today, however, we have to say that a state is a human community that (successfully) claims the monopoly of the legitimate use of physical force within a given territory.[39]

Weber's lecture is often used as a way to define what the state is: the state is the institution that has a monopoly on legitimate use of force within a territory. But it also says something important about the effectiveness of law. Weber suggests that the ultimate source of legal authority is force. A government can lay down as many laws and proclaim as many rules as it likes, but if it does not have the means to enforce these precepts, it cannot claim to be a functioning state. A functioning state, in the final analysis, has authority only to the extent that it can legitimately force people to obey it.

Similarly, in order to make a legal regime for blockchain work, government authorities need to be able to sanction wrongdoing on the blockchain. Of course, they need not command perfect compliance. No legal regime could aspire to that. But they do need to have the capability to sanction some reasonable proportion of acts of noncompliance. And just like the other elements of legal effectiveness, decentralization makes the act of sanctioning noncompliance problematic.

To understand this point, it may be useful to compare how sanctioning works in a centralized industry with how it works in a decentralized one. Imagine, for example, that the government discovers that a bank is committing a crime, say, engaging in money laundering. Punishing the bank for doing so, once the facts have been discovered, is not a particularly difficult thing to do. The government can prosecute the bank in a court, levy fines on it, seize its assets and send its officers to prison. It can effectively force the bank out of business and thereby stop the problematic behavior.

But these tools are much blunter, and less effective, when applied to a decentralized virtual currency like bitcoin. If the government discovers that bitcoin is being used to launder money, it cannot simply go to a court and prosecute bitcoin. There is no bitcoin company. Certainly, the government can target individuals and companies that operate within the bitcoin world, such as the cryptocurrency exchanges that allow bitcoin holders to convert their bitcoin into real currency. But, as mentioned before, many of these exchanges are located abroad (some of the most popular are in Korea and Japan), and thus the government may struggle to reach them. But even if it did, and even if it managed to shut down all the cryptocurrency exchanges in the world, it would still not shut down bitcoin itself. Bitcoin continues to operate as long as someone, somewhere, has a computer that has downloaded the latest version of the blockchain. Shutting down a single company or exchange has little (in fact, in most cases, no) effect on the blockchain ecosystem as a whole. If the government wants to shut down bitcoin, or some other decentralized virtual currency, where does it go? The answer, governments are increasingly discovering, is that there is nowhere to go.

***

So the blockchain raises a set of difficult problems for the law. It is unclear how it fits into current legal regimes. It is unclear that regulators can adequately monitor behavior connected to the blockchain. And it is unclear how the government can sanction bad behavior on the blockchain. But all of these challenges and difficulties pale in comparison with a final challenge presented by the blockchain. What if the blockchain does not just challenge the law, but seeks to replace it?

The idea of computer code functioning as law is not particularly new. As early as 1999, Harvard scholar Lawrence Lessig devoted an entire book (*Code and Other Laws of Cyberspace*) to the subject. In it, Lessig argued that computer code acts as a kind of law within the newly developing world that he called "cyberspace." To Lessig, code looked a lot like law, and performed many of the same functions.

The software and hardware that make cyberspace what it is constitute a set of constraints on how you can behave. The substance of these constraints may vary, but they are experienced as conditions on your access to cyberspace. In some places (online services such as AOL, for instance) you must enter a password before you gain access; in other places you can enter whether identified or not. In some places the transactions you engage in produce traces that link the transactions (the "mouse droppings") back to you; in other places this link is achieved only if you want it to be. In some places you can choose to speak a language that only the recipient can hear (through encryption); in other places encryption is not an option. The code or software or architecture or protocols set these features; they are features selected by code writers; they constrain some behavior by making other behavior possible, or impossible. The code embeds certain values or makes certain values impossible. In this sense, it too is regulation, just as the architectures of real-space codes are regulations.

Just as law sets limits on behavior, permitting some actions while forbidding others, computer code can do the same. It limits what users can do with software, what websites they can access, what programs they can use. For Lessig, this was both a cause for concern and a cause for hope. "In cyberspace we must understand how code regulates – how the software and hardware that make cyberspace what it is regulate cyberspace as it is .... . This code is cyberspace's 'law.' Code is law."[40] But "we have every reason to believe that cyberspace, left to itself, will not fulfill the promise of freedom." As a result, Lessig concluded, code as law "will present the greatest threat both to liberal and libertarian ideals, as well as their greatest promise."[41]

While the idea of code as law has been around for some time, the idea of blockchain as law is something substantially new, and something substantially different from previous iterations. To be sure, just as AOL and Gmail condition access to their services on someone entering in a password, virtual currencies condition access to funds and transactions on someone entering in a "private key" that demonstrates that they own the currency. Just as the code that underlies AOL and Gmail determines the rules of the road for users, the code that underlies virtual currencies and other blockchain programs determines the rules of the road for use of these currencies and programs. But what is new about the blockchain is that it allows these rules of the road, these laws, to be set, not by a central administration, but by the users themselves. Rather than forcing users to rely on the beneficent coding of Time Warner or Google, the blockchain allows users themselves to encode only the laws that they desire. What is more, it allows them to alter and change these laws for individual transactions. This of course starts to look more like a contract than law; it is an agreement between two or more parties setting out the terms of their relationship. But, again, easy analogies are misleading. Unlike a contract, blockchain-based programs often do not need to rely on a judge in the event that one party breaks its promise. The smart contract can instead include in its code provisions setting forth how to determine a breach, and can automatically transfer funds or take other actions to recompense the injured party when a breach occurs.

The legal scholars Aaron Wright and Primavera De Filippi call this law-creating feature of the blockchain *"lex cryptographica."*[42] In their book *Blockchain and the Law*, Wright and De Filippi argue that "blockchains could accelerate a structural shift of power from legal rules and regulations administered by government authorities to code-based rules and protocols governed by decentralized blockchain-based networks." If blockchain structures end up being adopted as widely as some proponents predict, they could potentially undermine the rule of law itself. As Wright and De Filippi state:

> Systems deployed on a blockchain – especially those relying on *lex cryptographica* – are not subject to the same kinds of limitations [as traditional online activities are]. By relying on decentralized peer-to-peer networks, blockchain-based systems can be designed to operate autonomously and potentially independent of the whims of centralized intermediaries by implementing code-based rules that are more persistent and often harder to change than those deployed by traditional centralized operators . . . . These blockchain-based systems can serve as the foundation for more sophisticated types of decision making, allowing legal institutions to be created without voting or the designation of a central authority.[43]

In other words, by allowing individuals to write and enact code-based protocols that are self-executing and irreversible, blockchains could potentially become laws unto themselves. This law might circumvent, replace or subsume traditional law. This is a dramatic challenge to government-enforced order. "Like many other technologies, blockchains can be deployed both to support and undercut existing laws and regulations," Wright and De Filippi continue, "but what makes the technology particularly potent is its ability to facilitate the creation of resilient, tamper-resistant, and automated code-based systems that operate globally, providing people with new financial and contractual tools that could replace key societal functions."[44]

There are, however, strong reasons to doubt that the blockchain presents a true alternative to law as we know it. For one, much of the theorizing about blockchain remains in the world of imagination. There are few examples of large-scale smart contracts operating in the real world. Most of the projects remain in beta phase, or have very limited use. An airline company launching a blockchain-based insurance system that pays people when their planes are late (like the Fizzy smart contract mentioned in Chapter 3) hardly amounts to an existential challenge for legal systems themselves. Neither, for that matter, does bitcoin. One example that received significant press attention was Ujo Music's announcement in 2015 that it had created a smart contract to allow people to purchase Imogen Heap's song "Tiny Humans." Any time that someone paid $0.60 to download the song on Ujo Music's website, a smart contract was triggered that would automatically send a portion of the sales price to Imogen Heap and a portion to other collaborators who helped produce the song. But after significant media coverage, and months on the site, the total payments amounted to just $133.20. In 2016, Ujo Music abandoned the effort.[45] As Ujo Music would later explain in a blog post, they were "but a few bright-eyed technologists with a special hammer, looking for the right nail."[46] If anything, these examples appear to highlight the essential function that law continues to play in the blockchain. After all, if someone does not agree with a result on the blockchain, they can always challenge the result in court, regardless of what the blockchain itself might say.

What is more, it is unclear that the rules and structures of blockchain amount to anything akin to law. The smart contracts that can be created on the blockchain are much more akin to contracts than to law generally: the parties agree that in the event that some action is taken or some event occurs (the "condition"), then some consequence will automatically follow. The consequence typically involves the payment of some amount of virtual currency to one or more parties. This is how typical contracts work as well: one party agrees to pay the other party in the event the other party performs some service or takes some action, such as building a house for the first party or selling a company to the first party. Law, on the other hand, provides the backdrop around which contracts work. Law generally requires some authoritative decision-maker, like a president or a legislature, promulgating rules of conduct and a judge enforcing them. Private parties cannot simply agree among themselves that their actions are not subject to law. The law applies regardless.

Ultimately, while decentralization may make law more difficult to apply, it appears unlikely that it will supplant it. Similar hand-wringing among legal scholars occurred when the internet was first launched, but, by and large, legal structures muddled through. As Jack Goldsmith, a legal scholar at Harvard, and Tim Wu, a legal scholar at Columbia, argued in their book *Who Controls the Internet?*, the mere fact that activities take place on the internet does not mean that traditional laws do not apply.[47] It just requires changes in the way that those laws are applied. To be sure, the seeming "nowhere-ness" of internet activity made the legal community uneasy. Many worried that "territorial government seemed to be melting away and becoming increasingly irrelevant."[48] But, as Goldsmith and Wu demonstrated, governments found ways to govern the internet. They threatened internet providers, they targeted search engines and they filtered content. And, in some ways, the internet gave even more power to national governments than they had had in the pre-internet world. "[I]n the hands of a government like China, that does not share these values [of privacy and free speech], the Internet enables frighteningly unprecedented control by the government over individuals."[49]

In an uncanny echo of discussions today around the blockchain's effects on government and law, Goldsmith and Wu also addressed arguments about the undermining effect of the internet on law.

> The diminishing costs of moving information on the Internet have obviously made it harder for governments to suppress communications and related activities that they dislike. The Net has allowed talented technologists, dissatisfied groups, and various types of law evaders to take advantage of the difficulty of controlling information to achieve political, social, and commercial goals. This was also true, however, of the telegraph, the telephone, the radio, the television, and other earlier communication revolutions, all of which dramatically increased the number and speed of communications, and dramatically lowered their costs. These communication technologies produced radical changes in human organization and interaction, and required governments to develop new strategies for regulating human affairs. But they did not displace the central role of territorial government in human governance. And neither, we have argued in this book, will the Internet.[50]

It might equally be said that, while the blockchain presents tricky questions about where precisely it fits in our legal structure, it does not threaten the structure itself.

***

The blockchain has an uneasy relationship with the law. Because the technology is so innovative and new, it simply does not fall neatly into preestablished categories. This raises two opposing possibilities, both of them worrying. First, it might mean that the technology ends up falling into gaps in the law, leading to opportunistic behavior with no legal remedy. Alternatively, it might lead to the opposite situation, with overzealous regulators contorting the law in an effort to assert their jurisdiction over it. Thus, we might have underregulation, or we might have overregulation. Neither is desirable. The next Chapter will discuss how governments have sought to sort all of this out.

PART III

THE FUTURE OF DECENTRALIZATION

7

How to Govern Technology

It is because every individual knows so little and, in particular, because we rarely know which of us knows best that we trust the independent and competitive efforts of many to induce the emergence of what we shall want when we see it.

Friedrich Hayek, *The Constitution of Liberty*

Malta has an audacious plan.

Many countries have been slow to reform their laws in response to the spread of blockchain. Others have begun grudging efforts to tackle it. Malta, however, has leaped in headfirst. The small island nation in the Mediterranean Sea has dubbed itself "Blockchain Island," created a digital innovation authority and passed a slew of new laws to make itself more welcoming to blockchain companies. It has even researched ways to incorporate blockchain technologies into the running of government itself. As the Maltese prime minister, Joseph Muscat, has said (by way of a tweet), Malta "aims to be the global trailblazers in the regulation of blockchain-based businesses and the jurisdiction of quality and choice for world class fintech companies."[1]

The person charged with masterminding this effort is Steve Tendon, a Swedish-born software engineer turned international consultant from Gothenburg. If anyone has the cosmopolitan chops to pull off a project of the ambition and reach that Malta has tasked him with, Tendon does. Born in Sweden, Tendon moved to South Africa as a child, later studying at an English school in Sweden and completing his undergraduate studies – in computer science – at Milan's prestigious Politecnico University. After working for a time at Borland International, an early competitor of Microsoft and Lotus, he became a management consultant, where he invented his own methodology for making organizations more flexible and adaptable. In the course of his work, he became convinced that the best organizations were fluid ones, where dynamic teams could dissolve and reorganize quickly and efficiently. Eventually, his research led him to a new white paper, just published by Vitalik Buterin, proposing a new blockchain platform called Ethereum.

"After the first three sentences, I was completely sold," he told me. "This was going to change the world. I had to get into it."[2]

With his background in computer science and software engineering, Tendon quickly learned the basic mechanics of the blockchain, but he wanted to find out more before entering the industry in a more serious way. To that end, he enrolled in a course that the Massachusetts Institute of Technology was offering on fintech and blockchain. One of his assignments asked him to imagine how to redesign a system with the blockchain. But Tendon realized that the system at issue could be any kind of system.

"So I thought, how could you reorganize a *country* using the blockchain?"

Many things came to mind. It might improve election systems. It might improve identification systems, such as government IDs or licenses. It might improve government record-keeping. It might improve healthcare systems. All of these government services suffered from an inability to create secure databases that could be accessed in convenient ways. The blockchain, Tendon believed, could revolutionize the way that government worked.

A few weeks later, in June 2016, at a conference on financial services, Tendon happened to meet Christian Cardona, Malta's economy minister. Tendon explained his ideas about how a small jurisdiction could adopt the blockchain as a building block for its services and Cardona, intrigued, invited him to come visit him in Malta to discuss the idea more. At that meeting, Tendon explained in detail how the blockchain could be used, not just to make regulations and governments more efficient, but also the entire economy. The meeting, scheduled for just a half hour, ended up running for more than two hours. At the end, Cardona was sold. He tasked Tendon with drafting a national strategy for turning Malta into a blockchain hub.

Tendon realized early on that this would require a substantial rethinking of Malta's laws and government structure. "We saw that there was a problem with what was happening in the bitcoin space," Tendon told me. "We had financial services authorities coming out with certain positions and regulations, and then we had other authorities coming out with different, often conflicting, positions and regulations. That was something that just could not work. So we wanted a single regulator that could prevent multiple regulators from stepping on each other's toes and that could develop a cohesive view of the industry so as not to hinder development of the technology."

Eventually, Tendon's plan came into place. His national strategy would have three prongs. First, it would require the Maltese government itself to adopt the blockchain in its processes. Second, it would require a new regulator that had the expertise and oversight capacity to monitor private sector activities involving blockchain. And third, it would require new laws to clarify the legal treatment of blockchain-based activities. One of the primary goals of the strategy was to attract blockchain companies to the country.

In the process of drafting the national strategy, Tendon also found a name for the project. "I knew that the vision needed a name," he told me. "I immediately thought of Silicon Valley, and then started playing around with what was unique about Malta. 'Blockchain Island' was an easy choice. It was a deliberate design."

Tendon presented his draft national strategy to Cardona, Malta's minister for the economy, in October 2016. Cardona accepted it with enthusiasm and eventually asked him to turn the outlines contained in the strategy into the specifics of a legal framework, including actual statutory language to be implemented by Malta's parliament. This latter effort culminated in the passage of three bills: one creating a single regulator, the Malta Digital Innovation Authority; one establishing a framework for regulating blockchain-based "technology arrangements," such as smart contracts or autonomous organizations; and one setting forth rules for virtual currencies.[3]

From an advertising perspective, the strategy worked quite well. The content of Malta's new laws was widely viewed as "permissive," aimed primarily at attracting blockchain businesses to Malta, rather than constraining them. In the months after Malta announced the legislation, a series of cryptocurrency companies announced that they would be moving their operations to the island nation. The collection of companies included large exchanges, such as Binance, the world's largest cryptocurrency exchange; OKex, the world's second-largest exchange; and ZB.com, the world's fifth-largest exchange.[4] It also included companies that had run into trouble in their home jurisdictions. The virtual currency exchange BitBay, for example, moved to Malta after Polish banks refused to do business with it.[5] Binance itself had shuttered its operations in Japan after that country's Financial Services Agency warned the company that it lacked a proper license and faced criminal liability if it continued to operate.[6] The flood of companies and investments in Malta led one cryptocurrency trader to quip that "Malta is getting crowded."[7]

Malta's efforts to take the lead in creating a clear and permissive legal structure for blockchain technology received ample attention in the crypto-press. After the announcement of the legislation, the headlines told the story in unambiguous terms: "How Malta Is Becoming the Blockchain Hub of the

World";[8] "Another Exchange is Heading to Malta, the 'Blockchain Capital of the World'";[9] "Have a Cryptocurrency Company? Bermuda, Malta or Gibraltar Wants You."[10] International organizations, however, were more skeptical. The International Monetary Fund, in a visit to the island, informed the Maltese government that its blockchain activities created "significant risks" for the country's financial system; in particular, Malta could soon become a hotbed of money laundering and terrorism financing. It concluded that there was need for "immediate action" to improve the government's monitoring and enforcement capacities.[11]

And efforts to integrate blockchain into the fabric of government have proved slow and halting. One early project, launched in September 2017, aimed at putting academic diplomas on the blockchain. People who earned a degree from, say, the Malta College of Art, Science and Technology, could have their degree placed on a blockchain. In theory, the credential would then reside in a secure database, able to be accessed at any time by the proper authorities. Students would no longer need to go back to the university to request confirmation of their educational records. They could access them directly. As one official at Malta's Education Ministry stated at the time, "Think of Syrian universities and 5 million displaced Syrian who need to prove their credentials, this system does away with all of that."[12] In 2019, the Maltese government announced that it had signed a two-year contract with a blockchain company, Learning Machine, to put all of the country's academic certificates on a - blockchain.[13] Beyond this, however, ambitions to use the blockchain to transform government have overshot reality.

It remains to be seen whether Malta's efforts to incorporate blockchain into the very DNA of the country will bear fruit. But the very fact that they are trying to do so is telling. One explanation is that Malta's efforts to reduce the regulatory burdens on blockchain companies are a crass effort to undercut other countries and curry favor with tech executives. In this view, Malta's efforts are yet another example of a small jurisdiction becoming a haven for bad actors, whether they be tax evaders, money smugglers or corporate oligarchs. It is a race to the bottom, with Malta in the lead. But another explanation is that Malta is at the vanguard of a much-needed movement towards adapting national laws and policies to new technology. In this view, Malta is not so much undercutting other jurisdictions as it is besting them, in fair combat. In other words, it is a race to the top. Sorting out these competing narratives is difficult, not least because our views about the virtues of blockchain will likely color our opinions about what regulation should look like. But regardless of our views of the morality of Malta's actions, it is clear that Malta has been a leader in rethinking how to address technological change through law.

***

It is said that the Chinese premier Zhou Enlai once remarked, when asked his opinion of the significance of the French Revolution, that it was "too early to say." Modern regulators do not have that luxury with the blockchain. Virtual currencies, smart contracts and blockchain networks are rapidly spreading around the world. The benefits of these decentralized structures have been widely remarked upon, as have the dangers. Responsible governments have many options available to them to respond to these challenges, but whatever path they choose will have real consequences for citizens, businesses and technology.

So, with all that said, what should governments do? In general, governments faced with a potentially transformative new technology have three policy options available to them. First, they can rework their regulations to encourage development of the technology, in the hope that its growth will spur innovation and economic prosperity. Second, they can reform their laws to discourage use of the technology, out of concern for its harmful or risky consequences. And third, they can do nothing, letting markets, consumers and businesses do the hard work of sorting out the technology's costs and benefits. Each of these options brings with it its own unique set of risks and rewards.

Of course, governments might also choose to take bits and pieces of each of these approaches. In the blockchain context, this might mean deciding to do nothing with respect to the use of cryptocurrencies, cracking down on miners and encouraging enterprise-oriented blockchain start-ups. This sort of pragmatic, ad hoc approach to the blockchain, adopting shifting regulatory attitudes depending on the particular applications of the blockchain, has much to recommend it, including, perhaps primarily, avoiding the over-breadth problems that come with adopting widely applicable laws on diverse behaviors. It would allow regulators to pick and choose the right approach depending on the context. As a practical matter, most governments, most of the time, engage in this kind of ad hoc regulatory approach, addressing problems as they pop up. But doing so does not avoid the basic question of *what* to encourage, *what* to discourage, and *what* to leave alone.

***

Let us begin with the default approach of doing nothing, which, despite its name, actually has much to commend it. We often hear of governments adopting a wait and see approach to a problem – say, a growing conflict in a far-off region or a budding trade war or even, more prosaically, an emerging technology. Recent examples include President Trump taking a wait and see approach to North Korea's threats to call off a summit meeting between the two countries,[14] the city of Seattle taking a wait and see approach to shareable electric scooters like Lime,[15] and Germany adopting a wait and see approach to the United Kingdom's Brexit negotiations.[16] The term "wait and see," however, masks an important truth. In all these cases, the government has decided *not* to act. Thus, "doing nothing" is a more accurate term. Doing nothing does not, of course, mean taking no action at all. Governments may well be enforcing their laws and going about their ordinary affairs while doing nothing. What doing nothing means as a regulatory approach, then, is that a government has made a conscious decision not to revise its laws or regulations in order to target a particular problem. It means letting the current regulatory structure stand and continuing to apply it as it has always been applied.

The do nothing approach has many virtues as a regulatory paradigm.[17] For one, it allows a government to avoid the difficult and costly process of passing new laws and regulations. If an issue is not sufficiently problematic, and its harms to society are relatively limited, then it may simply not be worth rethinking regulations in a way to apply them to the new problem.

Another virtue of a do nothing approach is that it avoids unintended consequences. History is littered with the corpses of well-intentioned laws that end up doing more harm than good. Just look at President Bill Clinton's attempts to rein in executive compensation in the early 1990s. During his campaign, Clinton had denounced bloated CEO salaries that seemed to have no connection to the success of their companies. He blamed the problem on a tax system that rewarded "unlimited executive compensation" and pledged, instead, to create a system that would have "no incentives for executive compensation that is excessive or moving our plants overseas."[18] So, in 1993, after his election, he pushed a tax change through Congress that was directly addressed at excessive executive compensation. Under the revised tax code, companies could deduct CEO pay only if it was less than $1 million. Anything above that amount was nondeductible. It was believed that this change would put downward pressure on executive compensation, since it made it more expensive for companies to pay salaries that exceeded $1 million. This sounds like a reasonable assumption. The problem, though, was that the tax law also provided incentives for so-called pay for performance – that is, executive compensation tied to the success of the company. Although pay for performance could technically mean any compensation that was contingent on the attainment of performance goals, what it meant in practice was stock options. So, if a company paid a CEO $2 million in salary, it could not deduct all the CEO's pay as an expense. But if it paid the CEO $1 million in salary and $1 million in stock options, it could. So what happened after Clinton enacted these rule changes aimed at reducing CEO pay? CEO pay skyrocketed. Between 1992 and 1996, average CEO pay at S&P 500 companies rose from $3 million to $6.2 million. And it did not stop there. It kept going up in 1997 and 1998 and 1999. In 2000, it peaked at $14.6 million, almost five times as much as it had been in 1992.[19] And there are strong reasons to believe that Clinton's reform not only failed to prevent these increases but actually caused them. While CEO pay had been increasing before the passage of Clinton's tax reforms, it accelerated afterwards, much of it being in the form of stock options.[20] Even well-intentioned laws, then, sometimes do more harm than good. If we do not think we can come up with a reasoned and well-balanced law that will both solve the problem and not cause new ones, then governments may be better off not doing anything at all.

A final reason for adopting a do nothing approach when it comes to technological disruption is that it allows governments to gain more information before acting. Whether drafting laws or deciding on budget priorities or fashioning regulatory enforcement goals, it is essential for decision-makers to have accurate and comprehensive information about the field concerned. Otherwise, they are deciding on policy without knowing the facts. As an industry matures and develops, it can be expected to grow more stable. Governments will come to know the relevant actors and the ways they interact with one another. Imagine, for example, if Congress had developed a regulatory framework for social media back in 2003 when MySpace was launched. It would not have known about Facebook, and, more importantly, it would not have known the extent, or even the existence, of some of the most worrying problems in social media, such as social media addiction problems, privacy problems and political propaganda campaigns. By doing nothing, governments acquire more, and better, information about the particular industry and its benefits and harms.

Have any countries actually adopted a do nothing approach with respect to the blockchain? One surprising candidate here is the United States. As of the writing of this book, Congress had not passed any major laws related to the blockchain. Regulators had not written any major regulations relating to the blockchain, either. To be sure, regulators had not exactly been sitting on their hands with regard to cryptocurrencies and digital assets. The SEC, the CFTC and other government bodies have made public statements about the blockchain – for example, advising companies on how current laws might apply to the industry or how crypto-companies can comply. Still, they have largely shied away from issuing legally binding rules. Indeed, the lack of action by Congress and regulators has been widely criticized by both proponents and critics of the industry, with proponents arguing that the lack of clarity in blockchain regulation hinders innovation, and critics arguing that current regulations do not sufficiently contain blockchain's risks to investors.

To say that the United States has done nothing, however, is not to say that individual states within the United States have done nothing as well. In fact, much of the targeted regulation in the blockchain space has come from states. Delaware has revised its famed corporations law to allow corporations to issue their stock through a blockchain.[21] Ohio announced that it would accept bitcoin as payment for business taxes such as sales tax, cigarette tax and withholding tax.[22] Wyoming has passed thirteen blockchain-related statutes, including laws recognizing direct property rights in digital assets and authorizing banks to provide services to blockchain businesses.[23] New York even created an entire regulatory framework around virtual currency companies, providing a so-called BitLicense to entities engaged in transmitting, holding or buying virtual currencies for others.[24] But, in yet another example of unintended consequences, the New York BitLicense, originally intended to create a better framework for regulating blockchain-based companies, appears to have ended up actively discouraging companies from setting up operations there. ShapeShift, the virtual currency exchange mentioned in Chapter 4 for its connections to money laundering, left New York after the BitLicense framework was announced. Its CEO, Erik Voorhees, said at the time that "we're not going to spy on thousands of people purely to make their [law enforcement's] job a little bit easier."[25] Other virtual currency companies have followed suit, leaving the state after deciding that the BitLicense framework did more harm than good.[26] Jerry Brito, the executive director of Coin Center, had less than flattering things to say about the New York law. "It's a mixed bag, is the best that can be said about the BitLicense," he said. "We are working with [other states] to ensure they do not repeat the mistakes made here."[27] Perhaps with more information, governments will draft better laws.

✳✳✳

Another approach that governments have taken towards the blockchain – one that is most visibly on display in Malta – is a permissive approach. A group of scholars and industry proponents have long argued that current law does not provide a good structure for regulating the blockchain. In their view, old laws are too vague in application or restrictive in substance for blockchain companies to be able to operate profitably under them. In order to remedy these problems, this group of scholars argues that governments should take a permissive approach to blockchain regulation, adopting rules that are designed to free up the creative energy of blockchain start-ups, primarily by being less restrictive on the kinds of activities that blockchain companies can undertake.

There are a number of reasons why governments might want to relax their rules when dealing with new technologies like the blockchain. Start-ups in new industries tend to be small and capital-light. For that reason, they are typically very sensitive to regulatory costs. A large investment bank on Wall Street might be able to stomach a Sarbanes-Oxley Act that costs them $4.4 million per year in compliance costs.[28] A small start-up just trying to get off the ground on a strapped budget and a small bank account likely cannot. Even BitLicense, the New York version of a blockchain rule, carries a hefty cost; it is estimated that one cryptocurrency exchange spent $100,000 on its application.[29] If we believe that regulatory burdens are inhibiting companies from innovating in ways that benefit society more broadly, then governments have strong reasons to relax the rules that apply to the industry.

Another – perhaps more problematic – reason for relaxing the rules that apply to a new technology is to ensure that domestic companies establish a foothold in the industry. It has long been recognized that certain technologies benefit from so-called network effects.[30] Network effects generally refer to the benefits that accrue to current users of a product when new users start using it as well. A classic example is the telephone. Telephones are not particularly useful if only one or two people own them. But as the number of telephone owners grow, so too does the benefit of the technology itself. Entirely new uses emerge. Suddenly, people in an entire city or state or even country can seamlessly communicate with one another.

Network effects can be a good thing when they bring large benefits to lots of people, as in the case of telephones. But network effects can also mean that the first entrant into a market gains a sizable advantage over later entrants.[31] Once a particular company establishes a dominant position – say, by becoming the largest social network or the largest stock exchange – it can be hard for competitors to come in and compete with them, even if the competitors' products are arguably superior.

This is so for several reasons. For one thing, if everyone else is using one company's technology, then new companies with related but different technologies can be shut out. Users simply want to use the technology that everyone else is using, even if the new, somewhat different technology is better. Imagine, for example, trying to launch a social network that competes with

Facebook. Or a messaging platform that competes with Twitter. It might not be strictly impossible, but it is certainly difficult. Another reason why early entrants have an advantage over later ones is that, even when there are no true network effects at work, early entrants benefit from the many users who simply migrate to the platform that has more name recognition. This is particularly likely to occur in industries where consumers are uncertain about the quality of products or prone to inertia.[32] In cryptocurrencies, where the differences between products and exchanges and services are often only discernible by blockchain experts, and sometimes not even by them, the first mover advantage is particularly strong. In sum, network effects often mean that the first company to take a lead will keep that lead indefinitely.

The reason why this dynamic can be problematic is that it might lead to destructive competition between governments. After all, governments are not operating in a vacuum. International competition is a fact of life today for most large companies. A government that wants to ensure that its domestic companies become dominant within the industry might relax its rules in order to give its companies a competitive advantage over other companies. But once one government does so, other governments may follow suit in order to avoid having their companies disadvantaged. Or they might try to go even further, reducing their regulatory burdens to the absolute minimum in order to outcompete neighboring countries.[33] Countries might, for example, signal to blockchain companies that they are exempt from completing costly registration processes or paying certain business taxes. Doing so would give those companies located in the jurisdiction an advantage over competitors in other countries. Adopting a permissive approach to the blockchain, thus, should make it more likely that your country's companies win.

One version of a permissive approach that has been widely bandied about in blockchain circles is a so-called regulatory sandbox. The term, of course, conjures up images of toddlers at play in a sandbox under the watchful eye of their parents. Rambunctious as they may be, they are largely immune from causing serious injury, either to themselves or to others. The sand protects them from falls, and their parents can step in if things get really bad. Regulatory sandboxes are based on a similar idea: if we can establish a framework in which blockchain companies can play around with new ideas or products in a controlled environment and under the watchful gaze of regulators, we can encourage innovation while preventing harm. Under a regulatory sandbox, blockchain companies might, for example, be able to launch their products or services without going through all the usual authorizations. Or they might receive assurances that they would not be subject to fines or other penalties by regulators. In return, they would open up their businesses to regulators to give them a closer understanding of what they are doing.[34]

A number of countries have launched so-called sandbox initiatives. The United Kingdom was the first to do so. In 2015, its Financial Conduct Authority announced a sandbox program that allowed financial technology (or fintech) start-ups to offer new financial services without going through the costly authorization processes that normally attend such services.[35] While this effort was not specifically focused on the blockchain industry, crypto-companies have been a serious focus of the program. In 2018, for example, of the twenty-nine firms selected for inclusion in the sandbox, twelve involved some form of blockchain application.[36] The program has widely been regarded as a success, and other countries have followed suit. In 2016, Hong Kong's Monetary Authority launched a Fintech Supervisory Sandbox that allowed banks and technology firms to test out new financial products without complying with the panoply of registration and disclosure requirements that usually accompany such initiatives.[37] So did Singapore in 2016. Singapore's sandbox was so popular that the country decided to create a new, even faster, "express" sandbox that pared down the minimum requirements even more. Their stated goal was to grant approval for express sandbox applications within twenty-one days from the date of applying.[38] These initiatives have received praise from regulators and companies alike for greatly reducing the time and money that fintech companies must devote to regulatory compliance issues. What was once a trickle has since become a stampede. Countries around the world have rushed to launch their own sandboxes, attempting to draw financial industries to their jurisdictions. As of the writing of this book, Abu Dhabi, Bahrain, Brazil, India, Kazakhstan, Kuwait, Malaysia and Sri Lanka had all launched fintech sandboxes. So had Jersey (the island, not the state), Indonesia, Russia and Sierra Leone.

Some commentators have worried that in the rush to create sandboxes governments have forgotten about other priorities, including their duty to protect citizens from harm. These commentators have argued that countries are racing to the bottom in order to lure industry to their country. The critique also goes for states. When Arizona launched its fintech sandbox in 2018, it touted its program in outlandish terms. One message to the media bore the title "Arizona State Offering Regulation-free Access for UK Companies."[39] Not only were regulations relaxed, they didn't even exist. Two of the three companies that joined Arizona's sandbox were blockchain companies. One described itself as a "financial service platform implementing an array of avante garde [sic] technologies."[40] When the Consumer Financial Protection Bureau announced that it was considering launching a sandbox program, consumer rights advocates were so outraged that they published a letter denouncing the initiative. "As with some other proposals for fintech 'sandboxes,'" they wrote, "vague promises of the benefits of innovation and industry claims about the constraints or uncertainties of existing regulations do not justify special treatment or waiver of consumer protection rules for favored companies or industries."[41] They concluded that the sandbox proposal would lead to a "broad undermining of the consumer protections required by Congress."[42]

Others worry that a permissive approach to blockchain regulation will encourage unsavory actors. Kenneth Rogoff, an economist at Harvard and a world-renowned expert on currency, might not at first glance seem a likely proponent of this viewpoint. He has, after all, written an entire book on why we need to phase out paper currency. But it turns out that, despite his aversion to cash, he has a deeply skeptical view of cryptocurrency, at least in its current form. Rogoff argues that no right-minded government could embrace crypto-currencies, at least of the bitcoin variety. "Any single large advanced economy foolish enough to try to embrace cryptocurrencies, as Japan did last year," he wrote in an article in *The Guardian* in 2018, "risks becoming a global destina-tion for money-laundering." For Rogoff, governments cannot take this risk. "For the moment, the real question is if and when global regulation will stamp out privately constructed systems that are expensive for governments to trace and monitor."[43]

∗∗∗

As the criticism of sandboxes reveals, not everyone believes that governments should open their doors to the blockchain. Some believe that, far from loosen-ing our rules to regulate the blockchain, we need to be tightening them. They argue that regulatory sandboxes and regulation-lite initiatives are the exact opposite of what regulators need to be doing if they want to address the issues that blockchain technology raises. They point out that the blockchain poses a number of serious problems that existing regulatory frameworks leave largely unaddressed. In order to stamp out these problems, regulators must adopt new, more restrictive rules for the blockchain industry. Proposals span the gamut from imposing stronger gatekeeper rules on virtual currency exchanges to banning all uses of the technology. If the permissive approach to the blockchain represents an attempt to open the gates wide to blockchain technology, the restrictive one represents an attempt to slam them shut.

Restrictive approaches to regulating technology have a long pedigree, and for a number of reasons. For one, outlawing a technology is an obvious option when a government discovers that the technology is causing harm to citizens, and harms for which there is little redress. If a government believes that a technology imposes significant harms on society, without offsetting benefits to outweigh those losses, then it makes sense to ban it. If, say, the government believes that blockchain technology is primarily a means for criminals to launder their proceeds and fraudsters to scam investors, then a ban makes sense. But even if blockchain technology is viewed as a mixed-use technology, with some beneficial uses and some harmful ones, governments might still be justified in banning it if the government believes that widespread use of the technology will undermine other, more important policies. For example, even if blockchain technology provides a more secure and less expensive way for individuals to store and send value, a government might have justifiable reasons for banning it in order to uphold, say, currency controls of money-laundering filters.

Governments might also settle on the restrictive approach as a precautionary measure. When the harms from a technology are little understood but potentially significant, regulations might be justified simply in order to avoid the "unknown unknowns." Governments know, for example, that there is problematic behavior happening on the blockchain, and they know that there are people seeking to take advantage of others on the blockchain, but there are also other things that governments simply do not know, or even that they do not know that they do not know. Prior to the financial crisis, government policy-makers largely did not know that mortgages and mortgage-backed securities might be the source of systemic risk. What is more, they didn't know that they didn't know this; they simply were not thinking about it. Thus, when a new technology comes around, and there are conceivable and plausible risks that arise from it, risks that are difficult to calculate or assess, it might be better to restrict the technology until such a time when the risks are better understood.

This principle is known in the legal world as the "precautionary principle": when regulators do not know the potential harms from a new technology, they should attempt, where possible, to restrict its adoption until they are able to assess those harms. The precautionary principle has been used to justify any number of restrictions on new technologies. One that received much attention in the late 1990s and early 2000s was the European Union's severe restrictions on the use of genetically modified organisms or GMOs. These restrictions were so severe that most commentators viewed them as a de facto ban; it was effectively impossible to import genetically modified crops and foods into the European Union. This de facto ban on genetically modified organisms was, at least nominally, justified by concerns about the risks that GMO crops posed to humans. While the science related to these risks was uncertain, the EU and many of its member states believed that the precautionary principle justified their placing a ban on the use of GMO crops in their territories until more was known. The United States, which had significantly more relaxed regulations about the use of genetically modified organisms, disagreed. After long negotiations failed to reach agreement, the United States eventually challenged the EU's rules in the World Trade Organization, arguing that they violated international laws regarding free trade. The WTO's Dispute Settlement Body ultimately ruled that the EU's rules amounted to a "general de facto moratorium" on GMO products, and that the "undue delays" in approving GMO products violated the EU's international obligations.[44] The WTO's ruling led to some changes in the way the EU handled genetically modified organisms but, to date, the EU's rules still reflect a widely skeptical view of the technology.

China stands out as an exemplar of this kind of restrictive, draconian approach to blockchain regulation. While many of its rules have been handed down in an informal fashion, with government regulators simply informing relevant actors that they should stop using the technology, the general message of these rules is clear: cryptocurrencies are unwelcome. In 2013, China's central bank informed financial institutions that they could no longer handle bitcoin transactions. The bank stated that the directive was needed to "protect the status of the renminbi as the statutory currency, prevent risks of money laundering and protect financial stability."[45] At the same time, the order did not prohibit individuals from mining for bitcoin or using virtual currency; it stated that "[o]rdinary members of the public have the freedom to participate in Bitcoin transactions as a kind of commodity trading activity on the Internet, provided they assume the risks themselves." But, in 2014, the bank went further, ordering commercial banks and payment companies to close bitcoin trading accounts.[46] Then, in 2017, the Chinese government announced that it would shut down all cryptocurrency exchanges in the country, as well as ban initial coin offerings.[47] In 2018, the central bank took aim at another prong of the blockchain, notifying local governments that they should order cryptocurrency mining companies to begin an "orderly exit" from the country.[48] Then, as the final nail in the coffin, in 2019, China's National Development and Reform Commission, the country's economic planning body, formally added cryptocurrency mining to a list of industries it planned to eliminate.[49] The rationales behind these decisions are debated, but it is widely speculated that Chinese authorities worried that citizens were using virtual currencies to evade regulations on currency, undermining a key plank of China's mechanisms of control of the economy.

But China is not alone in adopting a restrictive approach to blockchain technology. Algeria, Bangladesh, Bolivia and Nepal have all banned bitcoin transactions.[50] The Central Bank of Bangladesh announced in 2014 that it considered "any transaction through bitcoin or any other crypto currency [to be] a punishable offense." Anyone caught using bitcoin could be sentenced to up to twelve years in jail.[51] It was later reported that Bangladeshi authorities were "on the hunt" for cryptocurrency users.[52]

Of course, bans and restrictions are difficult to administer when the technology at issue is as decentralized as blockchain is. It is hard to have an effective ban on a technology when there is no single administrator or company that runs it. Even if a country shuts down an exchange, it will not shut down bitcoin. As long as there are computers that serve as nodes to keep track of the blockchain ledger, the cryptocurrency will exist, and a record of who owns what will remain. The only way to destroy the currency would be to destroy all copies of it, which reside on thousands of computers around the world. It simply is not feasible for countries to implement total bans on the technology. This difficulty led at least one country, Kyrgyzstan, to back down from an initial plan to ban bitcoin from the country. As the chairman of Kyrgyzstan's National Bank explained at the time, "It is very difficult to prohibit what we did not let out."[53]

But restrictive approaches to blockchain have come in for their fair share of criticism as well. One prominent critic has been Hester Peirce, a commissioner at the Securities and Exchange Commission. She has earned the nickname "Crypto Mom" for her efforts to promote blockchain technologies. In 2016, for example, Cameron and Tyler Winklevoss, the Harvard-educated twins famous for their dispute with Mark Zuckerberg over Facebook, sought to create a bitcoin-based exchange traded fund (ETF). It was thought that an ETF would allow investors a convenient way to gain exposure to bitcoin without having to go through the complicated process of purchasing and storing the virtual currency. It was also hoped that the creation of an ETF would make the virtual currency more attractive to institutional investors. But in order to list the fund on an exchange, it first needed the approval of the SEC. After a lengthy review, the SEC rejected the application in 2018, finding that there was insufficient assurance that the ETF would be protected from fraud and manipulation.[54] But in a blistering dissent, Peirce argued that the SEC had it all wrong.[55] In rejecting the Winklevoss brothers' application, the SEC was not truly assessing the merits of the application, Peirce argued, but rather announcing a judgment on bitcoin itself. This was not what regulators were meant to do. Regulators should focus on the objective merits of the application, not on the technology itself. Investors would be the ultimate arbiters of whether bitcoin was something worth buying. And by rejecting the bitcoin ETF, the SEC was doing something even more pernicious: preventing reputable actors from entering the market.

More institutional participation would ameliorate many of the Commission's concerns with the bitcoin market that underlie its [rejection of the ETF application]. More generally, the Commission's interpretation and application of the statutory standard sends a strong signal that innovation is unwelcome in our markets, a signal that may have effects far beyond the fate of bitcoin [ETF]s.

By restricting access to cryptocurrencies, the SEC was preventing participants from improving the technology. "Greater participation by institutional investors in the bitcoin market would help to pressure exchanges to bolster their defenses against theft, encourage greater investment in custody solutions in the bitcoin space, and make it more difficult for market manipulators to escape the notice of their fellow market participants." And what is more, restrictive approaches to the technology would hamper innovation itself.

Peirce concluded her dissent with a remarkable screed against restrictive approaches to technology:

> More generally, the disapproval order demonstrates a skeptical view of innovation, which may have an adverse effect on investor protection, efficiency, competition, and capital formation well beyond this particular product. The disapproval order's broad interpretation of the Commission's statutory mandate signals that the Commission reserves for itself the authority to judge when an innovation is ripe enough, respectable enough, or regulated enough to be worthy of the securities markets. By suggesting that bitcoin, as a novel financial product based on a novel technology that is traded on a non-traditional market, cannot be the basis of an [ETF] the Commission signals an aversion to innovation that may convince entrepreneurs that they should take their ingenuity to other sectors of our economy, or to foreign markets, where their talents will be welcomed with more enthusiasm. By withholding approval of a bitcoin-based [ETF] because the underlying market insufficiently resembles the markets for other commodities, we set ourselves up as the gatekeepers of innovation. Securities regulators are ill-equipped to fill this particular role.

She also took a parting shot at the do nothing crowd, arguing that applying the nation's outdated laws to a technology as unique as the blockchain simply did not make sense. Rather than taking into account the "innovative characteristics of the bitcoin market," Peirce argued, the SEC "analyzes the [ETF] through a legal and regulatory framework derived from prior approval orders for commodities with very different characteristics." This was just bad policy, plain and simple.

✳✳✳

A close look at the regulatory paradigms for technology that governments have available to them shows the trade-offs that all of them involve. A do nothing approach allows governments more time to learn about the technology before acting, but it also leads to ambiguity and uncertainty. A permissive sandbox approach encourages companies to experiment and innovate, but it also may unleash harmful consequences on society at large. A restrictive precautionary approach may prevent these harms, but it also ensures that the technology will be slow to improve and mature.

Our intuitions about which approach is best depend heavily on our beliefs about other important values, from the role of democracy to the workings of capitalism. It is not uncommon to hear the argument (indeed, there are echoes of it in Hester Peirce's dissent) that we should just let markets do their work. If the technology is a useful one, then it will thrive in the marketplace. If it is not, then it will fade away.

But, of course, as any economist could tell you, it is more complicated than that. For one, markets do not always lead to results that we like. The dark web has shown that where government is absent, strong and enduring demands for drugs, guns and child pornography can develop and thrive. And just because a market exists does not mean that it is a fair or a functioning one. Cell phone companies have strong incentives to create monopolies. Health insurance companies have incentives to discriminate against people with preexisting health problems. The mere fact that these are the result of market forces does not mean that they are desirable. And finally, even if the market does eventually correct mistakes, and bubbles within an industry eventually burst, the process of correcting these inefficiencies can take time, and many people can be hurt in the process. The history of financial crises is littered with examples of fortunes destroyed, houses lost and companies bankrupted. This may all be chalked up to "creative destruction," but the collateral damage that accompanies it can be large and painful.

At the same time, government is not always the answer either. The knee-jerk reaction among many regulators is to say that if a technology raises concerns, we should pass new laws to solve them. But the turn to regulation in the face of technological change is just as problematic as the turn to markets. For one, we need to know what the regulation should look like. We might have some general ideas about this – it should encourage useful innovation while protecting consumers and preventing fraud and manipulation, etc. – but once we move out of the world of platitudes and into the nitty-gritty of specific laws, it is likely that substantial matters of disagreement will surface. Should initial coin offerings be subject to the securities laws? If so, which ones? Should virtual currency transactions be treated as taxable events under the tax laws? If not, why not? And even if reasonable observers can reach agreement about these difficult questions, it is another question entirely whether the legislative process would ever produce this "ideal" regulation. If there is a single belief that unifies both sides of the aisle today, it is that the U.S. legislature has become a paralyzed and partisan institution, one that is beholden to powerful special interest groups. Reasonable observers might well doubt, then, that any law that would be passed through this process would even come close to the "ideal" law that they had in mind. And even if it is, we would also need to trust that government regulators, once equipped with this "ideal" law, will do a better job of guiding the industry than the industry would do on its own. It is not unreasonable to think that where a technology is complicated, multifold and *sui generis*, as the blockchain is, regulators will have some serious trouble handling it.

Ultimately, governing technology requires a considered choice between these two opposing possibilities, one the market, the other democracy. The choice requires a careful balancing of the pathologies of the market and the pathologies of democracy. It likely requires a dose of both. The irony when it comes to the blockchain, of course, is that the blockchain itself was borne out of a distrust of both markets and democracy. The cypherpunks of the 1990s and 2000s worried about the corruption of both elected politicians and corporate executives alike. They sought refuge in a technology that promised to return power to the hands of the people. That markets and democracies are reasserting control should come as no surprise to those familiar with the history of technology.

8

Technology and the Rule of the Crowd

But when men have realized that time has upset many fighting faiths, they may come to believe even more than they believe the very foundations of their own conduct that the ultimate good desired is better reached by free trade in ideas – that the best test of truth is the power of the thought to get itself accepted in the competition of the market, and that truth is the only ground upon which their wishes safely can be carried out. That, at any rate, is the theory of our Constitution.

Oliver Wendell Holmes, Abrams v. United States

Visitors to Jerry Brito's Twitter page are greeted with a giant image of a man and a woman holding hands, staring out of a darkened window at a line of skyscrapers. One skyscraper is engulfed in blinding white light. Film aficionados, or Brad Pitt fans, will recognize the scene as the climactic ending to the movie *Fight Club*. They may also remember that the scene is set to the iconic score of the Pixies' "Where Is My Mind." And if they have a really good memory, they will know that that skyscraper is lit up, not with Christmas decorations, but rather with explosives. It is the culmination of the protagonist Tyler Durden's master plan to reset modern society. As he explains in the movie, "Advertising has us chasing cars and clothes, working jobs we hate so we can buy sh*t we don't need." Durden's solution to all this is to destroy the banks, thereby destroying money, and thereby freeing everyone from their unthinking addiction to meaningless possessions and achievements.

It is an appropriate image for the man who heads Coin Center, a cryptocurrency think tank focused on promoting free and open access to virtual currencies. Coin Center has quickly established itself as one of the most prominent and influential groups advocating for blockchain technology in government circles. It has lobbied Congress to create a tax exemption for small gains from virtual currency transactions.[1] It has argued that virtual currencies like bitcoin should not be regulated under the burdensome securities regime that governs stocks and bonds.[2] And it has promoted model state laws that would encourage the growth of blockchain start-ups.[3] In short, Coin Center has become a leader in pressing for meaningful legal change to address block-chain technology.

Brito himself studied law at George Mason and afterwards worked for the Mercatus Center, a market-oriented research institute at the university. Always interested in technology and its implications for society, he came to regret that he had missed out on the crypto wars of the 1990s, when programmers and governments first started tussling over the difficult issues of online privacy and internet surveillance. So when he heard about bitcoin, he leapt at the chance of getting involved.

"I thought we had fought all the battles that had to be fought. Then along comes bitcoin, and it was right in my wheelhouse," he told me.[4]

Bitcoin really was in Brito's wheelhouse. Anyone who interacts with him can see that he lives and breathes technology. When I first reached out to him, he told me that his assistant, Amy, would find a good time for us to talk. A few minutes later, I received an email from Amy.

> Hi William,
> Happy to find a time for you and Jerry.
> Would Monday, Aug 20 at 1:30 PM EDT (Eastern Daylight Time) work?
> Jerry is also available for a 30 minute call:
> Monday Aug 20 at 2 PM
> Wednesday Aug 29 from 12:30 to 4 PM
> If these times don't work, feel free to select another time that might work better for you.

I wrote back that I was available, and Amy quickly thanked me and told me she would be sending a calendar invitation for the call. The whole process was smooth and seamless, one of those commonplace interactions that barely register in your memory of the day. But something about the interaction made me go back and look at the original message from Amy. On second reading, I noticed something that I had not noticed on first reading. At the bottom of the message, in barely noticeable small type, came the signature block. I rarely read signature blocks, but this time I did.

> Amy Ingram | Personal Assistant to Jerry Brito
> x.ai – an artificially intelligent assistant that schedules meetings

Brito's assistant, Amy, was not a real person. She was a computer program. And a remarkably good one at that. Her language was precise and natural, if a bit formal. There was nothing particularly that would have distinguished her from a diligent assistant in real life.

Later, I mentioned that I was surprised to discover that his assistant was a computer.

"How'd you find out?" Brito asked.

He explained that most people never realized Amy was a computer, and it would take too long to describe her to everyone he spoke to, so he had taken to just referring to her as Amy, no qualifications included. At one point, he told someone that Amy would reach out to find a time for them to talk, and the person replied that Amy could speak with their own assistant, Nancy. Nancy and Amy emailed back and forth and quickly set up a mutually convenient time to talk. Nancy, it turned out, was a real person.

"But Nancy never knew that she was training her replacement," Brito said.

Brito's belief in technology and its capacity to improve human life has informed his take on the blockchain. The blockchain, Brito argues, is akin to a public good, something that everyone benefits from, and from which no one can be excluded. "To me, the most important benefit of the blockchain is that it is censorship-resistant," Brito said. "In the physical world, we have the ability to engage in peer-to-peer transactions. But in the digital world, our interactions are typically intermediated, and by necessity. You have to have intermediaries to make them work. What that means is that you lose some of the beneficial features of peer-to-peer transactions. One party can view all transactions, or block some of them, or choose not to do business with a person, or even a whole class of persons."

Blockchain solved these problems by reinstating the power of the crowd.

You want to decentralize where you don't want to have one party of a handful of parties being in control of something. We don't like monopolies. We don't like oligopolies. The internet is a good example of this. Originally, individuals had to access email through individual companies. With Compuserve, you could email anyone in the world, so long as they had Compuserve too. But if you decentralize email, and simply have one standard that is known to all, then you are opening it up to everyone.

But Brito is aware that the blockchain has some in-built limits, that decentralization is not a panacea. For one, there are risks in handing over control to groups.

"For a number of reasons, some regulatory, some business-related, many folks have said that we can't use an open network where we have no idea who the validators are, who the counterparties are."

Similarly, there are risks to making data accessible and viewable by the public.

"Bitcoin is not private at all, but it's going to have to be," Brito said. "Just look at J.P. Morgan's Quorum project, or R3's Corda platform [two blockchain projects focused on financial institutions]. For practical purposes, you can't live in a world where firms can see each other's trades, or employees can see their co-workers' salaries." For those reasons, Brito foresees that the bitcoin industry's next focus will be on promoting privacy to an even greater degree than it already does.

> One of the main effects to date of the rise and success of bitcoin and cryptocurrencies has been to spark interest in the idea of a shared ledger in the minds of CTOs everywhere. That's been one of the most influential ideas. ... Hash-linked data and shared databases have been around for a long time, but bitcoin has put wind in the sails of CTOs. If you go to a board of directors and tell them, "We need to upgrade our back office," it sounds boring. But if you go to them and say, "We need to blockify," now that, that's exciting.

Brito also believes that digital currencies are essential to the future of democracy.

> Imagine if the only way to support unpopular causes was with easily controlled e-money. Certain transactions could be disallowed by law, political pressure or corporate fiat, and anonymous giving would be impossible. Each of your transactions would be tied to your identity. One could not make a purchase at a gay bookstore or a pregnancy clinic without knowing that somewhere there's a permanent record of the transaction. And there might not be any transaction that couldn't be subpoenaed in a divorce or other legal proceeding.

Blockchain-based virtual currencies like bitcoin could help solve this problem. "Bitcoin employs no user-identifiable accounts, relying instead on public key cryptography, so there is no way to know who gave money to whom. And because no intermediaries are needed for bitcoin transactions, governments have no intermediaries to regulate."[5]

In short, if you want democracy to work in an age of technology, you need more than just the outward trappings of democracy from previous eras, such as constitutions, elections and legislatures. You need a technology that *itself* incorporates democratic norms. This is what the blockchain is intended to do.

***

Will the blockchain save democracy, or will it destroy it? In recent years, commentators have weighed in ad nauseam on the question. To some, the technology promises to restore power to the many and, in the process, rejuvenate democratic governance. To these observers, blockchain is "the ultimate democratic tool,"[6] a technology for "bolstering political accountability."[7] But to others, blockchain technology presents a dire threat to democratic principles. It is a "path to authoritarianism,"[8] a "super tax haven"[9] and a "boon for extremist groups."[10]

Most of these claims are overblown. Blockchain's potential to revolutionize the political process has, time and again, failed to materialize. And while virtual currencies have certainly challenged law enforcement agencies in important ways, there is little evidence that it has led to dramatic increases in crime rates, let alone the "world without law" that some doomsayers have predicted.

But the focus on blockchain as either the savior or executioner of democracy obscures a more important point: that many of the benefits and pitfalls of blockchain mirror the benefits and pitfalls of democracy. They are both, in the final analysis, methods for decentralizing power. Democracy aims at decentralizing political power, while the blockchain aims at decentralizing currency, business, finance and other aspects of daily life. It should come as no surprise, then, that decentralized governance in the virtual world faces many of the same problems that decentralized governance in the real world does. Their shared experiences in confronting these problems shed light on the benefits and costs of group decision-making in modern society. They give us insight into the problems that crowds create, but also the problems that crowds can solve.

Let us begin by looking at the demand for crowd rule. Any observer of politics today is keenly aware of the strong undercurrent of distrust of corporate and political elites in today's landscape. This distrust has in turn driven demands for more inclusive forms of decision-making, both in politics and in technology. Recent years have witnessed calls to "drain the swamp" of political elites in Washington, to "occupy Wall Street" to demand more accountable banks, and to reempower the middle class (as most recently evidenced by the "yellow vests" protests in France). At the same time, hand-wringing about the growing power of a few large technology companies, such as Amazon, Facebook and Google, has led to investigations and hearings on how tech companies protect (or, more often, fail to protect) the interests and data of their consumers. Both trends suggest a deep-seated and widely held instinct that individuals have lost, and somehow need to recover, control over the decisions that matter in their lives. The blockchain fits neatly into this instinct. As the cypherpunks put it in their manifesto, "[p]rivacy is necessary for an open society in an electric world," and privacy requires decentralization. "Software can't be destroyed and ... a widely dispersed system can't be shut down."[11] The cypherpunks' demands have become more relevant today, as evidence grows of the entrenched power of tech giants and global elites.

But any system that attempts to decentralize power has to deal with a basic problem: group decision-making can be inefficient. Centralized systems have the advantage of only requiring one person to act. A monarch can simply legislate by decree. A company can simply adopt new policies. But groups do not have this luxury. Once we introduce multiple actors into the decision-making process, the possibility of disagreement and dissension arises. Discussions must occur. Negotiations must take place. And if power is spread out widely, to thousands or even millions of people, these negotiations and discussions are quite difficult. You cannot simply have the entire population of the United States sit down in a forum and debate with one another. As a result, modern democracies have effectively given up on decentralizing the vast majority of government decisions. Instead, citizens exert their control over government through periodic elections, at which they choose representatives. Once they have done so, they then relinquish control back to the state. The blockchain's efficiency problem is even greater: in order to make the technology work, a majority of all the computers on the network must reach consensus on the rules and actions taken on the blockchain. This inefficiency has only been magnified by the fact that bitcoin and many other virtual currencies rely on a proof-of-work system that incentivizes miners to expend massive amounts of energy in order to manage the currency.

Given the inefficiencies of decentralized systems, the turn to decentralization needs to be justified by some other external rationale. In other words, there must be some distinctive benefit furnished by group decision-making (as opposed to single-actor decision-making) that is sufficiently valuable that it offsets the costs of its distinctive inefficiency. One commonly cited benefit concerns the quality of the decisions themselves: proponents of decentralization often contend that groups make better decisions than individuals do. They might do so either because their constituent members have information that single decision-makers do not, or because the process of deliberation and discussion leads to more informed decisions, or simply because the brute mathematics of collective action improves the likelihood of high-quality outcomes. Aristotle wrote that:

> the many ... when they meet together may very likely be better than the few good, if regarded not individually but collectively .... For each individual

among the many has a share of virtue and prudence . . . . Some understand one part, and some another, and among them they understand the whole.[12]

The French philosopher Nicolas de Condorcet famously demonstrated in his "jury theorem" that, when voters must decide between two options, one of which is correct and the other of which is not, their probability of opting for the correct choice increases as more voters participate.[13] Friedrich Hayek similarly argued that capitalist systems, with decentralized decision-making, were superior to state-run economies with centralized planning, because it was simply impossible for a single actor to gather and process all the information that was spread out among market actors.[14] When knowledge is diffuse and widely available, allowing crowds to participate in decisions may help those decisions become more accurate or informed.

Another important rationale for crowd rule is grounded less on instrumental reasons and more on moral ones. We may be willing to accept the inefficiencies of decentralized decision-making if other external values are more important, such as a belief in the virtues of self-government or the dignity of individual choice. John Stuart Mill, for example, argued in favor of democracy because of its effect not just on the quality of decisions but also on the moral fiber of citizens. In his *Considerations on Representative Government*, he wrote that the justification for democracy rested on two principles. First, "the rights and interests of every or any person are only secure from being disregarded when the person interested is himself able, and habitually disposed to stand up for them." And second, "the general prosperity attains a greater height, and is more widely diffused, in proportion to the amount and variety of the personal energies enlisted in promoting it." The first is a straightforward instrumentalist justification of democracy – the only way to ensure that an institution protects the interests of all is for all to participate in it. But the second goes to the effects of voting on the characters of the voters themselves. And of these two principles, Mill was clear that this latter reason was the most powerful. On voting, he wrote:

Still more salutary is the moral part of the instruction afforded by the participation of the private citizen, if even rarely, in public functions. He is called upon, while so engaged, to weigh interests not his own; to be guided, in case of conflicting claims, by another rule than his private partialities; to apply, at every turn, principles and maxims which have for their reason of existence the general good; and he usually finds associated with him in the same work minds more familiarized than his own with these ideas and operations, whose study it will be to supply reasons to his understanding, and stimulation to his feeling for the general interest. He is made to feel himself one of the public, and whatever is their interest to be his interest.[15]

For Mill, one of the great benefits of spreading out power was its tendency to improve the character of those who received it. By granting citizens the right to vote in elections, democracies force individuals to think about things beyond their day-to-day affairs and their narrow self-interests. Democracies instill in their citizens a belief in, and a devotion to, the public good.

More recent studies have cast some doubt on Mill's conclusions about the virtuous effects of crowd decision-making. In 1998, two psychologists at the Hebrew University of Jerusalem, Gary Bornstein and Ilan Yaniv, ran a study to test the differences between how groups and individuals reached decisions. To do so, they used something called the "ultimatum game." The ultimatum game is a classic way of testing people's competing senses of fairness and rationality. The game works as follows. One side, the proposer, is given a set amount of money, say, $10. The proposer is then told that he may offer to give the other side, the responder, some of that money, anywhere from $0 to $10. The responder, then, has a choice: he may either accept the offer or reject it. If he accepts, the proposer keeps his portion of the money, and the responder keeps his. But, and here is the twist, if he rejects the proposer's offer, then neither side gets to keep any of the money. So, if a proposer offers to give the responder $3 and the responder accepts, the proposer will keep $7 and the responder will keep $3. But if the proposer makes the same offer and the responder refuses, then both the proposer and the responder will receive nothing.

Now, the rational thing for the responder to do is to accept any amount offered that is above zero – any money is better than no money, right? Similarly, the rational thing for the proposer to do is to offer an amount that is just above zero – the responder will have to prefer something to nothing, right? But studies have shown, again and again, and in cultures around the world, that neither side acts in the way this rational model predicts. Instead, individuals tend to offer substantially more than zero (they generally offer somewhere between 40 and 50 percent of the money), and they tend to reject sums that are viewed as too small (any offer below 20 percent of the money is frequently rejected), even if the offered amount is above zero.[16] These results have been interpreted to suggest that individuals have a strong sense of fairness (and vengeance), which may override their purely economic interests.

So far, so good. But Bornstein and Yaniv wanted to know whether the propensities revealed by the ultimatum game would change when the players participated as a collective assembly. Would individuals act differently in a group setting? In order to test this out, they conducted two experiments. The first experiment was a traditional ultimatum game with a single proposer and a single responder. The second experiment was a modified ultimatum game in which both the proposing group and the responding group were made up of three people. In order to ensure that the incentives were similar, the amounts offered in the group game were tripled (from a total of 50 Israeli shekels to a total of 150 Israeli shekels – a shekel was worth approximately 34 cents at the time of the study, so the total amount at stake in the group game was around $50). Any resulting rewards for the proposing group or the responding group were to be shared equally among the team members. The proposing group was given a few minutes to discuss their offer, and the responding group was given a few minutes to decide whether or not to accept it.

The results of the study were stark. Individuals offered, on average, 50 percent of the total sum of shekels. Groups, on the other hand, offered only 40 percent. Groups, in other words, were significantly stingier than individuals were. And while groups offered significantly less than individuals, their stinginess did not affect the willingness of the responders to accept their offers. The rejection rate was the same for both groups and individuals. The results suggested that groups acted more rationally than individuals – they hewed closer to the rational, homo economicus model of behavior than individuals did.[17] And they were also more selfish.

Bornstein and Yaniv's findings about increased selfishness in group decision-making dovetail neatly with the findings of psychologists studying the phenomenon of group polarization. In a series of studies beginning in the 1960s, social psychologists demonstrated a startling tendency among individuals, when acting in groups, to gravitate, not toward more moderate consensus positions, but rather towards more extreme ones. Individual members might begin with a slight belief in favor of some position regarding, say, abortion, but once they were placed within a group, even a group with similar beliefs, they would end up with much more vehement beliefs on that same position. For example, moderately feminist individuals, when joined in a group, tended to become more stridently feminist.[18] The same went for racial prejudice.[19] And while many of the initial studies relied on looking at groups in close physical proximity, more recent studies have shown that group polarization can also occur over the internet, in contexts such as Facebook and Twitter, where filtered news can lead to an "echo chamber" of similar opinions.[20] The intuition behind these studies is that, when people discuss an issue with one another, they will tend to give more weight to the arguments and information that supports their side. Similarly, they will discount or disbelieve the arguments and information that contradict their prior beliefs.

The end result is that decentralization can lead to more extreme positions and results.

The burgeoning literature on group polarization, and Bornstein and Yaniv's findings about group decision-making, cast light on some of the drawbacks of decentralized systems in today's world. Crowd rule may lead to more selfish, and less other-regarding, behavior. It may also lead to division and discord. Anyone who has witnessed the rise of nativism and populism in both the United States and Europe in recent years is fully aware of the power of appeals to people's baser instincts. So is anyone who is active on Twitter or Instagram today. The blockchain has witnessed its own fair share of this division, with widely reported schisms within the community on the future of virtual currencies and the structure of their systems. These have at times led to forks in the network, in which entire groups wall themselves off from the remaining members.

✱✱✱

But one other important obstacle that any decentralized system must overcome is the difficulty of keeping a decentralized system truly decentralized. It is one thing to set up a system that starts out decentralized. It is another thing entirely to ensure that the system stays that way. After all, there are strong incentives for individuals to attempt to centralize power. In fact, in many decentralized systems participants are actively seeking to undermine the very decentralization that the system was designed for.

Take, for example, markets in capitalist economies. One of the fundamental requirements for a functioning market is that there are many different competitors seeking to sell the relevant goods or services. It is thought that this competition between companies will force companies to provide better goods or services, or provide them more cheaply. But, of course, the underlying mechanism for this pressure is competition. Companies provide higher quality goods and sell them for less, not because they want to in the abstract, but because they are forced to. If they do not, others will. As Adam Smith wrote, the only way to ensure that a corporation is run well is "that free and universal competition which forces every body to have recourse to [good management] for the sake of self defence."[21] And what exactly are companies competing for? Market share. Companies in modern economies are constantly seeking to amass greater and greater shares of the market. If they are successful at this, they can turn a profit. But if they are *very* successful at this, they can end up eliminating their competitors and, as a result, eliminating competition itself. If they do so, then they are called monopolies. But even if they do not become monopolies, they may still achieve a dominant position that gives them many of the same benefits in terms of greater profits and reduced pressure on quality, price and innovation. Indeed, this desire to amass market share is one of the primary driving forces behind the merger waves of recent years. If companies cannot continue to grow revenue through internal changes, they often resort to simply purchasing their competitors.

The irony, of course, is that the decentralized system of capitalism assumes, and indeed requires, that its participants actively seek to undermine the principles of decentralization. Adam Smith himself recognized this, bemoaning the rise of "oppressive monopolies" that sought to eliminate their competitors. As he described it, "people of the same trade seldom meet together, even for merriment and diversion, but the conversation ends in a conspiracy against the public, or in some contrivance to raise prices."[22] To be sure, concentration is not always bad. Economies of scale may justify some degree of concentration within an industry. But it can be dangerous and it leads to less decentralization. It is for this reason that modern economies have developed robust antitrust rules that seek to prevent companies from merging to create monopolies that threaten competition and decentralization.

In politics, similarly, groups constantly seek to concentrate power. Democracy is premised on the idea of mass participation in government through the mechanism of elections. This ensures a certain degree of decentralization. Interest groups, however, have found ways to limit this decentralization by channeling it into centralized structures that are easier to control. Political parties – those bedrocks of modern democracy – are in essence organizations for concentrating and enhancing the power of their members. The United States has two dominant parties, the Democratic Party and the Republican Party, that have held unrivaled sway over the country for decades.[23] The last time the United States elected a president that was neither a Democrat nor a Republican was in 1850. The path to political office, thus, remains firmly within the grasp of two parties. The stranglehold that political parties hold over elections also means that voters have a limited range of options when they head to the polls. To be sure, parties have not eliminated crowd control. We still hold elections, after all, as well as primaries. But they have certainly done much to undermine the power of the crowd, including in ways that appear motivated by a desire to limit the power of individual voters. The history of political parties in the United States is closely tied to the history of gerrymandering, the practice of shaping voting districts in ways that allow a party to win more than its fair share of elections. Advances in polling, big data and statistical methods have allowed parties to fine-tune gerrymandering to such an extent that elections in many geographical districts are effectively predetermined. This leads to ever more imbalanced results. For example, in North Carolina, a state that is more or less split evenly between Republican and Democratic voters, Republican legislators drew voting districts in a way that led to the Republicans winning ten out of thirteen available seats in 2016. As one Republican legislator said at the time, "I propose that we draw the maps to give a partisan advantage to 10 Republicans and three Democrats, because I do not believe it's possible to draw a map with 11 Republicans and two Democrats."[24] This is a remarkable level of centralized decision-making in a system that is designed to allow the crowd to rule.

The blockchain has struggled with similar problems. It is a system purpose-built for decentralization, but it has struggled to prevent centralization from creeping in in unexpected places. A number of factors have driven this move to centralization. First, as a practical matter, many users have simply preferred using centralized administrators, such as digital exchanges, to handle their virtual currencies, rather than trusting their own technical competence. Exchanges simplify the process of acquiring, storing and selling cryptocurrencies; users can download an app, pay with a normal credit card and connect with their real-world bank account. These steps are difficult or impossible to do in most cryptocurrencies without the aid of an intermediary. One-stop shops are appealing to consumers, but the resulting crypto-exchanges bring a level of centralization into the blockchain. They require users to trust a single institution for their access to the currency.

Aside from the demand for simplicity and ease of use, another driver of centralization in the blockchain is profit. It turns out that, as in most markets, there is profit to be made from controlling large swathes of the blockchain market – in this case, the mining infrastructure that underlies virtual currencies. Bitcoin's proof-of-work system (a system that is widely used in other virtual currencies as well) requires nodes to expend computational power solving hash equations in order to win new bitcoin. This structure incentivizes miners to build bigger and faster mining farms that are able to win larger shares of bitcoin payouts. These farms, with specialized equipment, located in geographically ideal locations and maintained by experts, can solve hashing algorithm problems much faster than any run-of-the-mill miner using his home laptop could ever hope to achieve. At one point in 2018, the world's largest miner was estimated to control nearly 51 percent of the entire network's computing power.[25] Under any normal metric of industry concentration, this is extraordinarily high.

A final driver of centralization within the blockchain is trust. This rationale is somewhat ironic; the whole point of bitcoin was to create a virtual currency that did not require users to trust a single administrator with their money. But it turns out that the problem of trust also goes the other way. Just as many people do not trust banks and governments to handle their money, many banks and governments do not trust crowds either. Many institutions are simply unwilling to entrust their data and transactions to a public blockchain. Public blockchains, after all, can be viewed by anyone and are maintained by shadowy miners located around the world. As Amber Baldet, the former head of J.P. Morgan's blockchain team, explains:

> You might have heard the joke that the cloud is just somebody else's computer. The blockchain is just all of our computers. So when these things have some vulnerability or exploit that goes to one node, it could potentially go to all of them and you end up with catastrophic failure. So it's hard. Product and security development is hard here.[26]

It certainly does not help matters when Russian intelligence agents are heard saying that just as "the internet belongs to the Americans ... blockchain will belong to us."[27] The distrust of public blockchains has driven many institutional actors to develop their own private blockchains, sometimes referred to as "permissioned" blockchains, that have only a few, or even one, administrator. Thus, what began as a decentralized technology quickly turned centralized.

***

But if decentralized systems are slow, cumbersome and prone to falling apart, they are still ascendant. Globally, democracy has never been more dominant. In 2016, a study by the Pew Research Center concluded that nearly 60 percent of the world's countries were democracies, a post-World War II record.[28] And despite all the hand-wringing about backsliding in democracies, even authoritarian regimes at least pay lip service to democratic ideals. North Korea holds elections, after all. Similarly, capitalism, a system premised on the decentralized decision-making of economic actors around the globe, is likewise unchallenged as an ideal (even if it may be limited or guided in places like China that opt for a form of "state" capitalism). And, of course, one of the great appeals of the internet is that it spreads out access to power, knowledge and information.

The blockchain is yet another example of these efforts to allow the crowd to rule. Throughout its history, it has been guided by appeals to our senses of fairness and equality. Even if the results of the technology are that decisions are slow and cumbersome, blockchain enthusiasts have, at least for now, been willing to live with it, given their broader moral commitments to decentralization as an ethical principle. This does not, however, mean that hard questions about whether virtual currencies and other blockchain technologies are efficient solutions to the world's problems should not be asked. The pathologies and shortcomings of democracy have been studied and refined for millennia. The pathologies of the blockchain have only just begun to be studied. But it does suggest that the technology is based on much more than just algorithms. If blockchain were simply computer code and math problems, with nothing more, it could never have achieved the level of attention and passion that it has. The blockchain's great promise is that it is inspired by the same principles that inspire democracy itself. This also happens to be its greatest flaw.

Conclusion

If we want everything to remain as it is, it is necessary for everything to change.

Giuseppe Tomasi di Lampedusa, *The Leopard*

At the beginning of this book, I wrote that the blockchain stands at the intersection of three great themes of modern society: technology, money and democracy. At its heart, the blockchain is a technology for democratizing money – along with many other aspects of our daily lives. Its aim is to use advances in cryptography and computing power to improve the way that our economy works and to give us all greater control over our information, our data and, ultimately, our lives. In the Age of Technology, this is what democracy is supposed to look like. Not a day goes past that we do not hear laments about the stranglehold that big technology firms like Apple, Google and Facebook have over our online identities. Giving power back to the people is an elegant solution to this problem. But decentralization also has its drawbacks. It can be chaotic. It can be confusing. And, at times, it can cause tremendous harm. The blockchain has had its fair share of all of these.

It is tempting to say that when Satoshi Nakamoto first created bitcoin, he could hardly have known how it would all turn out. And, of course, on some level this is true. He could not have predicted the "bitcoin pizza," the Silk Road, Mt. Gox or the dizzying bull market of 2017. At the same time, Nakamoto displayed an uncanny prescience about where his technology was heading. He wrote, for example, that while blockchain technology would not eliminate privacy concerns on the internet, if it were successful, users would "win a major battle in the arms race and gain a new territory of freedom for several years." He foresaw that the blockchain would be difficult to shut down; he wrote, for example, that "[g]overnments are good at cutting off the heads of a centrally controlled networks [sic] like Napster, but pure [peer-to-peer] networks like Gnutella and Tor seem to be holding their own." He also saw that the blockchain was an inherently flexible technology that could be molded by its users into a potentially infinite variety of uses. As he wrote, "once it gets boot-strapped, there are so many applications if you could effortlessly pay a few cents to a website as easily as dropping coins in a vending machine."

At the same time, Nakamoto had his worries about what he had unleashed on the world. He worried about how governments would react to his virtual currency. After users started pushing for WikiLeaks to use bitcoin to get around government sanctions, Nakamoto disagreed vehemently, saying that "the heat you would bring would likely destroy us at this stage." He also worried about superpowered miners. "We should have a gentleman's agreement to postpone the GPU arms race as long as we can for the good of the network," he wrote. And he worried, perhaps most of all, about cybersecurity. In his final public message, after detailing improvements he had made to the virtual currency, he concluded, "There are still more ways to attack than I can count."

The abiding mystery that surrounds Nakamoto's identity only deepens the curiosity about him and his technology. Notwithstanding the considerable efforts of enterprising journalists to identify him, we may never know who he is. There would certainly be a kind of poetic justice in this. The inventor of blockchain, a technology for removing trusted intermediaries from our lives and decentralizing power to everyone, refuses to stand at the center of his invention. He refuses to occupy the limelight. Blockchain must stand or fall on its own merits – on the features of the technology itself and on the efforts of its users to make it work.

The idea of virtual currency, of course, did not begin with Nakamoto. Its philosophical roots lie much further back, in ancient debates about the proper relationship between the state and the individual, and the proper limits on governmental intrusion into the lives of its citizens. Thomas Hobbes, in *Leviathan*, famously argued that because the state of nature was nasty and brutish, individuals were forced to submit to an all-powerful state. Hobbes' position justified limitless government power and the elimination of individual rights. John Locke, on the other hand, argued that individuals only consented to government in order to protect their lives, liberties and fortunes, and if government sought to take these things away, then individuals were justified in resisting. This central debate about the substance and limits of government power and individual freedoms has informed political theory for centuries. And to an emerging group of libertarians and computer scientists concerned with privacy in the internet age – a group led by Timothy May, John Gilmore and Eric Hughes, who eventually earned the moniker the "cypherpunks" – Locke's ideology was attractive. They found in cryptology and algorithms a potential solution to the problem of tyrannical government. The cypherpunks believed that, in order to reduce the power of governments and corporations, what was needed was new technology, better computers and more encryption. But their plans ran smack into a seemingly insoluble wall: at the end of the day, all of their projects needed money, and governments and banks controlled it. If they were to realize their project, they would need a form of money that was resistant to government control. And thus began the great race for virtual currency.

The race was fitful and paved with failure. The first efforts crashed and burned, including the legendary cryptographer David Chaum's ECash, as well as other virtual currencies with colorful names such as hashcash, B-Money and Bit Gold. But with each new effort, and each new failure, the community learned more about the obstacles they were facing. So, when Satoshi Nakamoto launched his virtual currency, bitcoin, on October 31, 2008, he was able to revise and improve on all the groundwork that had been laid down before by his predecessors. The answer, he believed, lay in something called the blockchain.

Bitcoin was something new in the world of virtual currency. It was a form of digital ledger that would be maintained not by a single entity, but rather by all its users. As Nakamoto described it, it was a system that was "fully peer-to-peer, with no trusted third party." Nakamoto's bitcoin, thus, would be the world's first democratic form of money, run by its community of users. As a result, it would be free of government and corporate interference. In order to ensure trust, Nakamoto designed the blockchain to be public, allowing people to go in and check to ensure that they still had their money. In order to protect privacy, bitcoin used a cryptographic private key system that allowed users to tell others about their accounts without also broadcasting their identity. In order to incentivize users to maintain the system, bitcoin introduced the concept of mining, in which users could create new blocks of transactions and be rewarded for their efforts with newly minted bitcoin. In order to prevent hacking, bitcoin blocks were cryptographically linked with previous blocks, making the historical record of transactions effectively immutable.

Nakamoto's invention may have been innovative, but there was nothing inevitable about its rise. Time and again, Nakamoto and other backers had to resort to begging and pleading to convince others of bitcoin's merit. One of their constant refrains was that potential users should imagine what would happen if bitcoin became the world's currency. Imagine how much each bitcoin would be worth then! And they could earn hundreds of them just for downloading the software and running it on their home computer. Eventually, Nakamoto's efforts paid off, and people began to use and accept bitcoin in the real world (including, famously, Laszlo Hanyecz, who bought a Papa John's pizza for 10,000 bitcoins).

Once people started using bitcoin in the real world, an ecosystem sprang up around it. Bitcoin exchanges such as Mt. Gox were created to make it easier to buy and sell the currency. Professional miners started building mining farms around the world, and chipmakers started fabricating specialized chips to handle the difficult math problems that underlay the currency. Bitcoin marketplaces emerged to allow people to buy goods and services with their newly valuable bitcoin. Some of these marketplaces, such as the Silk Road, existed on the dark web and catered to people interested in buying illegal things, a group that naturally appreciated the ability to pay with anonymous currency. Despite these early warning signs of the virtual currency's potential attractiveness to criminals, more and more investors grew interested in bitcoin and its technology. Entrepreneurs and venture capitalists like the Winklevoss brothers and Marc Andreesen invested heavily in the virtual currency, believing that the technology was as innovative as the internet and personal computers had been when they were first created. Other investors such as Wences Casares viewed it as a way for citizens in countries with volatile or unpredictable currencies, such as Venezuela and Argentina, to park their money in a safe haven.

The explosion of interest in bitcoin spurred two related developments. First, the value of bitcoin soared. In 2010, it was worth less than a penny. By the end of 2017, it was worth $20,000. The extraordinary price spike led outside observers to compare it to historical bubbles, such as tulip mania in the seventeenth century and the South Sea Bubble in the eighteenth century. Worries of a crash spread. The second development was the emergence of competing cryptocurrencies. Seeing bitcoin's success, a number of entrepreneurs, with varying degrees of computer literacy, launched their own virtual currencies based on the blockchain. Some of these, like Ethereum, were much more than just currencies. They leveraged the inherent flexibility of the blockchain technology to create systems that could serve many purposes, such as forming smart contracts and decentralized organizations that ran themselves. Initial coin offerings, in which individuals or groups raised money through the sale of virtual currencies or "tokens," exploded onto the scene in 2017. Large swathes of these failed miserably. Around half of ICOs went out of business within a year.[1] But while virtual currencies garnered much of the media attention, other larger, more reputable companies started looking at blockchain as a way to improve their operations. IBM created an entire blockchain platform for enterprise use. Maersk launched a blockchain for shipping. Walmart looked into using the blockchain to track its supply chain. Big banks looked into creating a blockchain to settle complicated financial transactions. And many smaller companies started looking into using the blockchain for elections.

But as blockchain broke into the mainstream, so too did its flaws. One of these was its capacity to enable crime. Even from the days of the cypherpunks, this was a very real presence in the field. One of the most popular conversation topics in cypherpunk chat rooms was an assassination market, enabled by anonymous currencies paid to potential assassins. And while full-fledged assassination markets may not have materialized (although there are instances of people, including the founder of the Silk Road, paying others bitcoin in return for murder), criminal opportunities most certainly did. The hacking of cryptocurrency exchange Mt. Gox, which led to staggering losses for investors, was just the first of a string of high-profile cyberintrusions into exchanges. The Silk Road, the dark web marketplace that sold drugs and other illicit goods, was eventually shuttered by the U.S. government, but other marketplaces replaced it. Ransomware hackers asked for payment in bitcoin in return for returning infected data. Russian spies used bitcoin to finance their efforts to affect the U.S. election in 2016. The anonymity that bitcoin enabled fed into a widely held perception that the blockchain represented the Wild West of the internet.

Another major problem for the blockchain was its seemingly insatiable hunger for energy. The security of bitcoin and other virtual currencies depended on the miners that devoted computing power to solving difficult cryptographic problems. But computing power required energy. And as the number and power of miners soared in the 2010s, so too did bitcoin's energy use. Studies concluded that, at one point in 2018, the bitcoin network was consuming the amount of energy used by the entire country of Ireland. Bitcoin was tremendously inefficient from a transactional standpoint. What is more, many of the miners that powered the blockchain were based in China, where coal is used heavily as a source of electricity, making the carbon footprint of the crypto-industry enormous. Some miners relocated to more environmentally friendly locations, such as Sweden and Iceland, where renewable energy was abundant and cheap. Others sought to find more efficient ways to run a blockchain, through different mining mechanisms such as proof-of-stake systems. But the inefficiency remained.

Finally, blockchain technology eluded easy categorization under the law. It looked a bit like currency, but also a bit like a security, and, at the same time, a bit like a commodity. Outdated rules were simply not built to handle systems that looked like the blockchain. Inevitably, problematic behavior fell between the cracks in the law. Unscrupulous operators took advantage of these legal ambiguities to launch products outside the scrutiny of government regulators, such as fraudulent initial coin offerings that duped unsophisticated investors. Regulators slowly recognized the severity of the problem and started reacting. Some launched studies and consultations on how to regulate the industry. Others issued white papers and public statements on their views of how legal frameworks applied in their area. And yet, despite all this flurry of activity, regulators struggled to keep up with the pace of change.

Internationally, governments took wildly different approaches to the technology. Some, like Malta, welcomed it with open arms. They launched sandbox projects and incentive packages for blockchain companies to come to their jurisdictions, and they lowered their regulatory burdens for blockchain-related technologies. Other jurisdictions took the opposite approach, banning or severely limiting the ability of citizens and companies to use blockchain technology or even be associated with virtual currencies. Countries like China forbade banks from handling virtual currencies and cracked down on miners. Still other countries adopted a wait and see approach, deciding not to take action before learning more about how the technology developed. The United States still has not adopted any federal statutes related to virtual currency or the blockchain. These varying approaches reflected the wide divergence of opinions on blockchain and cryptocurrencies. Some call it the next internet, others call it rat poison.

It is easy to assume that the blockchain is unprecedented in its innovation and significance. Money, long the domain of governments and banks, can suddenly be managed by the people. Corporations, those bastions of executive privilege, can now be run by the masses. Smart contracts can (maybe) step in to replace courts, the ultimate arbiter of government power. Cryptocurrencies, decentralized applications and other blockchain technologies are breaking down the walls of power and disrupting long-staid industries. These are powerful claims.

But it is worth remembering that the blockchain is simply a technology that allows us to decentralize things that we have typically thought of as requiring centralization. Many other technologies have done the same. Indeed, some of the greatest technologies in history have had at their core this same promise. The internet promised to allow individuals to communicate with anyone in the world, simultaneously, and without boundaries. The automobile promised to move people further and faster than ever before, leveling geographic barriers and spreading out economic activity. The printing press promised to disseminate knowledge and information on a scale previously unimaginable. Any student of the history of technology can rattle off many more examples. Even democracy, not typically thought of as a "technology," can be viewed in this light, a mechanism for aggregating citizen preferences in an efficient way.

But just because the claims of blockchain are not new does not mean that the claims themselves are wrong. Technology can and does lead to dramatic changes in relative economic and political power. The printing press really did allow knowledge to spread outside to people who had never had access to it. Cars really did give individuals unprecedented flexibility in where they lived and moved. The internet really did disseminate communication and information and data on unprecedented levels. Democracy really did change the way that societies governed themselves.

If anything, the suggestion that the blockchain is not radically novel, but rather follows in a long tradition of technologies aimed at spreading out knowledge and power, is a more helpful one than the claim that blockchain is so revolutionary that it has no precedents. If blockchain is *sui generis*, and thus without precedent, we are forced to examine it in a vacuum. Analysis in a vacuum is hard. But once we view blockchain and cryptocurrencies as part of a trend, not the exception to one, we can assess them in historical context. We can look back at other efforts and examine how they turned out. We can draw comparisons. We can take accounts.

And the lessons of history can tell us much. For one, they tell us that people have a great appetite for more access to information, more control over their daily lives, more of a say on the matters of importance to them. Technologies that promise to satisfy these desires have a great appeal, both emotionally and, just as importantly, in the market. This appeal is broad and diverse, and it defies class, politics and ideology. We can have Edwin Meese, a prominent conservative thinker and devoted federalist, say that "by allowing the states sovereignty sufficient to govern, we better secure our ultimate goal of political liberty through decentralized government," and at the same time Bill Clinton, that apostle of progressive politics today, say that in the twenty-first century "there will be a lot more decentralization . . . [and] in the information age, the role of government is to empower people with the tools to make the most of their own lives, to tear down the barriers to that objective, and to create the conditions within which we can go forward together."² By now, access to the internet has become so ingrained in our daily life that we feel bereft when we see that our cell phone has no connection. Cars were once thought of as the ultimate pathway to individual freedom and self-realization (and now, with the rise of Uber and other ridesharing companies, we have seen that even they can be further decentralized). The overwhelming interest in the blockchain, with its promise of mass control over our financial, economic and material world, thus should come as no surprise. It satisfies this deep desire for a "say" in all our fundamental interactions.

At the same time, decentralization is not without its drawbacks. Spreading out power can be chaotic. It can transfer decision-making authority from the orderly few to the disorderly many. And while this transfer of power limits the power of elites, it also strengthens the power of the uninformed or the disinterested. The masses can be prone to problematic emotions like hysteria or panic anger, and they can be swayed by appeals to their worst instincts, such as nativism or selfishness.

And for another, there are powerful forces at work against decentralization. There will always be groups that seek to concentrate power back into their own hands. They may be driven by ostensibly, or even truly, altruistic motivations. They might think that they are better at running things, or that individuals would prefer some measure of central authority and organization. But they may also be driven to undermine decentralization for more self-interested reasons. Monopoly is good if you are the monopolist. These forces towards centralization are powerful and relentless. The rise of the tech giants (Facebook, Google, Amazon, Apple and a few other) are evidence enough of just how thoroughly a purportedly decentralizing innovation – the internet – can lead instead to unprecedented centralization.

Politicians, citizens and philosophers have been working to improve and tweak the basic model of democracy for thousands of years. They have attempted to identify its weaknesses and problematic tendencies, its pressure points where it might fall apart or lead to injustice. Democracy itself is as close to a pure good as one can find in the world – a system devised around principles of freedom and equality – and yet even it has its limits. Even with democracies, most modern societies have come to the conclusion that pure, unfiltered collective decision-making by direct citizen action is undesirable in the vast majority of cases. As James Madison wrote in *The Federalist Papers*, the system of government they aimed to create was not so much a democracy as a republic, where citizens delegate decision-making to representatives. The purpose of Congress was not simply to take the views of the people and then act on them. Instead, it was to "refine and enlarge the public views, by passing them through the medium of a chosen body of citizens, whose wisdom may best discern the true interest of their country, and whose patriotism and love of justice will be least likely to sacrifice it to temporary or partial considerations." Under this system, Madison concluded, "it may well happen that the public voice, pronounced by the representatives of the people, will be more consonant to the public good than if pronounced by the people themselves . . . ."[3] And, of course, the work did not stop with the creation of the constitution. Our system of democracy is constantly evolving in response to changing norms and technologies.

If democracy has had thousands of years to amend and revise its ways, the blockchain has had just a decade. Its founding father, Satoshi Nakamoto, wrote in his final message that the technology had too many flaws to count. In the years since, many of these flaws have been identified and, at times, exploited. Without a doubt, more flaws will be found, and the blockchain, like any technology, must change if it is to survive. Programmers, users and governments have only just begun the hard work of understanding and, then, improving on it.

The blockchain is not an ideal deliberative body. It has flaws and quirks and vulnerabilities. But it is a remarkable effort to rethink how our democracy works. Its popularity stands as a testament, on the one hand, to the depth of distrust of authority and government in today's world and, on the other, the fervent and undying belief that technology and the world of cyberspace can provide an answer. Its failings show how, time and again, the blockchain, like other technologies, has run up against the stubborn realities of law, markets and human nature. But even if the blockchain has not lived up to its greatest aspirations, it has accomplished something even more important. It has captured the imagination of individuals across the globe and inspired people to question how the basic building blocks of society work, and how they don't. This, perhaps, will be its greatest legacy.

Notes

INTRODUCTION

1. *See* Cyrus Farivar, *Why the Head of Mt. Gox Bitcoin Exchange Should Be in Jail*, ARSTECHNICA (Aug. 1, 2014), https://arstechnica.com/tech-policy/2014/08/why-the-head-of-mt-gox-bitcoin-exchange-should-be-in-jail; Nathalie-Kyoko Stucky, *Vilified Bitcoin Tycoon After Losing $500 Million: My Life Is at Risk*, DAILY BEAST (Sept. 17, 2014), https://www.thedailybeast.com/vilified-bitcoin-tycoon-after-losing-dollar500-million-my-life-is-at-risk.

2. Takashi Mochizuki & Eleanor Warnock, *Mt. Gox Shows Bitcoin's Growing Pains*, WALL ST. J., Feb. 17, 2014.

3. *See* NATHANIEL POPPER, DIGITAL GOLD: BITCOIN AND THE INSIDE STORY OF THE MISFITS AND MILLIONAIRES TRYING TO REINVENT MONEY 200 (2015)

4. *See Arrest of Alexander Vinnik*, MAGICALTUX (July 27, 2017), https://blog.magicaltux.net/article/Arrest-of-Alexander-Vinnik; POPPER, *supra* note 3, at 207.

5. Fesnavarro, *Where Are My Bitcoins MTGOX?*, REDDIT (Feb. 4, 2015), https://www.reddit.com/r/Bitcoin/comments/1x21bq/where_are_my_bit coins_mtgox/.

6. Jermwerty, *MtGox Withdrawal Delays*, BITCOINTALK (Feb. 6, 2014), https://bitcointalk.org/index.php?topic=179586.msg4981012#msg4981012.

7. Smoothie, *MtGox Withdrawal Delays*, BITCOINTALK (Feb. 8, 2014), https://bitcointalk.org/index.php?topic=179586.msg5008907#msg5008907.

8. TheButterZone, *Do You Think Mt. Gox Will Survive?*, BITCOINTALK (Feb. 24, 2014), https://bitcointalk.org/index.php?topic=483905.msg5326811#ms g5326811.

9. *See* POPPER, *supra* note 3, at 310–11.

10. *See* Tim Hornyak, *Despite Mt. Gox Fiasco, Karpeles Still Has Bitcoin Plans*, PCWORLD (Nov. 11, 2014), https://www.pcworld.com/article/2846252/despite-mt-gox-fiasco-karpeles-still-has-bitcoin-plans.html.

11. *See* Robert McMillan, *The Inside Story of Mt. Gox, Bitcoin's $460 Million Disaster*, WIRED (Mar. 3, 2014), https://www.wired.com/2014/03/bitcoin-exchange/. Karpeles later discovered a number of the missing bitcoin in one of the company's wallets, bringing the number of stolen bitcoin down to 650,000. *See* Brian Feldman, *Mt. Gox Found 200,000 Missing Bitcoins*, ATLANTIC, Mar. 21, 2014.

12. There is some debate about precisely when Karpeles learned that the coins were missing. Some have claimed that he knew as early as 2011, shortly after acquiring the company, and that he hid the fact from his investors in order to turn a quick profit. *See* PAUL VIGNA & MICHAEL J. CASEY, THE AGE OF CRYPTOCURRENCY: HOW BITCOIN AND THE BLOCKCHAIN ARE CHALLENGING THE GLOBAL ECONOMIC ORDER 268 (2015).

13. PLATO, THE REPUBLIC bk. VIII.

1 THE ORIGINS OF THE BLOCKCHAIN

1. https://bitcoin.org/bitcoin.pdf.

2. The archives of the Cryptography Mailing List can be found at http://www.metzdowd.com/pipermail/cryptography/. Nakamoto's first message to the list, and thus his first announcement to the world, can be found here: Satoshi Nakamoto, *Bitcoin P2P E-cash Paper*, METZDOWD (Oct. 31, 2008), http://www.metzdowd.com/pipermail/cryptography/2008-October/014810.html.

3. James A. Donald, *Bitcoin P2P E-cash Paper*, METZDOWD (Nov. 2, 2008), http://www.metzdowd.com/pipermail/cryptography/2008-November/014814.html.

4. Ray Dillinger, *Bitcoin P2P E-cash Paper*, METZDOWD (Nov. 6, 2008), http://www.metzdowd.com/pipermail/cryptography/2008-November/014822.html.

5. John Levine, *Bitcoin P2P E-cash Paper*, METZDOWD (Nov. 3, 2008), http://www.metzdowd.com/pipermail/cryptography/2008-November/014817.html.

6. James A. Donald, *Bitcoin P2P E-cash Paper*, METZDOWD (Nov. 3, 2008), http://www.metzdowd.com/pipermail/cryptography/2008-November/014819.html.

7. Hal Finney, *Why Remailers . . .*, Email to the Cypherpunk Mailing List, dated Nov. 15, 1992, https://cryptome.org/2014/09/hal-finney-cpunks-1992.htm.

8. For more information on Hal Finney, see Andy Greenberg, *Nakamoto's Neighbor: My Hunt for Bitcoin's Creator Led to a Paralyzed Crypto Genius*, FORBES (Mar. 25, 2014), https://www.forbes.com/sites/andygreenberg/2014/03/25/satoshi-nakamotos-neighbor-the-bitcoin-ghostwriter-who-wasnt/#481873594a37; NATHANIEL POPPER, DIGITAL GOLD: *BITCOIN AND THE*

INSIDE STORY OF THE MISFITS AND MILLIONAIRES TRYING TO REINVENT MONEY, chs. 1–5 (2015).

9. Hal Finney, *Bitcoin P2P E-cash Paper*, METZDOWD (Nov. 7, 2008), http://www.metzdowd.com/pipermail/cryptography/2008-November/014827.html; Hal Finney, *Bitcoin P2P E-cash Paper*, METZDOWD (Nov. 13, 2008), http://www.metzdowd.com/pipermail/cryptography/2008-November/014848.html.

10. Satoshi Nakamoto, *Bitcoin P2P E-cash Paper*, METZDOWD (Nov. 6, 2008), http://www.metzdowd.com/pipermail/cryptography/2008-November/014823.html.

11. Satoshi Nakamoto, *Bitcoin P2P E-cash Paper*, METZDOWD (Nov. 14, 2008), http://www.metzdowd.com/pipermail/cryptography/2008-November/014853.html.

12. For further discussion of the life and times of both Hobbes and Locke, see A.P. MARTINICH, HOBBES: A BIOGRAPHY (1999); ARNOLD A. ROGOW, THOMAS HOBBES: RADICAL IN SEARCH OF REACTION (1986); ROGER WOOLHOUSE, LOCKE: A BIOGRAPHY (2007); MAURICE CRANSTON, JOHN LOCKE: A BIOGRAPHY (1957); RICHARD ASHCRAFT, REVOLUTIONARY POLITICS & LOCKE'S TWO TREATISES OF GOVERNMENT (1986).

13. A number of excellent biographies of Thomas Hobbes exist. Among them are John Aubrey's classic *Brief Lives* (Oliver Lawson Dick ed., 1969), Alfred Edward Taylor's *Thomas Hobbes* (1908), Richard Tuck's *Hobbes* (1989) and A.P. Martinich's *Hobbes: A Life* (1999).

14. THOMAS HOBBES, LEVIATHAN 76 (Edwin Curley ed., Hackett 1994) (1651).

15. *Id.* at 135.

16. *Id.*

17. *Id.* at 212.

18. *Id.*

19. *Id.* at 135.

20. Among the excellent biographies of John Locke are Henry Richard Fox Bourne's *The Life of John Locke* (1876), Maurice Cranston's *John Locke: A Biography* (1957) and Roger Woolhouse's *Locke: A Biography* (2007).

21. JOHN LOCKE, TWO TREATISES OF GOVERNMENT 377 (Peter Laslett ed., Cambridge 1960) (1689).

22. *Id.* at 139.

23. *Id.* at 430.

24. *Id.* at 430–31.

25. *Id.* at 431–33.

26. HOBBES, *supra* note 14, at 80.

27. LOCKE, *supra* note 21, at 289.

28. *Id.* at 139.

29. FREDERICK MUNDELL WATKINS, THE POLITICAL TRADITION OF THE WEST: A STUDY IN THE DEVELOPMENT OF MODERN LIBERALISM x (1948).

30. Louis Rossetto, *The Original Wired Manifesto*, WIRED (Jan. 1993), https://www.wired.com/story/original-wired-manifesto/.

31. K.G. Coffman & Andrew Odlyzko, *The Size and Growth Rate of the Internet*, FIRST MONDAY (Oct. 5, 1998), https://firstmonday.org/ojs/index.php/fm/article/view/620/541.

32. John Perry Barlow, *A Declaration of the Independence of Cyberspace*, ELECTRONIC FRONTIER FOUND. (Feb. 8, 1996), https://www.eff.org/cyberspace-independence.

33. For an excellent and eminently readable history of the group, see ANDY GREENBERG, THIS MACHINE KILLS SECRETS: HOW WIKILEAKERS, CYPHERPUNKS, AND HACKTIVISTS AIM TO FREE THE WORLD'S INFORMATION (2012). *See also* STEVEN LEVY, CRYPTO: HOW THE CODE REBELS BEAT THE GOVERNMENT (2002).

34. GREENBERG, *supra* note 33, at 79–81.

35. Timothy May, *The Crypto Anarchist Manifesto*, https://www.activism.net/cypherpunk/crypto-anarchy.html.

36. *See* Robert Manne, *The Cypherpunk Revolutionary*, MONTHLY, Mar. 2011.

37. Thomas Rid, *The Cypherpunk Revolution: How the Tech Vanguard Turned Public-Key Cryptography into One of the Most Potent Political Ideas of the 21st Century*, CHRISTIAN SCIENCE MONITOR, July 20, 2016.

38. Steven Levy, *Crypto Rebels*, WIRED (Feb. 1, 1993), https://www.wired.com/1993/02/crypto-rebels/.

39. Eric Hughes, *A Cypherpunk's Manifesto* (Mar. 1993), https://www.activism.net/cypherpunk/manifesto.html.

40. For a collection of Julian Assange's posts to the Cypherpunk Mailing List, see https://cryptome.org/0001/assange-cpunks.htm.

41. JULIAN ASSANGE & JACOB APPELBAUM, CYPHERPUNKS: FREEDOM AND THE FUTURE OF THE INTERNET 19 (2012).

42. Jim Bell, *Assassination Politics*, OUTPOST OF FREEDOM BLOG, http://www.outpost-of-freedom.com/jimbellap.htm.

43. *Id.*

44. Jack Hammer, *Anonymous Trashing of Assassination Politics*, Email to the Cypherpunk Mailing List, dated Jan. 28, 1996, https://cypherpunks.venona.com/date/1996/01/msg01854.html.

45. Bill Frantz, *Assassination Politics Was V-Chips, CC, and Motorcycle Helmets*, Email to the Cypherpunk Mailing List, dated Feb. 15, 1996, https://cypherpunks.venona.com/date/1996/02/msg01294.html.

46. Jean-Francois Avon, *Assassination Politics*, Email to the Cypherpunk Mailing List, dated Feb. 14, 1996, https://cypherpunks.venona.com/date/1996/02/msg01236.html.

47. Rich Graves, *Anonymous Trashing of Assassination Politics*, Email to the Cypherpunk Mailing List, dated Jan. 26, 1996, https://cypherpunks.venona.com/date/1996/01/msg01728.html.

48. *See* David E. Kaplan, Douglas Pasternak & Gordon Witkin, *Terrorism's Next Wave: Nerve Gas and Germs Are the New Weapons of Choice*, U.S. NEWS & WORLD REP., Nov. 17, 1997.
49. *See* John Branton, *Anti-Government Figure Will Be Free*, COLUMBIAN, Dec. 13, 2009.
50. Timothy C. May, *The Cyphernomicon* (1994), http://www.kreps.org/hack ers/overheads/11cyphernervs.pdf.
51. Hal Finney, Email to the Cypherpunk Mailing List, dated Oct. 10, 1992, https://cryptome.org/2014/09/hal-finney-cpunks-1992.htm.
52. *See* Hal Finney, *Misc. Items*, Email to the Cypherpunk Mailing List, dated Nov. 28, 1992, https://cypherpunks.venona.com/raw/cyp-1992.txt.
53. Timothy May, *Some (Pseudo)Random Thoughts*, Email to the Cypherpunk Mailing List, dated Oct. 14, 1992, https://cypherpunks.venona.com/raw/cyp-1992.txt.
54. So, it turns out, did many powerful figures in government. Alan Greenspan, the chairman of the Federal Reserve, remarked in 1996 that "[w]e could envisage proposals in the near future for issuers of electronic payment obligations, such as stored-value cards or 'digital cash,' to set up specialized issuing corporations with strong balance sheets and public credit ratings." Alan Greenspan, Remarks at the U.S. Treasury Conference on Electronic Money & Banking (Sept. 19, 1996), https://www.federalreserve.gov/boarddocs/speeches/1996/19960919.htm.
55. May, *supra* note 53.
56. For an excellent history of the cowrie shell's use in West Africa and its particular merits as a form of currency, see Marion Johnson, *The Cowrie Currencies of West Africa*, 11 J. AFRICAN HIST. 17 (1970).
57. *See* JACK WEATHERFORD, THE HISTORY OF MONEY: FROM SANDSTONE TO CYBERSPACE 17–20 (1997).
58. JOHN KENNETH GALBRAITH, MONEY: WHENCE IT CAME, WHERE IT WENT 18 (1975)
59. *See* LEWIS MANDELL, THE CREDIT CARD INDUSTRY: A HISTORY (1990).
60. For a study on the effects of the switch to electronic deposits, see Joseph Bondar, *Social Security Beneficiaries Enrolled in the Direct Deposit Program, December 1983*, SOCIAL SECURITY BULLETIN, May 1984. Among other things, Bondar found that you were more likely to switch to electronic deposits if you were female, white, wealthy and lived in the West.
61. For a dramatic recounting of the difficulties PayPal ran into in creating its online payment system, see ERIC M. JACKSON, THE PAYPAL WARS: BATTLES WITH EBAY, THE MEDIA, THE MAFIA, AND THE REST OF PLANET EARTH (2012).
62. David Chaum, *Restoring Electronic Privacy*, SCIENTIFIC AMERICAN, Aug. 1992.

63. David Chaum, *Blind Signatures for Untraceable Payments, in* ADVANCES IN CRYPTOLOGY: PROCEEDINGS OF CRYPTO 82 (David Chaum, Ronald L. Rivest & Alan T. Sherman eds., 1983).

64. James Gleick, *Dead as a Dollar*, N.Y. TIMES, June 16, 1996.

65. Paul Fisher, *Electronic Cash: Smart Money Is on Plastic*, GUARDIAN, June 30, 1994.

66. Paul Mailment, *The Age of Cybercash*, NEWSWEEK, Dec. 26, 1994. *See also* John Vidal, *Bank to the Future*, GUARDIAN, Jan. 28, 1995.

67. *See* Kimberley A. Strassel, *Deutsche Bank to Test "E-Cash" with DigiCash in Pilot Project*, WALL ST. J., May 7, 1996.

68. Jeffrey Kuttler, *Credit Suisse, Digicash in E-Commerce Test*, AMER. BANKER, June 16, 1998.

69. *See* Frank Bajak, *Electronic Cash Hits the Internet*, ASSOCIATED PRESS, Oct. 22, 1995.

70. *See* Aaron van Wirdum, *The Genesis Files: How David Chaum's ecash Spawned a Cypherpunk Dream*, BITCOIN MAGAZINE, Apr. 24, 2018.

71. *Id.*

72. Ian Grigg, *How DigiCash Blew Everything* (Feb. 10, 1999), https://cryptome.org/jya/digicrash.htm.

73. Finney,*supra* note 7.

74. *See* POPPER, *supra* note 8, at 17–22.

75. *Id.* at 18–19.

76. *See* FREDERIC S. MISHKIN, THE ECONOMICS OF MONEY, BANKING, AND FINANCIAL MARKETS 96–99 (2015)

77. A remarkable study from the 1980s demonstrates the effect that price has on consumer perceptions. In the study, participants were asked to estimate the value of a house. They could visit the house, inspect it, and tour the neighborhood if they liked. So they had extensive first-hand knowledge of the quality of the home. They were also, however, given a price that the sellers were supposedly asking for the home. Unbeknownst to them, this price was not the actual list price for the home. Instead, it was a price that was either substantially higher or substantially lower than the real list price. The results on the participants' perceptions of the house were striking. Participants who were given the high fictional asking price ($149,900) estimated the true value of the home 24 percent higher than participants who were given the low fictional asking price ($119,900). The asking price of the home had dramatically changed participants' estimates of the true value of the home. The study showed just how powerful a hold prices have on our understandings of the world around us. Gregory B. Northcraft & Margaret A. Neale, *Experts, Amateurs, and Real Estate: An Anchoring-and-Adjustment Perspective on Property Pricing Decisions*, 39 ORGANIZATIONAL BEHAV. & HUM. DECISION PROCESSES 84, 94–96 (1987)

78. OSCAR WILDE, LADY WINDERMERE'S FAN, Act I (1982).

79. Niall Ferguson, The Ascent of Money 104 (2008).
80. Bernd Widdig, Culture and Inflation in Weimar Germany 4 (2001).
81. The relationship between post-war Germany's hyperinflation and the Nazi party is a matter of substantial debate, and some recent studies have cast doubt on the theory that inflation caused, or even contributed in a meaningful way to, the rise of Hitler's party. *See* Frederick Taylor, The Downfall of Money: Germany's Hyperinflation and the Destruction of the Middle Class (2013).
82. *See* Steve H. Hanke & Alex K. F. Kwok, *On the Measurement of Zimbabwe's Hyperinflation*, 29 Cato J. 353, 354 (2009).
83. For a description of the steep obstacles Zimbabwe faces in turning around the situation, see *Going Cashless, Zimbabwe Style*, Economist, May 19, 2018;, *Zimbabwe Struggles to Keep Its Fledgling Currency Alive*, Economist, May 23, 2019.
84. Nakamoto, *supra* note 2 (emphasis added).
85. As we will discuss later, all of these assumptions are not perfectly true, as governments and/or companies may create new bitcoins, they have some say in its maintenance, and they certainly monitor its use in circumstances of crime or fraud. But the observation remains true in the broad sense that governments have no unique technological control over the blockchain, unlike the unique control they have over the traditional money supply.
86. Satoshi Nakamoto, Post to P2P Foundation (Feb. 15, 2009), http://p2pfoun dation.ning.com/forum/topics/bitcoin-open-source?commentI d=2003008%3AComment%3A9543.
87. Aristotle, Politics bk. 3, ch. 7.
88. Machiavelli, The Discourses bk. 1, sec. 2.
89. Plato, The Republic bk. VIII. As John Dunn put it, "*The Republic* is a book with many morals. It is also a deliberately teasing book, and open to an endless range of interpretations. But no serious reader could fail to recognize that it comes down firmly against democracy." John Dunn, Setting the People Free: The Story of Democracy 44–45 (2005).
90. *Id.*
91. Aristotle, Politics bk. 3, ch. 7.
92. *Id.*, ch. 11.
93. Machiavelli, The Discourses bk. 1, sec. 2.
94. Adam Smith, An Inquiry into the Nature and Causes of the Wealth of Nations bk. IV, ch. 2.
95. Seymour M. Lipset, Introduction, *in* Robert Michels, Political Parties: A Sociological Study of the Oligarchical Tendencies of Modern Democracy 33 (1968).
96. Plato, The Republic bk. VIII.
97. *Id.*

2 THE TECHNOLOGY OF THE BLOCKCHAIN

1. For an analysis of the events of that day, see Arvind Narayanan, *Analyzing the 2013 Bitcoin Fork: Centralized Decision-Making Saved the Day*, FREEDOM TO TINKER BLOG (July 28, 2015), https://freedom-to-tinker .com/2015/07/28/analyzing-the-2013-bitcoin-fork-centralized-decision-ma king-saved-the-day/.
2. Transcript of #bitcoin-dev chat, Mar. 11–12, 2013, http://bitcoinstats.com/ irc/bitcoin-dev/logs/2013/03/11.
3. Transcript of #bitcoin-dev chat, Mar. 11–12, 2013, http://bitcoinstats.com/ irc/bitcoin-dev/logs/2013/03/11.
4. *See* PAUL VIGNA & MICHAEL J. CASEY, THE AGE OF CRYPTOCURRENCY: HOW BITCOIN AND THE BLOCKCHAIN ARE CHALLENGING THE GLOBAL ECONOMIC ORDER 151 (2015).
5. *See* Nick Marinoff, *Bitmain Nears 51% of Network Hash Rate: Why This Matters and Why It Doesn't*, BITCOIN MAGAZINE (June 28, 2018), https:// bitcoinmagazine.com/articles/bitmain-nears-51-network-hash-rate-why-m atters-and-why-it-doesnt/.
6. *See* ARVIND NARAYANAN, JOSEPH BONNEAU, EDWARD FELTEN, ANDREW MILLER & STEVEN GOLDFEDER, BITCOIN AND CRYPTOCURRENCY TECHNOLOGIES: A COMPREHENSIVE INTRODUCTION 168–89 (2016). *See also* Angela Walch, *In Code(rs) We Trust: Software Developers as Fiduciaries in Public Blockchains, in* REGULATING BLOCKCHAIN: TECHNO-SOCIAL AND LEGAL CHALLENGES (Philipp Hacker et al. ed., 2019).
7. For a more thorough description of the process, see NARAYANAN ET AL., *supra* note 6, at 168–89.
8. Collision-resistant does not mean collision-proof. Even the best crypto-graphic hash functions will inevitably have points of collision where two different inputs have the same output. After all, hash functions turn informa-tion of different sizes and lengths into outputs of fixed length. Fixed-length outputs are necessarily finite, while the potential inputs are infinite. Thus, not only do hash functions have some points of collision, they have infinite points of collision. But cryptographers have concluded that this is not problematic from a security standpoint so long as it is practically impossible to find the points of collision. For example, for a hash function with a 256-bit output, on average, you would need to try 2^{128} guesses before you would find a different input with the same hash. For a longer discussion of the collision-resistant properties of hash functions, see *id.* at 2–5.
9. *See* Samuel Gibbs, *Passwords and Hacking: The Jargon of Hashing, Salting and SHA-2 Explained*, GUARDIAN, Dec. 15, 2016.
10. This is a greatly simplified version of the actual mechanics of a bitcoin transaction. One important complication is that all bitcoins in a given public address must be spent in every transaction, and thus, if Locke has

more than one bitcoin in his account, he must specify where the other bitcoins will go. *See* NARAYANAN ET AL., *supra* note 6, at 51–55.

11. *See id.* at 67.

12. Or at least nodes are supposed to ignore it when users attempt to spend more bitcoin than they have. But sometimes they don't. In one infamous case, now known as the "value overflow incident," a hacker managed to get around this limitation and create 184 billion bitcoin out of thin air. He did so using a known problem in computer science referred to as "integer overflow." The idea here is similar to an odometer that runs out of space. Once an odometer has maxed out at, say, 9,999 miles, it then flips back to zero. Similarly, when bitcoin was first written, if a user sent a transaction that purported to send more bitcoin than the software was programmed to handle, the software would react as if it had flipped back to zero. Thus, it would not register the transaction as invalid. In 2010, one hacker exploited this to send himself 184 billion bitcoin. Needless to say, when Nakamoto and others inevitably noticed the unusual transaction, they issued a software update to fix the flaw and also reversed the transaction. As bitcoin developer Wladimir Van Der Laan described it, "it was the worst problem ever." *See* Bruno Skvorc, *The Curious Case of 184 Billion Bitcoin*, BITFALLS, Jan. 14, 2018.

13. Technically, there is no requirement for blocks to contain actual transactions. As we will see below, miners are competing to solve difficult mathematical equations, and once they do, they can add a block to the chain. If it turns out that their block did not include any actual transfers of bitcoin from one address to another, this is fine. If this is the case, the only transaction in that block will be what is known as the coinbase transaction, which is the transaction that creates new bitcoins to reward the miner for solving the equation. *See* Pascal Gauthier, *Why Do Some Bitcoin Mining Pools Mine Empty Blocks?*, BITCOIN MAGAZINE, July 12, 2016.

14. In fact, not all nodes download the entire blockchain. Some nodes instead act as "lightweight nodes," meaning that they download only a portion of the blockchain such as the block headers. This makes it much cheaper to act as a node, but, because these lightweight nodes do not have the full history of the blockchain, they have to rely on full nodes to check the validity of previous transactions. *See* NARAYANAN ET AL., *supra* note 6, at 71.

15. The first block ever mined is known as the "genesis block." It was created by Satoshi Nakamoto when he first created the system and was therefore the only node on the system. The block won Nakamoto fifty bitcoins, which would have been worth nothing at the time but at bitcoin's height in 2017 would have been worth $1,000,000. Interestingly, perhaps as a sign of Nakamoto's motivations for creating the virtual currency, Nakamoto included in this block a reference to a story in *The Times* of London with

the headline *Chancellor on brink of second bailout for banks. See* VIGNA & CASEY, *supra* note 4, at 63.

16. *See* NARAYANAN ET AL., *supra* note 6, at 106–07.
17. *See* Alex de Vries, *Bitcoin's Growing Energy Problem*, 2 JOULE 801, 801 (2018).
18. *See* Press Release, Digiconomist, New Academic Paper: Bitcoin's Growing Energy Problem (May 16, 2018), https://digiconomist.net/bit coins-growing-energy-problem.
19. *See* de Vries, *supra* note 17.
20. Once all potential bitcoins have been issued, miners will need to find a new income source for performing the work of maintaining the block-chain. This source will likely come from transaction fees, which are effectively bitcoins that can be included by users in their transactions in order to incentivize miners to include those transactions in the next block. So far, these transaction fees have been relatively small – on July 24, 2018, the average transaction fee was $0.92 – but they will likely increase if they become the primary method for compensating miners. *See Bitcoin Avg. Transaction Fee Historical Chart*, BITINFOCHARTS.COM, https://bitinfocharts .com/comparison/bitcoin-transactionfees.html.
21. The maximum size of a block is currently one megabyte, the size that Satoshi Nakamoto set for bitcoin blocks in 2010. Block size limits are a matter of significant discussion within the blockchain community because they have important ramifications for the speed of the network. Larger block sizes means that more transactions can be included in each block, which in turn means that more transactions can be handled per second. Many proponents of increasing the maximum block size argue that if bitcoin is to become a truly global virtual currency, if it is to scale up, it must speed up its processing time. Critics, however, point out that increasing the size of blocks in the blockchain will make it more expensive to run the nodes that verify these blocks, thus giving an advan-tage to large, centralized miners that have the power and money to support large fixed costs. *See* Nathaniel Popper, *Bitcoin Expansion Is off the Table*, N.Y. TIMES, Nov. 8, 2017.
22. *See* NARAYANAN ET AL., *supra* note 6, at 35–36.

3 BLOCKCHAIN IN THE WORLD

1. For more information on the theoretical background of Jentzsch's proposal, see Christoph Jentzsch, *Decentralized Autonomous Organization to Automate Governance* (White Paper), https://download.slock.it/public/ DAO/WhitePaper.pdf.
2. *See* Nathaniel Popper, *A Venture Fund with Plenty of Virtual Capital, But No Capitalist*, N.Y. TIMES, May 21, 2016.

3. Jentzsch, *supra* note 1.
4. The DAO Frontpage, http://web.archive.org/web/20160622212302/https://daohub.org.
5. *See* U.S. Sec. & Exch. Comm'n, Report of Investigation Pursuant to Section 21(a) of the Securities Exchange Act of 1934: The DAO (July 25, 2017), https://www.sec.gov/litigation/investreport/34-81207.pdf.
6. *See* Matthew Leising, *The Ether Thief*, BLOOMBERG, June 13, 2017.
7. Christoph Jentzsch, *The History of the DAO and Lessons Learned*, Aug. 24, 2016, https://blog.slock.it/the-history-of-the-dao-and-lessons-learned-d06740f8cfa5.
8. Dino Mark, Vlad Zamfir & Emin Gün Sirer, *A Call for a Temporary Moratorium on "The DAO"* (Working Paper, May 26, 2016, rev. May 30, 2016), https://docs.google.com/document/d/10kTyCmGPhvZy94F7VWyS-dQ4lsBacR2dUgGTtV98C4o/.
9. Jentzsch, *supra* note 1.
10. Ledgerwatch, *I Think the DAO is getting drained right now*, REDDIT (June 17, 2016), https://www.reddit.com/r/ethereum/comments/4oi2ta/i_think_thedao_is_getting_drained_right_now/.
11. For a more in-depth discussion of the flaws in the DAO's code, see Emin Gün Sirer, *Thoughts on the DAO Hack*, HACKING, DISTRIBUTED (June 17, 2016), http://hackingdistributed.com/2016/06/17/thoughts-on-the-dao-hack/.
12. *See* Leising, *supra* note 6.
13. Jentzsch, *supra* note 1.
14. *Id.*
15. Bruce Fenton, *It is Better to Lose Your Investment Than Lose Your Blockchain*, MEDIUM (June 17, 2016), https://medium.com/@brucefenton/its-better-to-lose-your-investment-than-lose-your-blockchain-2907a59d5a4o.
16. *Id.*
17. *See* Nathaniel Popper, *A Hacking of More than $50 Million Dashes Hopes in the World of Virtual Currency*, N.Y. TIMES, June 17, 2016.
18. *See* Vote: *The DAO Hard Fork*, CARBONVOTE, http://v1.carbonvote.com/.
19. *See* Vitalik Buterin, *Hard Fork Completed*, ETHEREUM BLOG,(July 20, 2016), https://blog.ethereum.org/2016/07/20/hard-fork-completed/.
20. Emin Gün Sirer, in an essay posted to Hacking, Distributed, wrote:

> First of all, I'm not even sure that this qualifies as a hack. To label something as a hack or a bug or unwanted behavior, we need to have a specification of the wanted behavior. We had no such specification for The DAO. There is no independent specification for what The DAO is supposed to implement. Heck, there are hardly any comments in The DAO code that document what the developers may have been thinking at the time they wrote the code. The "code was its own documentation," as people say. It was its own fine print.

The hacker read the fine print better than most, better than the developers themselves.

Sirer, *supra* note 11.

21. As of June 11, 2019. *Compare* https://coinmarketcap.com/currencies/ether eum/, *with* https://coinmarketcap.com/currencies/ethereum-classic/.
22. *See* Leising, *supra* note 6.
23. M.I. FINLEY, DEMOCRACY: ANCIENT AND MODERN 11 (1985).
24. As Benoît Cœuré of the European Central Bank put it, "[i]n more ways than one, Bitcoin is the evil spawn of the financial crisis." *See* Josiah Wilmoth, *Bitcoin is the "Evil Spawn of the Financial Crisis": European Central Bank Board Member,* CCN (Nov. 15, 2018), https://www.ccn.com/bitcoin-is-the-evil-spawn-of-the-financial-crisis-eur opean-central-bank-board-member/.
25. *See* Eric Pfanner, *Meltdown of Iceland's Financial System Quickens,* N.Y. TIMES, Oct. 8, 2008.
26. http://www.metzdowd.com/pipermail/cryptography/2009-January/015004 .html.
27. Satoshi Nakamoto, Message to Cryptography Mailing List, dated Jan. 16, 2018, http://www.metzdowd.com/pipermail/cryptography/2009-January/o 15014.html.
28. http://www.metzdowd.com/pipermail/cryptography/2008-November/014 865.html.
29. *See* PAUL VIGNA & MICHAEL J. CASEY, THE AGE OF CRYPTOCURRENCY: HOW BITCOIN AND THE BLOCKCHAIN ARE CHALLENGING THE GLOBAL ECONOMIC ORDER 77 (2015).
30. https://bitcointalk.org/index.php?topic=137.0.
31. *Id.*
32. *See* VIGNA & CASEY, *supra* note 29, at 79.
33. https://bitcointalk.org/index.php?topic=137.0.
34. The pizzas have reached near mythic status in bitcoin lore. There is even a Twitter page, @bitcoin_pizza, which tracks on a daily basis how much the bitcoin pizza would be worth today.
35. *See* Mark Molloy, *The Unlucky Man Who Accidentally Threw Away Bitcoin Worth $100 Million,* TELEGRAPH, Dec. 3, 2018.
36. *See* VIGNA & CASEY, *supra* note 29, at 83-85.
37. *Id.* at 83.
38. There are two excellent books on the history of the Silk Road. The first, *Silk Road,* by Eileen Orsmby, tracks the history of the website through extensive research, including the author's own participation in the site. EILEEN ORMSBY, SILK ROAD (2014). The second, *American Kingpin,* by Nick Bilton, explores the wide cast of characters involved in the site and its eventual downfall, including Silk Road's notorious owner, Ross Ulbricht.

NICK BILTON, AMERICAN KINGPIN: THE EPIC HUNT FOR THE CRIMINAL MASTERMIND BEHIND THE SILK ROAD (2017).

39. *See* Archived Silk Road Website, http://web.archive.org/web/20110304201806/http://silkroadmarket.org/.

40. *See* Dylan Love, *Take a Tour of Silk Road, the Online Drug Marketplace the Feds Shut Down Today,* BUSINESS INSIDER (Oct. 2, 2013), https://www.businessinsider.com/silk-road-walkthrough-2013-10.

41. Adrian Chen, *The Underground Website Where You Can Buy Any Drug Imaginable,* GAWKER (June 1, 2011), http://gawker.com/the-underground-website-where-you-can-buy-any-drug-imag-30818160.

42. *Id.*

43. *See* Associated Press, *Schumer Pushes to Shut Down Online Drug Marketplace* (June 5, 2011), https://www.nbcnewyork.com/news/local/Schumer-Calls-on-Feds-to-Shut-Down-Online-Drug-Marketplace-123187958.html.

44. Sealed Complaint, United States v. Ross William Ulbricht, https://www.scribd.com/doc/172773561/Criminal-Complaint-Against-Silk-Road-and-Dread-Pirate-Roberts.

45. Satoshi Nakamoto, Post to BitcoinTalk.org, dated Dec. 5, 2010, https://bitcointalk.org/index.php?topic=1735.msg26999#msg26999.

46. *See* Keir Thomas, *Could the Wikileaks Scandal Lead to New Virtual Currency?,* PCWORLD, Dec. 10, 2010.

47. Satoshi Nakamoto, Post to BitcoinTalk.org, dated Dec. 11, 2010, https://bitcointalk.org/index.php?topic=2216.msg29280#msg29280.

48. *See* Laura Noonan, *J.P. Morgan's Jamie Dimon Calls Bitcoin "A Fraud," "Worse Than Tulip Bulbs,"* FINANCIAL TIMES, Sept. 12, 2017.

49. *See* Kate Rooney, *Goldman Sachs Sees More Price Pain Ahead for Bitcoin,* CNBC (Aug. 3, 2018), https://www.cnbc.com/2018/08/03/goldman-sachs-sees-more-price-pain-ahead-for-bitcoin.html.

50. *See* Jessica Roy, *BitInstant CEO Charlie Shrem Arrested for Alleged Money Laundering,* TIME, Jan. 27, 2014.

51. An excellent account of the Winklevoss brothers' dealings with bitcoin can be found in BEN MEZRICH, BITCOIN BILLIONAIRES: A TRUE STORY OF GENIUS, BETRAYAL, AND REDEMPTION (2019).

52. *See* Sissi Cao, *These Two Venture Capital Firms Are Responsible for the Success of Bitcoin,* OBSERVER (Dec. 1, 2017), http://observer.com/2017/12/these-two-venture-capitalists-are-responsible-for-bitcoins-success/.

53. *See* Marc Andreessen, *Why Bitcoin Matters,* N.Y. TIMES (Jan. 21, 2014), https://dealbook.nytimes.com/2014/01/21/why-bitcoin-matters/.

54. *Id.*

55. *See* Nathaniel Popper, *Can Bitcoin Conquer Argentina?,* N.Y. TIMES, Apr. 29, 2015.

56. *See* Samantha Chang, *Bitcoin's "Patient Zero": Crypto Is an Intellectual Experiment That May Fail (But Probably Won't)*, CCN (Oct. 30, 2018), https://www.ccn.com/bitcoins-patient-zero-crypto-is-an-intellectual-exper iment-that-may-fail-but-probably-wont.

57. *See* NATHANIEL POPPER, DIGITAL GOLD: BITCOIN AND THE INSIDE STORY OF THE MISFITS AND MILLIONAIRES TRYING TO REINVENT MONEY 154 (2015).

58. *See* VIGNA & CASEY, *supra* note 29, at 79.

59. For historical data on bitcoin's exchange rate, see *Historical Data for Bitcoin*, COINMARKETCAP, https://coinmarketcap.com/currencies/bit coin/historical-data/.

60. Comparing bitcoin's volatility to that of the stock market is illumi-nating. Through November 2018, there were only three days in the year when the S&P 500 lost more than 3 percent of its value. Bitcoin, on the other hand, had seven days where it lost more than 10 percent. During the same period, the S&P 500's biggest drop was 4 percent; Bitcoin's was 16 percent. *See* Klint Finley, *Why Bitcoin is Plunging (This Time)*, WIRED (Nov. 21, 2018), https://www.wired.com/ story/why-bitcoin-is-plunging-this-time/. Campbell Harvey, a finance professor at Duke University, explains bitcoin's volatility as a result of existential disagreements about its viability. "With bitcoin, you've got some people that fundamentally believe that it's worth zero. And others that fundamentally believe that it will soon be worth $1 million a coin. So that is a massive amount of disagreement and uncertainty. It translates into extreme volatility." *See* James Doubek, *Bitcoin Is Bouncing Around Again. Here Are Some Possible Causes*, NATIONAL PUBLIC RADIO (Nov. 28, 2018), https://www.npr.org/2018/11/2 8/671133977/bitcoin-is-bouncing-around-again-here-are-some-possible-causes.

61. Finney would later have this to say about his experience mining bitcoins:

> After a few days, bitcoin was running pretty stably, so I left [my computer] running. Those were the days when difficulty was 1, and you could find blocks with a CPU, not even a GPU. I mined several blocks over the next days. But I turned it off because it made my computer run hot, and the fan noise bothered me. In retrospect, I wish I had kept it up longer, but on the other hand I was extraordinarily lucky to be there at the beginning. It's one of those glass half full half empty things. The next I heard of Bitcoin was late 2010, when I was surprised to find that it was not only still going, bitcoins actually had monetary value. I dusted off my old wallet, and was relieved to discover that my bitcoins were still there. As the price climbed up to real money, I transferred the coins into an offline wallet, where hopefully they'll be worth something to my heirs.

Hal Finney, Post to Bitcoin Forum, dated Mar. 19, 2013, https://bitcoin talk.org/index.php?topic=155054.0. *See also* POPPER, *supra* note 57, at 4.

62. See POPPER, *supra* note 57, at 42.
63. See VIGNA & CASEY, *supra* note 29, at 138.
64. Satoshi Nakamoto, Post to BitcoinTalk.org, dated Dec. 12, 2009, https:// bitcointalk.org/index.php?topic=12.
65. VIGNA & CASEY, *supra* note 29, at 140.
66. See Nate Drake, *Best ASIC Devices for Bitcoin Mining in 2018*, BITCOIN MAGAZINE (July 11, 2018), https://www.techradar.com/news/best-asic-devi ces-for-bitcoin-mining-in-2018.
67. Historical data on bitcoin's hash rate can be found at https://www.block chain.com/en/charts/hash-rate.
68. See David Hamilton, *The Top 5 Largest Mining Operations in the World*, COINCENTRAL (May 4, 2018), https://coincentral.com/the-top-5-largest-mi ning-operations-in-the-world/.
69. See Nick Marinoff, *Bitmain Nears 51% of Network Hash Rate: Why This Matters and Why It Doesn't*, BITCOIN MAGAZINE (June 28, 2018), https:// bitcoinmagazine.com/articles/bitmain-nears-51-network-hash-rate-why-m atters-and-why-it-doesnt/.
70. See David Z. Morris, *Chinese Bitcoin Mining Firm Bitmain Made $3 to $4 Billion in Profits Last Year, Says Analyst*, FORTUNE (Feb. 24, 2018), h ttp://fortune.com/2018/02/24/bitcoin-mining-bitmain-profits/.
71. The Goldman Sachs Group 10-K, 2017, https://www.goldmansachs.com/ investor-relations/financials/current/10k/2017-10-k.pdf.
72. Amazon 10-K, 2017, http://services.corporate-ir.net/SEC.Enhanced/Sec Capsule.aspx?c=97664&fid=15414896.
73. For more on mining pools, see NARAYANAN ET AL., BITCOIN AND CRYPTOCURRENCY TECHNOLOGIES: A COMPREHENSIVE INTRODUCTION 125 (2016).
74. See *Features*, DASH, https://docs.dash.org/en/stable/introduction/features .html.
75. See Jackson Palmer, *My Joke Cryptocurrency Hit $2 Billion and Something Is Very Wrong*, MOTHERBOARD (Jan. 11, 2018), https://mother board.vice.com/en_us/article/9kng57/dogecoin-my-joke-cryptocurrency- hit-2-billion-jackson-palmer-opinion.
76. They were, in order of market capitalization: bitcoin, litecoin, peercoin, namecoin, terracoin, devcoin and novacoin. See *Historical Snapshot of April 28, 2013*, COINMARKETCAP, https://coinmarketcap.com/historical/20 130428/.
77. See *Historical Snapshot of January 5, 2014*, COINMARKETCAP, https://coinmar ketcap.com/historical/20140105/.
78. See *Historical Snapshot of January 4, 2015*, COINMARKETCAP, https://coin marketcap.com/historical/20150104/.
79. See *Historical Snapshot of January 3, 2016*, COINMARKETCAP, https://coin marketcap.com/historical/20160103/.

80. *See Historical Snapshot of January 1, 2017*, CoinMarketCap, https://coi nmarketcap.com/historical/20170101/.

81. *See Historical Snapshot of January 7, 2018*, CoinMarketCap, https://coi nmarketcap.com/historical/20180107/.

82. *See* Shannon Liao, *Here's What Happened to the Cryptocurrencies That Celebrities Vouched for*, Verge (July 22, 2018), https://www.theverge.co m/tldr/2018/7/22/17510130/cryptocurrencies-celebrities-scam-paris-hil ton-steven-seagal-akon-mayweather.

83. *See* Paul Vigna, Shane Stifflett & Caitlin Ostroff, *What Crypto Downturn? ICO Fundraising Surges in 2018*, Wall St. J., July 1, 2018.

84. *See* Paul Vigna, *Inside the Chaotic Launch of a $4 Billion Crypto Project*, Wall St. J., June 12, 2018.

85. Shane Shifflett & Coulter Jones, *Buyer Beware: Hundreds of Bitcoin Wannabes Show Hallmarks of Fraud*, Wall St. J., May 17, 2018.

86. This statement appears in section 1.4 of the sale contract, deemed a "EOS Token Purchase Agreement." The warning is repeated in section 7.1 of the contract, which provides that "EOS tokens have no rights, uses, purpose, attributes, functionalities, or features, express or implied." EOS Token Purchase Agreement, dated Sept. 4, 2017, https://eos.io/docu ments/block.one%20-%20EOS%20Token%20Purchase%20Agreement %20-%20September%204,%202017.pdf.

87. *See* Kai Sedgwick, *46% of Last Year's ICOs Have Failed Already*, Bitco in.com (Feb. 23, 2018), https://news.bitcoin.com/46-last-years-icos-failed- already/.

88. *See* Claire Brownell, *Vitalik Buterin: The Cryptocurrency Prophet*, Financial Post (June 27, 2017), https://business.financialpost.com/fea ture/the-cryptocurrency-prophet.

89. *See* Stefan Stankovic, *Who Is Vitalik Buterin, the Mastermind Behind Ethereum?*, Unblock (May 2, 2018), https://unblock.net/who-is-vitalik-b uterin/.

90. *See* Morgan Peck, *The Uncanny Mind That Built Ethereum*, Wired (June 13, 2016), https://www.wired.com/2016/06/the-uncanny-mind-that- built-ethereum/.

91. *See* Brownell, *supra* note 88.

92. *See* Vitalik Buterin, *A Next-Generation Smart Contract and Decentralized Application Platform* (White Paper), https://github.com/ ethereum/wiki/wiki/White-Paper.

93. *Id.*

94. *See* Vitalik Buterin, *So Where Did the Name Ethereum Come From?*, Ethereum Cmty. Forum, https://forum.ethereum.org/discussion/com ment/3389/#Comment_3389.

95. *See* Vigna & Casey, *supra* note 29, at 232.

96. *See* Paul Vigna, *Wall Street, City Banks Join Blockchain-Focused Consortium*, WALL ST. J., Sept. 15, 2015.
97. *See* Robert Hackett, *Why J.P. Morgan Chase Is Building a Blockchain on Ethereum*, FORTUNE, Oct. 4, 2016.
98. *See* Ian Allison, *Enterprise Ethereum Alliance Is Back – And It's Got a Roadmap to Prove It*, COINDESK, May 3, 2018.
99. *See* Avi Salzman, *Blockchain Is Starting to Show Real Promise amid the Hype*, BARRON, Aug. 17, 2018.
100. For more information on the Fizzy project, see AXA's website devoted to the project at https://fizzy.axa/en-gb/faq.
101. *See* Salzman, *supra* note 99.
102. *See* Maxime Biais, *Analyzing Smart Contract Public Data* (Jan. 22, 2019), https://bia.is/2019/01/22/fizzy-analysis/.
103. *See* Joseph Young, *7 Investors Back World's First Blockchain Demand from Institutions*, CCN (Aug. 26, 2018), https://www.ccn.com/7-investors-back-worlds-first-blockchain-bond-demand-from-institutions/.
104. *See* Laura Shin, *Industries, Looking for Efficiency, Turn to Blockchains*, N.Y. TIMES, June 27, 2018.
105. *See* Solution Brief, TRADELENS, https://tradelens.com/solution/.
106. *See* Ian Allison, *IBM and Maersk Struggle to Sign Partners to Shipping Blockchain*, CCN (Oct. 26, 2018), https://www.coindesk.com/ibm-block chain-maersk-shipping-struggling.
107. *See Butterfly Ballot*, BBC NEWS (Nov. 23, 2000), http://news.bbc.co.uk/2/hi/in_depth/americas/2000/us_elections/glossary/a-b/1037172.stm.
108. Bush v. Gore, 531 U.S. 98 (2000).
109. *See* Ford Fessenden & John M. Broder, *Examining the Vote: The Overview*, N.Y. TIMES, Aug. 29, 2001.
110. Indeed, many of these efforts were spearheaded by President Bush himself. In 2002, Bush signed into law the Help America Vote Act (HAVA), providing funding for states to update and upgrade their voting systems. For an overview of HAVA's structure, see Leonard M. Shambon, *Implementing the Help America Vote Act*, 3 ELECTION L.J. 424 (2004).
111. *See* Michael Harriott, *On Conspiracy Theories and Election Hacking*, ROOT (Aug. 1, 2018), https://www.theroot.com/evidence-shows-hackers-changed-votes-in-the-2016-electi-1827871206.
112. *See Hackers Break into Voting Machines Within 2 Hours at Defcon*, CBS NEWS (July 30, 2017), https://www.cbsnews.com/amp/news/hackers-break-into-voting-machines-defcon-las-vegas/?__twitter_impression=true.
113. *See* LAWRENCE NORDEN & CHRISTOPHER FAMIGHETTI, AMERICA'S VOTING MACHINES AT RISK (Brennan Center for Justice 2015).
114. *See* Jens Manuel Krogstad & Mark Hugo Lopez, *Black Voter Turnout Fell in 2016, Even as a Record Number of Americans Cast Ballots*, PEW RES. CTR., May 12, 2017.

115. *See* Domenico Montanaro, Rachel Wellford & Simone Pathe, *2014 Midterm Election Turnout Lowest in 70 Years*, PBS NEWSHOUR (Nov. 10, 2014), https://www.pbs.org/newshour/politics/2014-midterm-elec tion-turnout-lowest-in-70-years.

116. In the 2016 presidential elections, the voting rate for eligible white citizens was 65 percent. The comparable number for black citizens was 60 percent. The number for Asian and Hispanic citizens was even lower, at 49 and 48 percent, respectively. *See* Krogstad & Lopez, *supra* note 114.

117. In 2016, 63 percent of women voted, while 59 percent of men did. *Id.*

118. In the 2016 presidential elections, 49 percent of millennials (people between the age of eighteen and thirty-five) voted, while 70 percent of the Silent/Greatest Generation (people over seventy-one years of age) did. *Id.*

119. Agora later issued a revised version of the release that was entitled "Swiss-based Agora records first government election on blockchain as accredited observer in Sierra Leone." *See* Agora, *Swiss-Based Agora Records First Government Election on Blockchain as Accredited Observer in Sierra Leone*, MEDIUM (Mar. 9, 2018), https://medium .com/agorablockchain/swiss-based-agora-powers-worlds-first-ever-block chain-elections-in-sierra-leone-984dd07a58ee.

120. *See* National Electoral Commission of Sierra Leone, Twitter post of Mar. 19, 2018, https://twitter.com/NECsalone/status/975773726703804419/.

121. Agora, *Agora Official Statement Regarding Sierra Leone Election*, MEDIUM (Mar. 20, 2018), https://medium.com/agorablockchain/agora-official-statement-regarding-sierra-leone-election-7730d2d9de4e.

122. *See* Donie O'Sullivan, *West Virginia to Introduce Mobile Phone Voting for Midterm Elections*, CNN (Aug. 6, 2018), https://money .cnn.com/2018/08/06/technology/mobile-voting-west-virginia-voatz/in dex.html; Benjamin Freed, *West Virginia Says 144 People Voted Using Mobile Blockchain App*, STATESCOOP (Nov. 7, 2018), https://statescoop .com/west-virginia-says-144-people-voted-using-mobile-blockchain-app/; Brian Fung, *West Virginians Abroad in 29 Countries Have Voted by Mobile Device, in the Biggest Blockchain-Based Voting Test Ever*, WASHINGTON POST, Nov. 6, 2018.

123. *See* O'Sullivan, *supra* note 122.

4 CRYPTO-CRIMINALS

1. *See US Indicts Suspected Russian "Mastermind" of $4 Billion Bitcoin Laundering Scheme*, EKATHIMERINI (July 27, 2017), http://www.ekathimer ini.com/220437/article/ekathimerini/news/us-indicts-suspected-russian-mastermind-of-4-billion-bitcoin-laundering-scheme; Richard Chirgwin,

Greek Police Arrest Chap Accused of Laundering $4bn of Bitcoin, REGISTER (July 27, 2017), https://www.theregister.co.uk/2017/07/27/greek_police_arres t_alleged_russian_bitcoin_launderer/; Costas Kantouris, *Greek Police See Leads in Money Laundering Suspect's Phone*, ASSOCIATED PRESS (July 27, 2017), https://www.usnews.com/news/business/articles/2017–07-27/greek-police-see-leads-in-money-laundering-suspects-phone; Justin Scheck & Bradley Hope, *The Man Who Solved Bitcoin's Most Notorious Heist*, WALL ST. J., Aug. 10, 2018; Andy Greenberg, *Corrupt Silk Road Investigator Re-Arrested for Allegedly Trying to Flee the US*, WIRED (Feb. 1, 2016), https://www.wired.com/2016/02/corrupt-silk-road-investigator-re-arres ted-trying-to-flee-the-us/; Sarah Jeong, *Criminal Charges Against Agents Reveal Staggering Corruption in the Silk Road Investigation*, FORBES (Mar. 31, 2015), https://www.forbes.com/sites/sarahjeong/2015/03/31/force-and-bridges/#6c7b19b138c5; Exhibit A – Affidavit of Special Agent Tigran Gambaryan in Support of Documents Submitted at Detention Hearing, United States v. Force, No. 3 CR-15-70370 (N.D. Cal. Apr. 29, 2015), https:// www.documentcloud.org/documents/2070122-gov-uscourts-cand-286034– 22-0.html.

2. Indictment at 7, United States v. BTC-E & Vinnik, No. CR 16-00227 SI (N.D. Cal. Jan. 17, 2017).

3. *Id.*

4. Costas Kantouris, *Russia Blasts Greece over Cybercrime Suspect's Extradition*, ASSOCIATED PRESS, July 13, 2018.

5. *See Greek Police Uncover Plan to Kill Russian National Arrested in Greece*, SPUTNIK NEWS (Oct. 5, 2018), https://sputniknews.com/europe/201805101 064329910-greece-police-russian-national-plan-kill/.

6. *See* Joshuah Bearman & Tomer Hanuka, *The Rise and Fall of Silk Road*, WIRED (May 2015), https://www.wired.com/2015/04/silk-road-1/.

7. *See* Eleni Chrepa, Olga Kharif & Kartikay Mehrotra, *Bitcoin Suspect Could Shed Light on Russian Mueller Targets*, BLOOMBERG (Sept. 4, 2018), https://www.bloomberg.com/news/articles/2018–09-04/bitcoin-sus pect-could-shed-light-on-russians-targeted-by-mueller; Nathaniel Popper & Matthew Rosenberg, *How Russian Spies Hid Behind Bitcoin in Hacking Campaign*, N.Y. TIMES, July 13, 2018; Indictment, United States v. Netyksho, No. 1:18-cr-00215 (D.C. Dist. Ct. July 13, 2018), http s://int.nyt.com/data/documenthelper/80-netyksho-et-al-indictment/b a0521c1eef869deecbe/optimized/full.pdf.

8. Alex Hern, *Bill Gates: Cryptocurrencies Have "Caused Deaths in a Fairly Direct Way,"* GUARDIAN, Feb. 28, 2018.

9. Hugh Son, Hannah Levitt & Brian Louis, *Jamie Dimon Slams Bitcoin as a "Fraud,"* BLOOMBERG (Sept. 12, 2017), https://www.bloomberg.com/ne ws/articles/2017-09-12/jpmorgan-s-ceo-says-he-d-fire-traders-who-bet-on-fraud-bitcoin.

10. Paul R. La Monica, *Warren Buffett Says Bitcoin Is "Rat Poison,"* CNN (May 8, 2018), https://money.cnn.com/2018/05/07/investing/warren-buf fett-bitcoin/index.html.

11. See Sean Foley, Jonathan R. Karlsen & Talis J. Putnis, *Sex, Drugs, and Bitcoin: How Much Illegal Activity Is Financed Through Cryptocurrencies?* (Working Paper, Jan. 2018), https://papers.ssrn.com/sol3/papers.cfm? abstract_id=3102645.

12. See *Flaws in Bitcoin Make a Lasting Revival Unlikely*, ECONOMIST, Mar. 27, 2019.

13. See Joseph Young, *6 Million Bitcoin Is Lost or Stolen, Should the Real Value of BTC Higher?*, CCN (July 4, 2018), https://www.ccn.com/6-mil lion-bitcoin-is-lost-or-stolen-should-the-real-value-of-btc-higher/.

14. See Eric Larchevêque, *2018: A Record-Breaking Year for Crypto Exchange Hacks*, COINDESK (Dec. 29, 2018), https://www.coindesk.co m/2018-a-record-breaking-year-for-crypto-exchange-hacks. It is worth noting that traditional currencies are also the subject of much crim-inal activity, and indeed share many features with bitcoin. Cash is anonymous, largely untraceable and nearly instantaneous. Handing over dollar bills to a drug dealer is also significantly simpler than arranging a transfer of bitcoin to him. And it is not as if traditional currencies are not subject to hacking and cyberintrusions either. In 2016, fifteen million consumers were victims of identity theft or fraud, leading to the loss of $16 billion. See Kelli B. Grant, *Identity Theft, Fraud Cost Consumers More than $16 Billion*, CNBC (Feb. 1, 2017), https://www.cnbc.com/2017/02/01/consumers-lost-more-than-16b-to-frau d-and-identity-theft-last-year.html. This is many times the amount of losses from cryptocurrency thefts. Harvard economist Kenneth Rogoff has gone so far as to argue that cash is such a magnet for crime that it should be eliminated outright. "The 'profits' governments reap by blindly accommodating demand for cash are dwarfed by the costs of the illegal activity that cash, especially big bills, facilitates," he wrote in a 2016 book on the topic. "The effect of curtailing paper currency on tax evasion alone would likely cover the lost profits from printing paper currency, even if tax evasion fell by only 10–15%. The effect on illegal activities is probably even more important." KENNETH ROGOFF, THE CURSE OF CASH: HOW LARGE-DENOMINATION BILLS AID CRIME AND TAX EVASION AND CONSTRAIN MONETARY POLICY 2 (2016).

15. See Steven Russolillo & Eun-Young Jeong, *Cryptocurrency Exchanges Are Getting Hacked Because It's Easy*, WALL ST. J., July 16, 2018.

16. See Danny Palmer, *WannaCry Ransomware: Hackers Behind Global Cyberattack Finally Cash Out Bitcoin Windfall*, ZDNET (Aug. 3, 2017), https://www.zdnet.com/article/wannacry-ransomware-hackers-behind-gl obal-cyberattack-finally-cash-out-bitcoin-windfall/.

17. PLATO, REPUBLIC bk. II.
18. For an excellent introduction to the utilitarian approach to crime, see Gary S. Becker, *Crime and Punishment: An Economic Approach*, 76 J. POL. ECON. 169 (1968); Steven Shavell, *Criminal Law and the Optimal Use of Nonmonetary Sanctions as a Deterrent*, 85 COLUM. L. REV. 1232 (1985); ROBERT COOTER & THOMAS ULEN, LAW AND ECONOMICS (6th ed. 2016); RICHARD A. POSNER, ECONOMIC ANALYSIS OF LAW (9th ed. 2014).
19. *See* Becker, *supra* note 18, at 176.
20. Dan M. Kahan, *Social Influence, Social Meaning, and Deterrence*, 83 VA. L. REV. 349, 378 (1997).
21. *See* Chen-Bo Zhong, Vanessa K. Bhons & Francesca Gino, *Good Lamps Are the Best Police: Darkness Increases Dishonesty and Self-Interested Behavior*, 21 PSYCH. SCI. 311 (2010).
22. *See* Scheck & Hope, *supra* note 1.
23. *See* Kyle Baird, *Brian Armstrong Claims Coinbase Is Registering 50,000 New Users Per Day*, BITCOINIST.COM (Aug. 15, 2018), https://bitcoinist.com/brian-armstrong-coinbase-registering-50000-new-users-per-day/.
24. *See* FEDERAL BUREAU OF INVESTIGATION, BANK CRIME STATISTICS1 (2013)
25. *See* INTERNET CRIME COMPLAINT CENTER, INTERNET CRIME REPORT 6 (2010).
26. *See* ShapeShift Website, visited Sept. 28, 2018, https://info.shapeshift.io.
27. *See* Justin Scheck & Shane Shifflett, *How Dirty Money Disappears into the Black Hole of Cryptocurrency*, WALL ST. J., Sept. 28, 2018.
28. The literature on social norms and the law is voluminous. For a few canonical examples, see Kahan, supra note 20; Lawrence Lessig, *The Regulation of Social Meaning*, 62 U. CHI. L. REV. 943 (1995); Cass R. Sunstein, *Social Norms and Social Roles*, 96 COLUM. L. REV. 903 (1996).
29. *See* Kahan, *supra* note 20, at 359.
30. *See* Christine M. Schroeder & Deborah A. Prentice, *Exposing Pluralistic Ignorance to Reduce Alcohol Use Among College Students*, 28 J. APPLIED SOC. PSYCHOL. 2150 (1998).
31. *See* Kahan, *supra* note 20, at 362.
32. *See* Charisse Jones, *Crack and Punishment: Is Race the Issue?*, N.Y. TIMES, Oct. 28, 1995.
33. For a comprehensive analysis of the rationale behind the crack-cocaine disparity and its disproportionate impact on African Americans, see David A. Sklansky, *Cocaine, Race, and Equal Protection*, 47 STAN. L. REV. 1283 (1995).
34. *See* Gertrude Chavez-Dreyfuss, *Cryptocurrency Thefts, Scams Hit $1.7 Billion in 2018*, REUTERS (Jan. 29, 2019), https://www.reuters.com/article/us-crypto-currency-crime/cryptocurrency-thefts-scams-hit-1-7-billion-in-2018-report-idUSKCN1PN1SQ.

35. KASPERSKY LAB, KSN REPORT: RANSOMWARE AND MALICIOUS CRYPTOMINERS 2016–2018 (2018), https://media.kasperskycontenthub.com/wp-content/up loads/sites/58/2018/06/27125925/KSN-report_Ransomware-and-malicious-cryptominers_2016–2018_ENG.pdf.

36. *Id.*

37. KASPERSKY LAB, KASPERSKY SECURITY BULLETIN: THREAT PREDICTIONS FOR CRYPTOCURRENCIES IN 2018 (Nov. 15, 2017), https://securelist.com/ksb-thr eat-predictions-for-cryptocurrencies-in-2018/83188/.

38. DAVID AXELROD, THE EVOLUTION OF COOPERATION 21 (2006).

39. *Id.* at 60–61.

40. Didicito, *Can somebody tell me how anybody with money on MtGox was not a greedy awful and stupid speculator?*, REDDIT (Feb. 28, 2014), https:// www.reddit.com/r/Bitcoin/comments/1z7y2d/can_somebody_tell_me_ how_anybody_with_money_on/.

41. Ittay Eyal & Emin Gün Sirer, *Majority Is Not Enough: Bitcoin Mining Is Vulnerable*, ARXIV (Nov. 2013), https://www.cs.cornell.edu/~ie53/publica tions/btcProcFC.pdf.

42. @el33th4xor, TWITTER (May 29, 2018, 6:13 PM), https://twitter.com/el33t h4xor/status/1001632762561007621.

43. Matt Blaze, *Stop Ignoring Those "Update Your Device" Messages*, N.Y. TIMES, Mar. 27, 2019.

44. See NATHANIEL POPPER, DIGITAL GOLD: BITCOIN AND THE INSIDE STORY OF THE MISFITS AND MILLIONAIRES TRYING TO REINVENT MONEY 55–56 (2015).

45. Satoshi Nakamoto, Post to bitcointalk.org, dated Dec. 12, 2010, https://bi tcointalk.org/index.php?action=profile;u=3;sa=showPosts.

46. Max Weber, *Politics as a Vocation, Lecture Delivered in 1918, in* FROM MAX WEBER: ESSAYS IN SOCIOLOGY 79 (H.H. Gerth & C. Wright Mills eds., London, Routledge 1948).

47. George L. Kelling & James Q. Wilson, *Broken Windows: The Police and Neighborhood Safety*, ATLANTIC, Mar. 1982.

48. See Philip Zimbardo, *Anonymity of Place Stimulates Destructive Vandalism*, LUCIFER EFFECT, http://www.lucifereffect.com/about_conten t_anon.htm.

49. See Bernard E. Harcourt & Jens Ludwig, *Broken Windows: New Evidence from New York City and a Five-City Social Experiment*, 73 U. CHI. L. REV. 271 (2006); Hope Corman & Naci Mocan, *Carrots, Sticks, and Broken Windows*, 48 J.L. & ECON. 235 (2005). Anthony A. Braga et al., *Can Policing Disorder Reduce Crime? A Systematic Review and Meta-Analysis*, 52 J. RES. CRIME & DELINQ. 567 (2015); Adam M. Samaha, *Regulation for the Sake of Appearance*, 125 HARV. L. REV. 1563 (2012).

50. See Kees Keizer, Siegwart Lindenberg & Linda Steg, *The Spreading of Disorder*, 322 SCIENCE 1681 (2008).

51. *See* Neal Kumar Katyal, *Criminal Law in Cyberspace,* 149 U. PA. L. REV. 1003, 1008 (2001).

5 THE ENERGY HUNT

1. Interview with Nils Lindh, Oct. 16, 2018.
2. *See Bitcoin: The Magic of Mining,* ECONOMIST, Jan. 8, 2015.
3. *See* Stan Higgins, *Bitcoin Mining Firm KnCMiner Declares Bankruptcy,* COINDESK (May 27, 2016), https://www.coindesk.com/kncminer-declares-bankruptcy-cites-upcoming-bitcoin-subsidy-halving/.
4. *See* Natalie Obiko Pearson & Brandon Kochkodin, *Hive Switches from Mining Gold to Bitcoin, Surges Six-Fold,* BLOOMBERG (Oct. 12, 2017), htt ps://www.bloomberg.com/news/articles/2017–10-12/hive-switches-from-mi ning-gold-to-bitcoin-surges-six-six-fold.
5. *See* HIVE BLOCKCHAIN TECHNOLOGIES, *Take an Exclusive 360 ° VR Tour Inside HIVE,* YOUTUBE (May 14, 2018), https://www.youtube.com/watch? v=73fqVCH5F4U.
6. *See* Christoph Steitz & Stephen Jewkes, *Cryptocurrency Miners Seek Cheap Energy in Norway and Sweden,* REUTERS (Apr. 10, 2018), https://c a.reuters.com/article/businessNews/idCAKBN1HH13L-OCABS.
7. *Id.*
8. *HIVE Blockchain Commences Ethereum Mining Operations in Sweden,* HIVE BLOCKCHAIN TECHNOLOGIES (Jan. 15, 2018), https://www.hiveblock chain.com/news/hive-blockchain-commences-ethereum-mining-opera tions-in-sweden/.
9. *See* Anna Baydakova, *Genesis Mining to End Unprofitable Crypto Contracts,* COINDESK (Aug. 16, 2018), https://www.coindesk.com/genesis-mining-to-end-unprofitable-crypto-contracts/.
10. Aaron Hankin, *Bitcoin Mining Poses Threat to Paris Climate-Change Accord, Study Finds,* MARKETWATCH (Aug. 1, 2018), https://www.market watch.com/story/bitcoin-mining-poses-threat-to-paris-climate-change-acc ord-study-finds-2018–08-01.
11. Rebecca Pinnington, *Shock Claim: Bitcoin Is DESTROYING the Planet and Uses as Much Energy as DENMARK,* EXPRESS (Dec. 5, 2017), https:// www.express.co.uk/news/science/888535/bitcoin-environment-destroy ing-planet-fossil-fuels-energy-electricity-Denmark-US-2020.
12. Anthony Cuthbertson, *Bitcoin Mining on Track to Consume All of the World's Energy by 2020,* NEWSWEEK (Dec. 11, 2017), https://www.news week.com/bitcoin-mining-track-consume-worlds-energy-2020–744036.
13. Alex de Vries, *Bitcoin's Growing Energy Problem,* 2 JOULE 801, 801 (2018).
14. *Bitcoin Energy Consumption Index,* DIGICONOMIST, https://digiconomist .net/bitcoin-energy-consumption. Another study, published in *Nature Sustainability* in November 2018, concluded that bitcoin mining

consumes approximately 8.3 tWh per year. Max J. Krause & Thabet Tolaymat, *Quantification of Energy and Carbon Costs for Mining Cryptocurrencies*, NATURE SUSTAINABILITY (2018).

15. *Ethereum Energy Consumption Index*, DIGICONOMIST, https://digicono mist.net/bitcoin-energy-consumption.
16. *See How Much Electricity Does an American Home Use?*, U.S. ENERGY INFO. ADMIN. (Nov. 7, 2017), https://www.eia.gov/tools/faqs/fa q.php?id=97&t=3; *New Academic Paper: Bitcoin's Growing Energy Problem*, DIGICONOMIST (May 16, 2018), https://digiconomist.net/bit coins-growing-energy-problem.
17. *See* Adam Rogers, *The Hard Math Behind Bitcoin's Global Warming Problem*, WIRED (Dec. 15, 2017), https://www.wired.com/story/bitcoin-glo bal-warming/.
18. Camilo Mora et al., *Bitcoin Emissions Alone Could Push Global Warming Above 2°C*, 8 NATURE CLIMATE CHANGE 931 (2018).
19. *A Deep Dive in a Real-World Bitcoin Mine*, DIGICONOMIST (Oct. 25, 2018), https://digiconomist.net/deep-dive-real-world-bitcoin-mine.
20. Technically, the mining difficulty adjusts after every 2,016 blocks. This means that if new blocks are being mined at the desired rate of one every ten minutes, then the difficulty will be reset every two weeks. In practice, the difficulty has adjusted more frequently than that, due to the fact that new mining power continues to be added to the network and thus new blocks are being mined more often than every ten minutes. The difficulty is adjusted based on the following equation:

Next difficulty = (previous difficulty x 2016 x 10 minutes) / (time in minutes to mine last 2016 blocks)

As the equation shows, if it took less than two weeks to mine 2,016 blocks, then the difficulty level will be increased for the next period. If, on the other hand, it took more than two weeks to mine 2,016 blocks, then the difficulty level will be lowered. *See* ARVIND NARAYANAN, JOSEPH BONNEAU, EDWARD FELTEN, ANDREW MILLER & STEVEN GOLDFEDER, BITCOIN AND CRYPTOCURRENCY TECHNOLOGIES: A COMPREHENSIVE INTRODUCTION 107–10 (2016).
21. *See Antminer S9-Hydro*, BITMAIN, https://shop.bitmain.com/product/deta il?pid=00020180927145605797A1iDnSogo6BF.
22. For more data on the historical development of hash power on the bitcoin network, see https://www.blockchain.com/en/charts/hash-rate?timespan=all.
23. *See* Alison Sider, *Bitcoin Mania Triggers Miner Influx to Rural Washington*, WALL ST. J., Feb. 11, 2018.
24. *See Bitcoin: The Magic of Mining*, ECONOMIST, Jan. 8, 2015.
25. *See* Sider, *supra* note 23.
26. *See* Kimberlee Craig, *PUD Board Hears Comment on Proposed Cryptocurrency Rate*, CHELAN CTY. PUB. UTIL. DIST. (Aug. 6, 2018),

https://www.chelanpud.org/about-us/newsroom/news/2018/08/07/pud-bo
ard-hears-comment-on-proposed-cryptocurrency-rate.

27. *See* Kimberlee Craig, *Board Approves New Cryptocurrency Rate
Effective April 1, 2019,* CHELAN CTY. PUB. UTIL. DIST. (Dec. 3, 2018),
http://www.chelanpud.org/about-us/newsroom/news/2018/12/03/board-a
pproves-new-cryptocurrency-rate-effective-april-1-2019.

28. *See* Tom Banse *Cryptocurrency Miners Go to Federal Court to Block
"Crippling" Electric Rate Hike,* KLCC (Mar. 19, 2019), https://www.klcc
.org/post/cryptocurrency-miners-go-federal-court-block-crippling-elec
tric-rate-hike.

29. *See* JUNIPER RESEARCH, THE FUTURE OF CRYPTOCURRENCY: BITCOIN AND
ALTCOIN TRENDS & CHALLENGES 2018–2023 (2018).

30. *See Visa Acceptance For Retailers,* VISA, https://usa.visa.com/run-your-
business/small-business-tools/retail.html.

31. BANK FOR INTERNATIONAL SETTLEMENTS, ANNUAL ECONOMIC REPORT
99–100 (2018).

32. *See* Christine Kim & Nikhilesh De, *Bitmain Confirms New Crypto
Mining Facility in Texas,* COINDESK (Aug. 6, 2018), https://www.coin
desk.com/bitmain-confirms-new-texas-mining-facility/.

33. *See Private Investors Buying Electric Power Stations in Russia to Mine
Cryptocurrency,* RT (Jan. 12, 2018), https://www.rt.com/business/415811-ru
ssia-power-station-cryptocurrenct-mining/.

34. *See* David Pimentel, *IoT Blockchain, Mining Distributor RBG Sign
$190M AUD Crypto Mining Deal,* BLOCKTRIBUNE (May 8, 2019), htt
p://blocktribune.com/iot-blockchain-rbg-sign-142m-crypto-mining-deal/
.

35. *See* Rick Noack, *Cryptocurrency Mining in Iceland Is Using So
Much Energy, The Electricity May Run Out,* WASH. POST, Feb. 13,
2018.

36. *See* Nick Marinoff, *Bitmain Nears 51% of Network Hash Rate: Why This
Matters and Why It Doesn't,* BITCOIN MAGAZINE (June 28, 2018), https://
bitcoinmagazine.com/articles/bitmain-nears-51-network-hash-rate-why-
matters-and-why-it-doesnt/.

37. Bitmain also earned revenue from its mining pool and mining farm
services. These amounts were $43 million and $22 million,
respectively.

38. BitMain's draft prospectus can be found at http://www.hkexnews.hk/APP/
SEHK/2018/2018092406/Documents/SEHK201809260017.pdf.

39. *See* Zheping Huang, *This Could Be the Beginning of the End of China's
Dominance in Bitcoin Mining,* QUARTZ (Jan. 5, 2018), https://qz.com/117
2632/chinas-dominance-in-bitcoin-mining-under-threat-as-regulators-hit-
where-it-hurts-electricity/.

40. Charles LeCavalier, *Hydro-Québec face à une "spirale de la mort,"* Le Journal de Québec (Jan. 9, 2018), https://www.journaldequebec.com/20 18/01/09/hydro-pourrait-se-lancer-dans-les-maisons-intelligentes.

41. Garrick Hileman & Michel Rauchs, Global Cryptocurrency Benchmarking Study 85 (2017).

42. For the classic exposition of the tragedy of the commons, see Garrett Hardin, *The Tragedy of the Commons*, 162 Science 1243 (1968).

43. Alfred W. Tucker, *The Mathematics of Tucker: A Sampler*, 14 Two-Year C. Math. J. 228, 228 (1983).

44. Satoshi Nakamoto, Post to BitcoinTalk.org, dated Dec. 12, 2009, https:// bitcointalk.org/index.php?topic=12.

45. *See* Megan Geuss, *Construction to Begin on 36 Megawatt Moroccan Wind Farm for Bitcoin Mining*, Ars Technica (Sept. 18, 2018), https://arstech nica.com/information-technology/2018/09/construction-to-begin-on-36-megawatt-moroccan-wind-farm-for-bitcoin-mining/.

46. Nathaniel Popper, *There Is Nothing Virtual About Bitcoin's Energy Appetite*, N.Y. Times, Jan. 21, 2018.

47. *See* Vlad Zamfir, *The History of Casper – Part 1*, Medium (Dec. 6, 2016), https://medium.com/@Vlad_Zamfir/the-history-of-casper-part-1-59233819c9a9.

48. Socrates, Apology.

49. The Federalist, No. 74, at 500 (Alexander Hamilton) (Jacob E. Cooke ed., 1961).

50. The Records of the Federal Convention of 1787 318–19 (Max Farrand ed., 1937) [hereinafter Records].

51. James Madison, *Public Opinion*, Nat'l Gazette, Dec. 19, 1791.

52. The Federalist, No. 4, at 19 (Alexander Hamilton) (Jacob E. Cooke ed., 1961).

53. Joseph Story, Commentaries on the Constitution of the United States 60 (1833).

54. The Debates in the Several State Conventions on the Adoption of the Federal Constitution 528 (Jonathan Elliot ed., 1836–45).

55. Records, *supra* note 50, at 319.

56. Or, as John Hart Ely wrote in his book, *War and Responsibility*, "author-ization [of war] by the entire Congress was foreseeably calculated, for one thing, to slow the process down, to insure that there would be a pause, a 'sober second thought,' before the nation was plunged into anything as momentous as war." John Hart Ely, War and Responsibility: Constitutional Lessons of Vietnam and Its Aftermath 4 (1993).

57. Alexander M. Bickel, *Congress, The President, and the Power to Wage War*, 48 Chicago Kent L. Rev. 131, 144((1971).

6 THE PENUMBRA PROBLEM

1. The facts are drawn from various filings the Securities Exchange Commission and the Department of Justice made in their cases against Zaslavskiy and his companies. SEC v. REcoin Group Foundation et al., Civil Action No. 17-cv-05725 (E.D.N.Y. 2017); United States v. Zaslavskiy, 1:17-cr-00647-RJD (E.D.N.Y. 2017).

2. *See* Post to BITCOINTALK, dated July 11, 2017, https://bitcointalk.org/index .php?topic=2014062.0.

3. Interview of Maksim Zaslavskiy by the Securities and Exchange Commission (Sept. 20, 2017).

4. Rule 10b-5 of the Securities Exchange Act of 1934 provides, in full:

> It shall be unlawful for any person, directly or indirectly, by the use of any means or instrumentality of interstate commerce, or of the mails or of any facility of any national securities exchange,
>
> (a) To employ any device, scheme, or artifice to defraud,
> (b) To make any untrue statement of a material fact or to omit to state a material fact necessary in order to make the statements made, in the light of the circumstances under which they were made, not misleading, or
> (c) To engage in any act, practice, or course of business which operates or would operate as a fraud or deceit upon any person, in connection with the purchase or sale of any security.

   17 CFR 140.10b-5.

5. SEC v. W.J. Howey Co., 328 U.S. 293, 301 (1946).

6. *See Brooklyn Businessman Pleads Guilty to Defrauding Investors Through Two Initial Coin Offerings* U.S. ATTORNEY'S OFF. E DIST. N.Y. (Nov. 15, 2018), https://www.justice.gov/usao-edny/pr/brooklyn-businessman-plead s-guilty-defrauding-investors-through-two-initial-coin.

7. The hypothetical is drawn from a problem presented by H.L.A. Hart in his article *Positivism and the Separation of Law and Morals*. In it, Hart articulates the problem as follows:

> A legal rule forbids you to take a vehicle into the public park. Plainly this forbids an automobile, but what about bicycles, roller skates, toy automobiles? What about airplanes? Are these, as we say, to be called 'vehicles' for the purpose of the rule or not.

   H.L.A. Hart, *Positivism and the Separation of Law and Morals*, 71 HARV. L. REV. 593, 607 (1958).

8. Jacobellis v. Ohio, 378 U.S. 184, 197 (1964) (Stewart, J., concurring).

9. Hart, *supra* note 8, at 607.

10. For interested readers, *Carpenter v. United States*, 585 U.S. __ (2018), provides a good example of how the Supreme Court struggles to apply the

Constitution to new technology, in that case to mobile phones and location data.

11. When asked whether the quote is accurately attributed to him, Henry Kissinger replied, "I'm not sure I actually said it, but it's a good phrase." *See* Marcin Sobczyk, *Kissinger Still Lacks a Number to Call Europe*, WALL ST. J., June 27, 2012.

12. The SEC has recognized the difficulty of regulating blockchain. In a brief the SEC filed in the Zaslavskiy case, they categorized the problem as multifold:

> Several characteristics of how ICOs are conducted pose challenges for law enforcement in investigating fraud. For example, (1) tracing funds: traditional financial institutions (such as banks) often are not involved, making it harder to follow the flow of funds; (2) international scope: blockchain transactions and users span the globe and there may be restrictions on how the SEC can obtain and use information from foreign jurisdictions; (3) no central authority: as there is no central authority that collects blockchain user information, the SEC generally must rely on other sources, such as digital asset exchanges, for this type of information; (4) seizing or freezing digital assets: digital "wallets" (software that "stores" digital assets) may be encrypted and, unlike money held in a bank or brokerage account, may not be held by a third-party custodian; (5) anonymity: many digital assets are specifically designed to be pseudonymous or anonymous; thus, attribution of a specific digital asset to an individual or entity could be difficult or impossible, especially where additional anonymizing tools are employed; and (6) evolving technology: digital assets involve new and developing technologies.

Brief of SEC in Support of US in Opposition to Defendant's Motion to Dismiss Indictment, U.S. v. Zaslavskiy, 2018 WL 2016191 (Mar. 19, 2018).

13. FRANZ KAFKA, THE PROBLEM OF OUR LAWS (Michael Hoffman trans., 2015).

14. One of these hotels, the Hotel Floridan, was later blown up in an episode of the TV show *Thunder in Paradise*, a show whose primary claim to fame is that it starred Hulk Hogan. *See* Rick Reed, *Old Howey Hotel to Explode on Hulk Hogan Show*, ORLANDO SENTINEL, Mar. 15, 1994.

15. SEC v. W.J. Howey Co., 328 U.S. 293, 298–301 (1946).

16. *Get Started with Bitcoin*, BITCOIN (emphasis added), https://bitcoin.org (accessed Nov. 9, 2018).

17. *See* Jeffrey E. Alberts & Bertrand Fry, *Is Bitcoin a Security*, 21 B.U. J. SCI. & TECH. L. 1 (2015); Todd Henderson & Max Raskin, *A Regulatory Classification of Digital Assets: Towards an Operational Howey Test for Cryptocurrencies, ICOs, and Other Digital Assets*, SSRN Working Draft, https://www.ssrn.com/abstract=3265295.

18. William Hinman, *Digital Asset Transactions: When Howey Met Gary (Plastic)*, Remarks at the Yahoo Finance All Markets Summit: Crypto (June 14, 2018), https://www.sec.gov/news/speech/speech-hinman-061418.

19. *See* U.S. Securities & Exchange Commission, Framework for "Investment Contract" Analysis of Digital Assets (2019), https://www.sec.gov/corpfin/framework-investment-contract-analysis-digital-assets#_edn1.

20. Jay Clayton, *Statement on Cryptocurrencies and Initial Coin Offerings* (Dec. 11, 2017), https://www.sec.gov/news/public-statement/statement-clayton-2017-12-11.

21. *See* PriceWaterhouseCoopers, Considering an IPO: The Costs of Going and Being Public May Surprise You (2012), https://www.strategyand.pwc.com/media/file/Strategyand_Considering-an-IPO.pdf.

22. 31 U.S.C. § 5312(a)(2).

23. 31 C.F.R. § 1010.100(m).

24. 31 C.F.R. § 1010.100(ff)(5)(i)(A) (emphasis added).

25. Dep't of the Treasury, Fin. Crimes Enf't Network, Application of FinCEN's Regulations to Persons Administering, Exchanging, or Using Virtual Currencies (Mar. 18, 2013), https://www.fincen.gov/resources/statutes-regulations/guidance/application-fincens-regulations-persons-administering.

26. 31 U.S.C. §§ 5318(a)(2) and 5318(h); 31 C.F.R. § 1011.210.

27. *See generally* Peter Van Valkenburg, Bank Secrecy Act, Cryptocurrencies, and New Tokens: What Is Known and What Remains Ambiguous (2017), https://coincenter.org/files/2017–05/report-bsa-crypto-token1.pdf.

28. *See* IRS Notice 2014–21 (Apr. 14, 2014), https://www.irs.gov/irb/2014%2616_IRB/ar12.html; Order Re Petition to Enforce IRS Summons, United States v. Coinbase, Inc., No. 17-cv-01431-JSC, 2017 WL 5890052.

29. 7 U.S.C. § 1(a)(9).

30. Commodity Futures Trading Commission v. McDonnell, 321 F.Supp.3d 366 (E.D.N.Y. July 16, 2018).

31. Anatole France, The Red Lily 91 (W. Stephens trans., 1894).

32. *See U.S. Bank CEOs Get Grilled by Congress on Blockchain Technology*, Tokenist (Apr. 15, 2019), https://thetokenist.io/u-s-bank-ceos-get-grilled-by-congress-on-blockchain-technology/.

33. The Monero system was designed to be a black box to observers, but some commentators have argued that it is not quite as anonymous as some of its proponents claim. One study found that a "chain-reaction" analysis could allow outside observers to guess transaction information with 80 percent accuracy. Malte Moser et al., *An Empirical Analysis of Traceability in the Monero Blockchain*, arXiv (2018), https://arxiv.org/abs/1704.04299.

34. Justin Scheck & Shane Shifflett, *How Dirty Money Disappears into the Black Hole of Cryptocurrency*, Wall St. J., Sept. 28, 2018.

35. The Supreme Court made this process slightly more complicated in *Luis v. United States*, 136 S. Ct. 1083 (2016), where it held that pretrial freezing

of the bank accounts assets of accused individuals could violate the Sixth Amendment right to counsel if it deprived the defendant of a fair opportunity to secure counsel.

36. *See* Order Re Petition to Enforce IRS Summons, United States v. Coinbase, Inc., No. 17-cv-01431-JSC, 2017 WL 5890052.

37. *See* Suzanne Katzenstein, *Dollar Unilateralism: The New Frontline of National Security*, 90 IND. L. J. 293 (2015).

38. For an inside look at the case, see BRADLEY C. BIRKENFELD, LUCIFER'S BANKER: THE UNTOLD STORY OF HOW I DESTROYED SWISS BANK SECRECY (2016).

39. MAX WEBER, POLITICS AS A VOCATION, LECTURE DELIVERED IN 1918, in FROM MAX WEBER: ESSAYS IN SOCIOLOGY 78 (H.H. Gerth & C. Wright Mills eds., London, Routledge 1948).

40. LAWRENCE LESSIG, CODE AND OTHER LAWS OF CYBERSPACE 6 (1999).

41. *Id.*

42. PRIMAVERA DE FILIPPI & AARON WRIGHT, BLOCKCHAIN AND THE LAW: THE RULE OF CODE (2018).

43. *Id.* at 52.

44. *Id.* at 5.

45. *See* DAVID GERARD, ATTACK OF THE 50 FOOT BLOCKCHAIN: BITCOIN, BLOCKCHAIN, ETHEREUM & SMART CONTRACTS (2017).

46. Ujo Music, *Emerging from the Silence*, MEDIUM: UJO (Aug. 29, 2016), https://blog.ujomusic.com/welcome-back-1addcco6bcc6.

47. JACK GOLDSMITH & TIM WU, WHO CONTROLS THE INTERNET? ILLUSIONS OF A BORDERLESS WORLD (2006).

48. *Id.* at 28.

49. *Id.* at 67.

50. *Id.* at 130–31.

7 HOW TO GOVERN TECHNOLOGY

1. @JosephMuscat_JM, TWITTER (Mar. 23, 2018), https://twitter.com/Joseph Muscat_JM/status/977115588614086656.

2. Interview with Steve Tendon (Aug. 21, 2018).

3. *See* Molly Jane Zuckerman, *Malta Approves Three Blockchain, Crypto Bills in Second Parliamentary Reading*, COINTELEGRAPH (June 27, 2018), https://cointelegraph.com/news/malta-approves-three-blockchain-crypto-bills-in-second-parliamentary-reading.

4. *See* Malta Chamber of Commerce, *ZB.com Is the Latest Cryptocurrency Exchange Heading to Malta*, MALTA CHAMBER COM. ENTER. & INDUS. (Aug. 20, 2018), https://www.maltachamber.org.mt/e n/zb-com-is-the-latest-cryptocurrency-exchange-heading-to-malta.

5. *See* Avi Mizrahi, *Bitbay Exchange Moves to Malta After Last Polish Bank Stops Service*, BITCOIN.COM (May 30, 2018), https://news.bit

coin.com/bitbay-exchange-moves-to-malta-after-last-polish-bank-stops-service/.

6. *See Japan Regulator Warns Cryptocurrency Exchange Binance over Unregistered Operations*, REUTERS, Mar. 22, 2018.

7. *See* Zuckerman, *supra* note 3.

8. Catherine Ross, *How Malta Is Becoming the Blockchain Hub of the World: A Talk with Leading Law Firm*, COINTELEGRAPH (July 13, 2018), https://cointelegraph.com/news/how-malta-is-becoming-the-bl ockchain-hub-of-the-world-a-talk-with-leading-law-firm.

9. Bill DeLisle, *Another Exchange Is Heading to Malta, the "Blockchain Capital of the World*," CRYPTOINSIDER (Aug. 20, 2018), https://cryptoinsi der.21mil.com/another-exchange-heading-malta-blockchain-capital-world/.

10. Nathaniel Popper, *Have a Cryptocurrency Company? Bermuda, Malta or Gibraltar Wants You*, N.Y. TIMES, July 29, 2018.

11. *See* Philip Leone Ganado, *Blockchain Carries "Significant Risks*," TIMES OF MALTA, Jan. 24, 2019.

12. *See* Ivan Martin, *Malta Becomes First Country to Explore Blockchain Education Certificates*, TIMES OF MALTA, Sept. 22, 2017.

13. *See* Kurt Sansone, *Malta Is First Country to Put Education Certificates on Blockchain*, MALTA TODAY, Feb. 21, 2019.

14. Jessica Dye, *Trump on North Korea Summit: "We'll See What Happens*," FINANCIAL TIMES, May 16, 2018.

15. *Lime Is Fighting Back Against Seattle's Resistance to Scooters*, MYNORTHWEST (Oct. 5, 2018), http://mynorthwest.com/1134905/seattle-sc ooter-lime-email-campaign/.

16. *See "Let's Wait and See": Merkel to Watch UK Closely After Latest Brexit Offer*, AGENCE FRANCE-PRESSE, Mar. 12, 2019.

17. *See* Sharon B. Jacobs, *The Administrative State's Passive Virtues*, 66 ADMIN. L. REV. 565 (2014)

18. BILL CLINTON, PREFACE TO THE PRESIDENCY: SELECTED SPEECHES OF BILL CLINTON 1974–1992 172 (Stephen A. Smith ed., 1996).

19. *See* Carola Frydman & Dirk Jenter, *CEO Compensation*, 2 ANN. REV. FIN. ECON. 75 (2010).

20. *See* Michael Doran, *Uncapping Executive Pay*, 90 S. CAL. L. REV. 815 (2017).

21. Delaware's so-called Blockchain Amendments revised a number of sections of Delaware's General Corporation Law with the stated purpose of "provid[ing] specific statutory authority for Delaware corporations to use networks of electronic databases (examples of which are described currently as 'distributed ledgers' or a 'blockchain') for the creation and maintenance of corporate records, including the corporation's stock ledger." Delaware State

Senate, Senate Bill No. 69, https://legis.delaware.gov/json/BillDetail/
GenerateHtmlDocument?legislationId=25730&legislationTypeId=1&
docTypeId=2&legislationName=SB69.

22. Information about Ohio's program to accept business taxes in cryptocurrency can be found at ohiocrypto.com, the website set up by the Treasurer
of Ohio.

23. See Wyo. Stat. Ann. §§ 34-29-101, 13-12-101 (the "Special Purpose
Depository Institutions Act").

24. See Regulation of the Conduct of Virtual Currency Businesses, 37 N.Y.
Reg. 7 (June 24, 2015) (codified at N.Y. Comp. Codes R. & Regs. tit. 23, pt.
200), http://docs.dos.ny.gov/info/register/2015/june24/pdf/rulemaking.pdf.

25. See Everett Rosenfeld, *Company Leaves New York, Protesting
"BitLicense,"* CNBC (June 11, 2015), https://www.cnbc.com/2015/06/10/c
ompany-leaves-new-york-protesting-bitlicense.html.

26. See Joseph Young, *BitQuick and Local Bitcoins Terminate Service in NY
Due to BitLicense Compliance Costs,* BITCOIN MAGAZINE (Aug. 12, 2015),
https://bitcoinmagazine.com/articles/bitquick-local-bitcoins-terminate-ser
vice-ny-due-bitlicense-compliance-costs-1439414074/.

27. See Michael J. de la Merced, *Bitcoin Rules Completed by New York
Regulator,* N.Y. TIMES, June 3, 2015.

28. See Carl Bialik, *How Much Is It Really Costing to Comply with Sarbanes-
Oxley,* WALL ST. J., June 16, 2005.

29. See Yessi Bello Perez, *The Real Cost of Applying for a New York
BitLicense,* COINDESK (Aug. 13, 2015), https://www.coindesk.com/real-cos
t-applying-new-york-bitlicense.

30. See S.J. Liebowitz & Stephen E. Margolis, *Network Externality: An
Uncommon Tragedy,* 8 J. ECON. PERSP. 133 (1994); Mark A. Lemley &
David McGowan, *Legal Implications of Network Economic Effects,* 86
CALIF. L. REV. 479 (1998).

31. See S.J. Liebowitz & Stephen E. Margolis, *Path Dependence, Lock-In,
and History,* 11 J.L. ECON. & ORG. 205 (1995); Paul A. David, *Clio and the
Economics of QWERTY,* 75 AMER. ECON. REV. 332 (1985).

32. For a discussion of the first-mover advantage in technology, see Mark
A. Lemley & David W. O'Brien, *Encouraging Software Reuse,* 49 STAN.
L. REV. 255 (1997).

33. The idea of a "race to the bottom" among states or countries is one
of the most debated ideas in legal academia. The discussion often
centers around the state of Delaware, which has adopted some of the
most permissive business law rules in the country. Needless to say,
scholars disagree vehemently about whether Delaware's laws represent a "bottom," that is, an undeniably bad legal structure, or
a "top," that is, an undeniably good one. For a sampling of the
contributions to this literature, see William L. Cary, *Federalism and*

Corporate Law: Reflections Upon Delaware, 83 YALE L. REV. 663 (1974); Ralph Winter, *State Law, Shareholder Protection, and the Theory of the Corporation*, 6 J. LEGAL STUD. 251 (1977); Lucian Arye Bebchuk, *Federalism and the Corporation: The Desirable Limits on State Competition in Corporate Law*, 105 HARV. L. REV. 1435 (1992); Marcel Kahan & Ehud Kamar, *The Myth of State Competition in Corporate Law*, 55 STAN. L. REV. 679 (2002); Mark Roe, *Delaware's Competition*, 117 HARV. L. REV. 588 (2003); Mark Roe, *Delaware's Politics*, 118 HARV. L. REV. 2491 (2005).

34. For a discussion of regulatory sandboxes, see Hilary J. Allen, *Regulatory Sandboxes*, 87 GEO. WASH. L. REV. 579 (2019).
35. *See Regulatory Sandbox*, FIN. CONDUCT AUTH., https://www.fca.org.uk/firms/regulatory-sandbox.
36. *See* Jimmy Aki, *FCA Chooses Blockchain Companies for Fourth Cohort of Regulatory Sandbox*, BITCOIN MAGAZINE (July 4, 2018), https://bitcoinmagazine.com/articles/fca-chooses-blockchain-companies-fourth-cohort-regulatory-sandbox/.
37. *See Fintech Supervisory Sandbox*, HONG KONG MONETARY AUTH., https://www.hkma.gov.hk/eng/key-functions/international-financial-centre/fintech-supervisory-sandbox.shtml.
38. *See MAS Proposes Fintech Sandbox Scheme with Fast-Track Approvals*, STRAITS TIMES (Nov. 14, 2018), https://www.straitstimes.com/business/banking/mas-proposes-fintech-sandbox-scheme-with-fast-track-approvals.
39. *See* Jemima Kelly, *A "Fintech Sandbox" Might Sound Like a Harmless Idea. It's Not.*, FINANCIAL TIMES (Dec. 4, 2018), https://ftalphaville.ft.com/2018/12/05/1543986004000/A–fintech-sandbox–might-sound-like-a-harmless-idea–It-s-not/.
40. *See* Website of the Office of the Arizona Attorney General, *Sandbox Participants*, https://www.azag.gov/fintech/participants.
41. *See* Letter to Consumer Financial Protection Bureau, Re: Opposition to Policy to Encourage Trial Disclosure Programs (Oct. 10, 2018), http://ourfinancialsecurity.org/2018/10/afr-letter-public-interest-groups-criticize-cfpb-proposal-regulatory-sandbox/.
42. National Consumer Law Center, Comments on Policy to Encourage Trial Disclosure Programs Proposed Rules (Oct. 10, 2018), https://www.nclc.org/images/pdf/regulatory_reform/group-comments-to-CFPB-trial-disclosure-programs-oct2018.pdf.
43. Kenneth Rogoff, *Cryptocurrencies Are Like Lottery Tickets That Might Pay Off in Future*, GUARDIAN, Dec. 10, 2018.
44. *See* Debra M. Strauss, *Feast or Famine: The Impact of the WTO Decision Favoring the U.S. Biotechnology Industry in the EU Ban of Genetically Modified Foods*, 45 AM. BUS. L. J. 775 (2008).

45. *See* Gerry Mullany, *China Restricts Banks' Use of Bitcoin*, N.Y. Times, Dec. 5, 2013.
46. *See* Chao Deng & Linglin Wei, *China Cracks Down on Bitcoin*, Wall St. J., Apr. 1, 2014.
47. *See* Chao Deng & Paul Vigna, *China to Shut Bitcoin Exchanges*, Wall St. J., Sept. 11, 2017.
48. *See* Chen Jia & Ren Xiaojin, *PBOC Gets Tougher on Bitcoin*, China Daily, Jan. 5, 2018.
49. *See* Cao Li, *China, a Major Bitcoin Source, Considers Moving Against It*, N.Y. Times (Apr. 9, 2019), https://www.nytimes.com/2019/04/09/business/bitcoin-china-ban.html.
50. *See Banco Central de Bolivia Prohibe el Uso del Bitcoin y Otras 11 Monedas Virtuales*, Enlaces Bolivia (Apr. 2017), http://www.enlaces boli via.net/9263-Banco-Central-de-Bolivia-prohibe-el-uso-de-bitcoins-y-otras-11-monedas-virtuales; *Bitcoin Notice* [in Bengali], Nepal Rastra Bank, h ttps://nrb.org.np/fxm/notices/BitcoinNotice.pdf; Atit Babu Rijal, *The Future of Cryptocurrencies*, Kathmandu Post (Dec. 27, 2017), http://kath mandupost.ekantipur.com/news/2017–12-27/the-future-of-cryptocurren cies.html; Benjamin A.T. Graham& Allison Kingsley, *Why Bitcoin's Success Could Be Its Downfall*, Wash. Post, Dec. 11, 2017.
51. *See* AFP, *Why Bangladesh Will Jail Bitcoin Traders* (Sept. 15, 2014), https://www.telegraph.co.uk/finance/currency/11097208/Why-Bangladesh-will-jail-Bitcoin-traders.html.
52. *See* Golam Mowla, *Police on the Hunt for Bitcoin Users in Bangladesh*, Dhaka Tribune (Feb. 19, 2018), http://www.dhakatri bune.com/bangladesh/crime/2018/02/19/police-hunt-bitcoin-users-ban gladesh/.
53. *See* Maksat Elebesov, *Will Cryptocurrency Be Banned in Kyrgyzstan?*, Sputnik Kyrgyzstan (Jan. 17, 2018), https://ru.sputnik.kg/economy/20180 117/1037290672/zapretyat-li-kriptovalyutu-v-kyrgyzstane-otvet-glavy-nac banka.html.
54. For the text of the SEC's order, see SEC Release No. 34-83723 (July 26, 2018), https://www.sec.gov/rules/other/2018/34-83723.pdf?mod=article_on line.
55. *See* Dissent of Commissioner Hester M. Peirce to Release No. 34–83723 (July 26, 2018), https://www.sec.gov/news/public-statement/peirce-dissent-34-83723.

8 TECHNOLOGY AND THE RULE OF THE CROWD

1. *See* Jerry Brito, *Bitcoin Taxation Is Broken. Here's How to Fix It.*, Coin Center (Apr. 12, 2017), https://coincenter.org/entry/bitcoin-taxation-is-bro ken-here-s-how-to-fix-it.

2. *See* Peter Van Valkenburgh, Framework for Securities Regulation of Cryptocurrencies (Coin Center, 2018), https://coincenter.org/entry/fra mework-for-securities-regulation-of-cryptocurrencies.

3. *See* Peter Van Valkenburgh & Jerry Brito, State Digital Currency Principles and Framework (Coin Center 2017), https://coincenter.org/e ntry/state-digital-currency-principles-and-framework.

4. Interview with Jerry Brito (Aug. 20, 2018).

5. *See* Jerry Brito, *A Shift Toward Digital Currency*, N.Y. Times (Oct. 16, 2012), https://www.nytimes.com/roomfordebate/2012/04/04/bringing-dol lars-and-cents-into-this-century/a-shift-toward-digital-currency.

6. Josh Zerlan, *Bitcoin as the Ultimate Democratic Tool*, Wired (Apr. 2014), https://www.wired.com/insights/2014/04/bitcoin-ultimate-demo cratic-tool/.

7. Usman W. Chohan, *Blockchain Enhancing Political Accountability? Sierra Leone 2018 Case*, SSRN Working Paper (Mar. 29, 2018), https://pa pers.ssrn.com/sol3/papers.cfm?abstract_id=3147006.

8. Ian Bogost, *Cryptocurrency Might Be a Path to Authoritarianism*, Atlantic, May 30, 2017.

9. Omri Marian, *Are Cryptocurrencies Super Tax Havens?*, 112 Mich. L. Rev. First Impressions 38 (2013).

10. Craig Timberg, *Bitcoin's Boom Is a Boon for Extremist Groups*, Wash. Post, Dec. 26, 2017.

11. Eric Hughes, *A Cypherpunk's Manifesto* (Mar. 9, 1993,) https://www.acti vism.net/cypherpunk/manifesto.html.

12. Aristotle, Politics bk. III.

13. One important assumption here is that each voter has a greater than 50 percent chance of being correct. For an excellent demonstration of the ways that the Condorcet jury theorem has been used in political theory, see Christian List & Robert E. Goodin, *Epistemic Democracy: Generalizing the Condorcet Jury Theorem*, 9 J. Pol. Phil. 277 (2001).

14. *See* Friedrich A. Hayek, *The Use of Knowledge in Society*, 35 Am. Econ. Rev. 519 (1945).

15. John Stuart Mill, Considerations on Representative Government ch. 3 (1861).

16. The ultimatum game was first devised by Werner Güth, Rolf Schmittberger and Bernd Schwarze. *See* Werner Güth, Rolf Schmittberger & Bernd Schwarze, *An Experimental Analysis of Ultimatum Bargaining*, 3 J. Econ. Behav. & Org. 367 (1982). It has since been used extensively by other psychologists and economists, and indeed has become a common way of testing cultural values. For example, one study conducted the ultimatum game in small-scale societies and found that in gift-giving societies the proposer often offered

more than half of the sum to the responder, while in relatively independent societies the proposer tends to offer substantially less than half, with the Machiguenga society in Peru offering on average just 26 percent. In all, the cooperation rates of the societies studied ranged from 26 to 58 percent. Joseph Henrich et al., *In Search of Homo Economicus: Behavioral Experiments in 15 Small-Scale Societies*, 91 AM. ECON. REV. 73 (2001).

17. Gary Bornstein & Ilan Yaniv, *Individual and Group Behavior in the Ultimatum Game: Are Groups More 'Rational' Players?*, 1 EXP. ECON. 101 (1998).

18. David G. Myers, *Discussion-Induced Attitude Polarization*, 28 HUM. REL. 699 (1975).

19. ROGER BROWN, SOCIAL PSYCHOLOGY: THE SECOND EDITION 224 (1986).

20. Sarita Yardi & Danah Boyd, *Dynamic Debates: An Analysis of Group Polarization over Time on Twitter*, 30 BULL. SCI. TECH. & SOC'Y 316 (2010). On the other hand, at least one study has suggested that Facebook users are exposed to significant amounts of "cross-cutting" content, that is, content that is ideologically opposed to their own ideological alignment. *See* Eytan Bakshy, Solomon Messing & Lada A. Adamic, *Exposure to Ideologically Diverse News and Opinion on Facebook*, 348 SCIENCE 1130 (2015). The study, it should be noted, was conducted by Facebook employees.

21. ADAM SMITH, THE WEALTH OF NATIONS, bk. I, ch. XI, pt. 1.

22. *Id.*, bk. I, ch. X, pt. 2.

23. For an excellent, and readable, history of American political parties, see DANIEL SCHLOZMAN, WHEN MOVEMENTS ANCHOR PARTIES: ELECTORAL ALIGNMENTS IN AMERICAN HISTORY (2015).

24. *See* Robert Barnes, *North Carolina's Gerrymandered Map Is Unconstitutional, Judges Rule, and May Have to Be Redrawn Before Midterms*, WASH. POST, Aug. 27, 2018.

25. *See* Nick Marinoff, *Bitmain Nears 51% of Network Hash Rate: Why This Matters and Why It Doesn't*, BITCOIN MAGAZINE (June 28, 2018), https:// bitcoinmagazine.com/articles/bitmain-nears-51-network-hash-rate-why-m atters-and-why-it-doesnt/.

26. Interview with Amber Baldet by *The Ledger* (June 1, 2018), https://finance .yahoo.com/video/balancing-ledger-amber-baldet-gives-175336929.html.

27. *See* Nathaniel Popper, *Blockchain Will Be Theirs, Russian Spy Boasted at Conference*, N.Y. TIMES, Apr. 29, 2018.

28. *See* Drew DeSilver, *Despite Concerns About Global Democracy, Nearly Six-in-Ten Countries Are Now Democratic*, PEW RES. CTR. (Dec. 6, 2017), http://www.pewresearch.org/fact-tank/2017/12/06/despit e-concerns-about-global-democracy-nearly-six-in-ten-countries-are-no w-democratic/.

CONCLUSION

1. *See* Aaron Hankin, *Nearly Half of All 2017 ICOs Have Failed,* MarketWatch (Feb. 26, 2018), https://www.marketwatch.com/story/nearl y-half-of-all-2017-icos-have-failed-2018–02-26.
2. *See* PUBLIC PAPERS OF THE PRESIDENTS OF THE UNITED STATES: WILLIAM J. CLINTON, 1999 471 (1999).
3. THE FEDERALIST, No. 10, at 62 (James Madison) (Jacob E. Cooke ed., 1961).

Acknowledgments

Leo Tolstoy once said that if he were to try to say in words everything that he intended to express in *Anna Karenina*, he would have to write the same novel again from the beginning. I might equally say that if I were to try to thank everyone who contributed to this book in one way or another, I would have to write an entirely new book from the beginning. *Blockchain Democracy* has benefited from countless conversations, phone calls, emails, texts and conferences, with friends and strangers, colleagues and family members, computer scientists and philosophers. I am grateful to so many, for so much. But I would be remiss if I were not to name a few people who contributed in special ways: my father, for inspiring me to write; my mother, for a warm home and warm meals; my wife, for constant support; my daughter, for bringing endless joy to our lives; Michael Coenen, for slogging through the early drafts; Jacob Eisler, for daily briefings; Steve Tarsa, for teaching me computers; and Jack Goldsmith, for guiding me through the Scylla and Charybdis of the academic market.

Index